The Civilisation of the Crowd

POPULAR CULTURE IN ENGLAND 1750–1900

J M Golby and A W Purdue

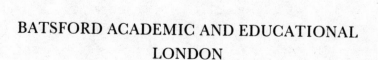

BATSFORD ACADEMIC AND EDUCATIONAL

LONDON

Published by Batsford Academic and Educational
an Imprint of B.T. Batsford Ltd
4 Fitzhardinge Street, London W1H 0AH

British Library Cataloguing in Publication Data
Golby, J.M.
The civilisation of the crowd.
1. England—Popular culture   2.England—
Social life and customs—19th century
I. Title   II. Purdue, A.W.
306'.1   DA533
ISBN 0–7134–1412–X
ISBN 0–7134–1413–8 Pbk

The Civilisation of the Crowd

Contents

Acknowledgements

Our interest in popular culture and its modern English history was greatly stimulated by our involvement in the preparation of the Open University's course on *Popular Culture*. Although our views on the subject are very different to those of many of our colleagues on that course, the discussions and debates we had with our fellow course team members were invaluable in helping us to formulate our ideas.

We wish to thank Norman McCord, Peter Bailey, Clive Emsley and Arthur Marwick for reading the manuscript in whole or in part; we have implemented many of their helpful suggestions. We are also deeply indebted to Tony Coulson for assistance with the selection of the illustrations, Mags Golby for preparing the index, Mrs. Susan Dowson for helping with the preparation of the typescript and, especially, Gill Cook who typed the last two drafts of the book with an efficiency and speed which ensured that the manuscript was handed over on time.

Our thanks are due to the following for permission to reproduce the illustrations on pages 111–14: John Johnson Collection, Bodleian Library (1, 2), Oxfordshire County Libraries (3), Mrs C. Milburn (4).

Introduction

The hero of this drama is Punch – the English Punch – perfectly different from the Italian Pulcinella. I send you a faithful portrait of him in the act of beating his wife to death; – for he is the most godless droll that ever I met with; and as completely without conscience as the wood out of which he is made; – a little, too, the type of the nation he represents.

Punch has, like his namesake, something of rum, lemon and sugar in him; he is strong, sour and sweet, and withal pretty indifferent to the confusion he causes. He is, moreover, the most absolute egotist the earth contains, 'et ne doute jamais de rien'. He conquers everything by his invincible merriment and humour, laughs at the laws, at men, and at the devil himself; and shows in part what the Englishman is, in part what he wishes to be.

A Regency Visitor. The English Tour of Prince
Pückler-Mushau, 1826–28

G.M. Trevelyan's well known definition of social history as 'the history of the people with the politics left out' would not describe much of the writing on the subject which has appeared in the last decades. Indeed, many recent publications might be better described as the history of the people with the politics brought in everywhere. Certainly, marxisant political theory has been ubiquitous in the many books and essays that have appeared on the history of popular culture, and the fair, the public house and the music hall have come to be seen as the arenas of class conflict and the frontiers of social control. To the political zealot with a holistic philosophy politics is everywhere, because so is capitalism, just as sin is to the religious

9

zealot. The editors of a recent collection of essays on popular culture have written:

> ... even where involvement is not aggressive, private
> (economic) and public (political) contrivance from above
> saturates any form that one examines in capitalism, from
> Butlin's to Brighton and Hove Albion Supporter's Club (before
> its abolition by the directors in 1978), from Whitsun in an
> Oxfordshire village in 1890, to the Canterbury Arms in the
> 1850s. No such cultural form can be seen as natural, or
> spontaneous, or as the simple product of popular demand.[1]

As G.M. Young wrote in relation to Evangelicalism, 'The world is very evil'.

Popular culture has a political dimension, for the recreations and pastimes of the people, and even their private lives and domestic arrangements, have in recent history rarely been matters of indifference to the authorities of the day and have concerned those who wished to reform or transform society. No doubt demotic culture has always been a subject for concern, but it seems likely that distaste for it among influential sections of the educated increased during what is conventionally known as the modern period. Religious reformers strove to make men more godly while the effect of the Enlightenment was to raise hopes that they might become more rational. Popular culture appeared neither godly nor rational.

The activities of successive waves of reformers who attempted to proselytise, cajole or discipline the populace into the acceptance of a remodelled way of life, marked by more suitable, more moral and more abstinent habits, are in part the subject of this book, though we suggest their impact was slight in proportion to their efforts. On the whole the English public has demonstrated an admirable immunity to the blandishments of missionaries and reformers, whether their message has been Christianity, temperance or Socialism. Nor were the attempts of employers to persuade or enforce the acceptance of a more disciplined and diligent life-style, both within and without the workplace, much more successful. If, as has been suggested, 'an industrialising bourgeoisie . . . wages a holy war on all popular pursuits which were felt to impede the formation of the new forms of work discipline required by industrial production',[2] its bellicosity was hardly crowned with success.

The major changes that occurred in popular culture have, of course, to be located within the parameters set by massive economic and social changes. This should not, however, lead us to view the majority of the population as helpless pawns in the grip of great historical forces which transformed their way of life. Not only did certain tendencies innate in the pre-existing culture make a substantial contribution to industrialisation and economic expansion, but the largely urban popular culture that had emerged by the mid-century was to a considerable degree a culture created by the people themselves.

Individualism, both social and economic, was already by the early eighteenth century deeply implanted in English society. The mobility of the population, its relative freedom from the restraints of custom, and the spirit of emulation which reached far down the social hierarchy were reflected in popular culture. Demand as a cause of industrialisation has often been neglected, but the effects of a slow, extremely patchy but highly significant rise in real wages, to which manufacturers of consumer goods and entrepreneurs of leisure responded, provided much of the dynamism of the home economy. This commercialisation of eighteenth century England, as described in a recent collection of essays[3], makes nonsense of the discredited but lingering view that somehow England moved at the turn of the eighteenth and nineteenth centuries from being a 'traditional', customary and uncommercial society to become an individualistic and capitalist one.

'Commercialisation' has tended in the historiography of popular culture to be a pejorative word. The study of the subject begins with the folklorists of the eighteenth century, inevitably interested in and attracted towards that which was old, traditional and fast disappearing, and ineluctably drawn to regret that which was new. A pre-lapsarian vision therefore coloured the subject from the beginning and, as what was new in an economically dynamic society was often commercial, commercialisation became early established as the cause of the Fall. This notion of a fall from a society that was 'traditional', customary, organic and pre-capitalist to one that was modern, individualistic, commercial and capitalist has under-pinned theories of popular culture ever since. It has acted as a back-drop to the writings of cultural pessimists and conservatives like Matthew Arnold, F.R. Leavis and T.S. Eliot and has broadly dove-tailed with Marxist historical theory.

Even were the fancy of such a traditional pre-industrial England other than mythical, the notion that the life of a folk society, in which consumption is not separate from production nor performance from spectating nor work from leisure, is superior to that of modern society with its manifold separations, would be questionable. Certainly, members of peasant communities have not been slow to leave them for the attractions of urban capitalism, and it has usually been urban intellectuals who have retrospectively discovered the pleasures and sterling virtues of peasant life.

/ We would suggest both that the economic and technological revolutions which transformed English society during the eighteenth and nineteenth centuries led to a more varied and satisfying popular culture, based upon higher living standards and greater individual choice, and that the culture which had emerged by the middle of the nineteenth century owed much to the tastes and aspirations of the mass of the population. There was no sharp break with the past, for so many of the cultural phenomena of pre-industrial England were able, like the pub and the fair, to survive, adapt and thrive in new circumstances. A nexus of popular demand and commercial supply did, however, produce novel cultural forms which it is deeply condescending to dismiss as placebos or opiates. /

Those who sought so strenuously in the first half of the nineteenth century to reform popular culture were, whether they laboured under the influence of vital religion or of the Enlightenment, optimistic about their enterprise. In the later decades of the century, however, cultural pessimism became widespread. The new forms of popular culture – the popular press, the music hall and mass spectator sports – were seen as constituting a mass culture which was not only inferior to earlier forms of popular culture, but was a threat to high culture, which increasingly became defined in terms of a narrow set of values exemplified in certain great works of art. Not only did mass culture, the civilisation of the crowd, become a threat to the cultural values of the great tradition in the eyes of conservatives like Matthew Arnold, whose *Culture and Anarchy* (1869) was such a seminal work, but it was increasingly viewed by socialists as dulling the sensibilities of the proletariat and as a cataract preventing perception of the reality of exploitation.

Even by the 1880s, as we suggest in Chapter 8, socialists were beginning to identify commercialised leisure as a formidable bulwark against revolutionary consciousness, and Marxists, in their relentless search for reasons for the non-appearance of a proletarian revolution, have subsequently attributed greater importance to this factor. Antonio Gramsci's subtle modification of Marxism has been much employed by historians of English social history in the last decade. His theories ascribe great importance to intellectuals and many historians like to think of themselves as such. His application of the concept of hegemony is more flexible as a tool for corralling the myriad contradictions of English social history within a single historical theory than is classical Marxism. It is also more credible in that its emphasis upon consent and negotiation as essential elements within an expansive hegemony replace the crudities of earlier theories which see the working classes as either suppressed or malleable. The application of the concept of hegemony has resulted in popular culture being seen as a crucial arena in the contest for ideological hegemony. As has recently been argued:

> In the latter half of the nineteenth century . . . the ruling classes were again able to lead as opposed to merely rule as a consequence of the development of new ideologies – specifically, those of liberalism, and imperialism – which were able, through a variety of routes, to influence and modify working class culture. The development of new, commercial forms of popular culture . . . played an important part in this process.[4]

The utilisation of the concept of hegemony has, it can be argued, enabled Marxist historians drastically to modify previous descriptions of Victorian society and yet remain within a Marxist tradition. It has certainly produced in the hands of some historians a considerable extension of our knowledge of working class politics, work and leisure. We would argue, nevertheless, that in the final analysis it merely distances the classic Marxist context, of an economic base determining the social, political and intellectual superstructure and of class struggle between a dominant bourgeoisie and a subordinate proletariat. It is a brilliant attempt to span the chasm between the evidence and an unsatisfactory theory.

Our approach will no doubt be called populist. We would however question whether the popular culture of the day, however commercialised, does not broadly express the aspirations and desires of most men as most men are. Nor does such a view rule out the conclusion that increases in economic prosperity for the mass of people have resulted in a popular culture more varied, more generous and more rewarding. Its faults, and they are numerous, can be laid at the door not of the culture of the many but at that of a high culture which has lost not only its self-confidence but its connection with its populist relative; but that is another matter.

If this book has a hero it is Punch, the English Punch, for he appears to us to represent the indomitable spirit of English popular culture. Though in his traditional guise he is now to be found only on the margins of contemporary popular culture – at children's parties and occasionally at fairs or seaside promenades – he has undergone, like Dr Who, many metamorphoses without losing his essential characteristics.

There was much of him in Ally Sloper, as there is in Andy Capp and most of our popular comic characters. He is the sprite of English populism, albeit a middle-aged and leering sprite – a demotic incarnation of the mildest Englishman's *alter ego* with his chauvinism both national and sexual, his hedonism, his disrespect for law and authority, his courage and sheer bloody-mindedness.

By origin he was, of course, Italian, having arrived in England in 1662 and amused the court of Charles II, but by the early eighteenth century he had become almost completely anglicised though an Italian accent lingered for some time. At the beginning of our period he was essentially a countryman, accompanied on his rural per-ambulations by small entrepreneurs of leisure who put him through his paces at fairs and parish feasts. The linguistic and cultural unity of England, however, made him equally at home in the streets of London, where Prince Pückler-Mushau saw him in the 1820s, or in the expanding towns of the industrial revolution. Like so much of English popular culture he was able to adapt with ease to the increasingly urban environment of the nineteenth century, to become a frequenter of city streets and markets and to follow the trend to holidays at the seaside.

Glove-puppet performances of the story of Punch and his wife Judy (she had previously been known as Joan) had, by the 1890s, become part of the tradition of the English sea-side holiday. By this time, although Punch's cheerful brutality still amused children and elicited atavistic guffaws from adults, he was a somewhat dated figure, no longer characteristic of the popular culture of the day. That culture had been largely weaned from blood sports, had embraced a degree of respectability and become more domestic and family-orientated. But this was so only up to a point, for, if one important theme of the history of English popular culture during our period is its domestication and taming, another is the continuity of its almost anarchic dimension, its appetite for beer and sensation, its tendency to mock authority (especially pompous authority), its celebration of the war between the sexes and its refusal to be serious or rational. There continues to be a gallon or two of Punch in popular culture, however watered down, and it is that ingredient which has so confounded the hopes of reformers, of whatever religious or political persuasion, for a culture of the people that would be serious and rational. /

ONE

The 'old' popular culture

The people of this neighbourhood are much attached to the celebration of wakes; and on the annual return of these festivals, the cousins assemble from all quarters, fill the church on Sunday, and celebrate Monday with feasting, with musick, and with dancing. The spirit of old English hospitality is conspicuous among the farmers on these occasions; but with the lower sort of people, especially in the manufacturing villages, the return of the wake never fails to produce a week, at least, of idleness, intoxication and riot. . . .

Reverend A. Macaulay, *The History of Claybrook*, 1791

The adjective 'traditional' is a constant temptation to historians who set out to describe the popular culture of eighteenth century England, especially if they do so to prepare the ground for an analysis of the massive changes which were to lead to the largely urban popular culture of the late nineteenth century. All too easily an awareness of the magnitude of the changes that industrialisation, urbanisation and population growth were to bring can lead to a caricature of the pre-industrial society and its popular culture: the society is seen as 'commercially unsophisticated' and with many of the characteristics of a subsistence or peasant economy; the size and variety of the middle ranks of society are ignored in favour of a contrast between the upper orders and the people; while the culture becomes all Mumming, Plough Monday and harvest feasts, a world in which the people, not to say the folk, live out lives set to the immemorial rhythms of nature, only intermittently aware, amidst their rituals, carnivals and charivari, that a rationalising capitalism is waiting in the wings.

If culture is the sum of 'relationships between elements in a whole way of life,'[1] then just as the industrial revolution did not and could

17

not have occurred in the context of an unsophisticated and un-developed economy nor of an immobile society, so the popular culture of eighteenth century England, which was itself part of the womb of an industrial and urban society, was not exclusively traditional nor was it a peasant culture. And yet we are immediately confronted with the evidence of those most obvious aspects of popular culture, the major holidays, festive occasions and public recreations, which were tied to the agricultural and religious calendars. These were indeed traditional and exhibited both continuity with past centuries and parallels with other European societies.

To a considerable degree the question of how traditional eighteenth century popular culture was is a matter of perspective. In contrast to the late nineteenth century much of the society does appear parochial, immobile and tied to tradition while central features of its popular culture appear attuned to the agricultural year, uncommercial and focused on amusements and recreations which had formed the basis of rural culture for centuries. It is no mere marxist reductionism to argue that the major features of an economy place limitations upon the forms that popular culture can take. Eighteenth century England was a predominantly rural society and the major engine of the economy was agriculture. Agricultural societies can take very different forms and their popular cultures can be diverse and various but they quite clearly, at any rate before mechanisation and modern communications, have salient features in common which they do not share with industrial societies. We will later argue that pre-industrial England was a unique economy and society; it was capitalist and individualist and, as such, distinct from other contemporary European societies; the long tradition of economic individualism, the acceleration of social mobility and the conflict engendered by Puritanism had all stamped themselves on the culture of the people. But the enduring context of a rural and decentralised society, which embraced the lives of the majority, limited the changes that could be made in popular culture. It gave rise to traditional features which would have been instantly recognisable to that useful fellow, the time traveller from centuries earlier, and came as no surprise, though much else did, to those real visitors from contemporary Europe.

It is clear that the term 'traditional society', as used by sociologists and anthropologists and by many historians, means something more specific than simply a society heavily influenced by beliefs and customs passed on from generation to generation, though this remains part of the meaning. Theorists of social and cultural change have posited an antithesis between traditional and modern society which usually corresponds to a parallel antithesis between the rural and the urban. Ferdinand Tönnies has argued for a distinction between *Gemeinschaft* and *Gesellschaft*. He perceives the nineteenth century as witnessing the transition from a society characterised by close kinship, common customs and collective beliefs and aspirations to a society organised on a rational basis in which individuals pursue their goals accepting the necessity of social organisation and mechanisms for law and government.[2] Robert Redfield sees a folk society as having 'the characters which are logically opposite to those which are to be found in a modern society'.[3] His folk society is essentially a peasant society existing in a subsistence economy, with a largely static culture which has conventional and ritual festivals, ceremonies and recreations.

Peter Burke in his wide-ranging study of popular culture in early modern Europe[4] sees traditional popular culture as primarily the culture of a peasant society. He is ever conscious of the varieties of that culture, of differences between and within regions, between Catholic and Protestant areas, between uplands and lowlands, and between town and country, but it is clear that he considers the vast majority of the inhabitants of all parts of Europe to have been peasants and their culture a peasant culture. He sees this culture as co-existing with an elite culture and skilfully adapts a model of Redfield's, that of the 'great' and 'little' traditions:

> There were two cultural traditions in early modern Europe, but they did not correspond symmetrically to the two main social groups, the elite and the common people. The elite participated in the little tradition, but the common people did not participate in the great tradition. The asymmetry came about because the two traditions were transmitted in different ways. The great tradition was transmitted formally at grammar schools and universities. It was a closed tradition in the same sense that people who had not attended these institutions, which were not open to all, were excluded. In a quite literal sense they did not speak the same language. The little tradition on the other hand was transmitted informally. It was open to all, like the church, the tavern and the market place, where so many of the performances occurred.[5]

Burke sees traditional popular culture as substantially intact *circa* 1500 but to have been considerably eroded over the next three centuries by the repression of religious reformers, the progressive withdrawal of the upper orders of society and by a combination of such developments as commercial expansion and printing which modified cultural expression, making it more secular and political. He writes that, 'Even before the industrial revolution, the growth of towns, the improvement of roads and the spread of literacy were undermining traditional popular culture'.[6] This undermining is seen as an uneven phenomenon, with urban areas, the most commercial regions and those societies where elites and labouring classes shared a common language, exhibiting the greatest degree of erosion. In such a scenario English popular culture, despite regional peculiarities and variations, is part of a common European traditional culture although by the eighteenth century it is in the van of an equally common decline.

But does England really fit so neatly into a model of a pan-European peasant society gradually finding a common culture eroded by the forces of modernity, a process in which English popular culture was to be an early victim? Or was England a very different society in terms of its economy, its law and its social structure, differences which resulted in a similarly distinct popular culture? Many historians seem to be coming to the conclusion that there is something peculiar, not to say deviant, about the English and their history.[7]

Alan Macfarlane has argued in a provocative recent study[8] that England followed an individual and individualist path from at least the thirteenth century and that what demarcated England from European societies throughout this period was the absence of a peasantry and the presence of a legal system which emphasised individual rights and personal titles to land. He uses a sophisticated definition of a peasantry, as being characterised by: the primacy of the household and community interlocked by kinship; production by the family unit with little hired labour; the greater proportion of produce being consumed by the family unit; a strong sense of attachment to locality; and the conception of land as not a saleable product. Whatever the disputes over the accuracy of Macfarlane's thesis for the late Middle Ages or for Tudor England, there can be little doubt that by the eighteenth century, England had long since ceased to be a peasant society. Even if we use a less exacting description of a peasant and think of him as simply a small owner-occupier, it is clear that by the early decades of the century such men farmed a declining proportion of English land and that the proportion decreased thereafter.

Economic and social historians have become increasingly unhappy with purely economic explanations of England's industrial revolution, and emphasis is now placed upon those social characteristics of the nation which were favourable to economic enterprise and innovation. Harold Perkin has pointed to the structure of English society, the importance of wealth above rank, the degree of individual freedom, the absence of legal barriers between different strata of society and the consequent degree of social, occupational and geographic mobility. As he comments, younger sons in practically all of Western Europe '. . . were restricted by social as well as by economic barriers in their opportunities of employment and therefore of marriage . . . [while in England] the provision of income opportunities was very elastic: the early disappearance of a peasant society had necessitated an alternative outlet, notably in domestic out-work industry, for the surplus population, while the upflow of new men into the landed gentry opened up opportunities all the way down the scale for newcomers'.[9]

Both the English economy and the social structure do seem to have been significantly different to those found elsewhere in Europe. There was a different system of landholding and of property relations, while the Common Law contrasted with continental Roman Law. By the middle of the eighteenth century not only were the majority of the agricultural workforce landless labourers but it is probable that the majority of the workforce was no longer directly engaged in agriculture at all.

Quite clearly Macfarlane's view of an England which had not been a peasant society for many centuries is incompatible with a picture of English popular culture in the eighteenth century differing only in its degree of decomposition from the popular culture found in contemporary continental countries. Major differences in economic and social structure over such a period of time would have resulted in a distinctive popular culture. But, even if we accept the more conventional periodisation which locates the major socio-economic changes, which were to make England more socially mobile and more economically individualist and which were to transform agriculture, in the sixteenth and seventeenth centuries, can the culture of the people have remained simply a regional variation of a common European culture? It seems probable, on the contrary, that the popular culture of eighteenth century England reflected its economic and social uniqueness and that what appears at first sight to be a traditional culture, a variety of European peasant culture, eroded but still recognisable, is, in fact, despite certain common features with this, distinctive: more commercial, more individualistic, less corporate and more secular.

And yet we began by writing that there were many features of popular culture which were indeed traditional and exhibited continuity with past centuries and parallels with other European societies. Such features were in many ways the most noticeable, because the most public; they were the major holydays, the festive occasions and the public recreations. Here we find a continuity not just with the early sixteenth century but with medieval society.

In the first place there was the close association of leisure with work, especially with agricultural work. The holidays and festivals which liberally punctuated the working year arose naturally out of work, celebrating its beginning as with Plough Monday, or its completion, as with harvest feasts. Other holidays occurred in the slack periods of the agricultural year and lasted for days or even weeks. Some fairs were held purely for entertainment or pleasure but others were centred round that most important event in the year for labourers and farmers alike, the annual hiring.[10] Many holidays were, of course true to the word's original meaning of 'holydays' and celebrated the ecclesiastical calendar. Both work and play were engaged in with a consciousness of tradition and custom and were surrounded by much ritual.

The vast majority of the population lived out their lives in village communities and recreation and leisure, like work, were enclosed within the village. Although peripatetic and professional entertainers would add colour and glamour to local festivities, the villagers for the most part made their own amusements. Here work and leisure reflected the essentially decentralised nature of pre-industrial England; it was the local worthies and local institutions which mattered, whether in the economic, social or political spheres. This resulted in a great variety of regional and sub-regional differences in leisure patterns. The timing of holidays, the customs and rituals which surrounded both the peaks and troughs of the agricultural year and the births, marriages and deaths of the life cycle went through infinite variations, not simply between north and south, or between pastoral and crop farming areas, but within the same counties.

The sports and pastimes of this society were boisterous and sometimes bawdy; they were often, to our eyes at least, violent and cruel. They involved not only hard knocks and bloody heads for human participants but a great deal of cruelty to animals. No amount of Chestertonian romanticism about a merry England of beef, ale and physical exuberance can obscure the fact, for example, that cock throwing (which consisted of throwing missiles at a tethered cock until it was dead) was by any standards an example of gratuitous cruelty, without the redeeming features of a chance of escape for the bird or any danger to the perpetrators of the violence. Sport throughout the country was violent, crude and usually involved betting and blood. There were badger-baiting, cock-fighting, bull-running, dog-fighting, bear-baiting and, of course, barefisted boxing. Football was to be found almost everywhere but the requirement that some sort of ball be kicked, run with or thrown was the only common denominator in what was in the modern sense hardly a sport at all. At Derby there could be as many as 1,000 a side playing in the annual Shrove Tuesday match, while in many towns holiday games could have the whole town as the playing area. Indeed, many football matches appear to have been more like battles than sport; on the Borders they appear to have had their origin in a close connection with actual warfare in that it was sometimes under cover of football matches that reivers were called together for raids.

Such wild activity could often boil over into riot and indeed a degree of license for riot and damage to life, limb and property was tacitly written into certain annual festivities. These were seen as a time of carnival when normal rules were lifted, the Lord of Misrule took over and the local hierarchy was subjected to discomfiture or derision. Authority tolerated and often supported such festivities, partly because they were traditional (and a local squire regarded himself as part of the community even if he was its apex), and partly because of a half-conscious recognition of the necessity of a safety valve to release tensions built up during the working year.

These features of rural culture were undoubtedly, with variations, common to all of Europe and bear a considerable resemblance to Keith Thomas's description of medieval recreation:

> The recreational activities of the Middle Ages . . . recall the old primitive confusion as to where work ended and leisure began. Some of these recreations were obvious products of a society organised for war – the tournament for the upper classes, archery for the people, riding, wrestling and similar rehearsals for future conflict. . . . Some seem to be explicable only in terms of the periodic release necessary in a rigidly hierarchical society – the Saturnalia or Feasts of Fools, in which social roles were reversed, the holidays on which assaults were formally exempted from prosecution . . . sports involving the ritual slaughter of animals – bull and bear-baiting, cock-fighting – are perhaps the hardest to interpret, but other pastimes clearly reflect the web of kinship and neighbourhood, either in friendly form, as in the convivial

wakes and ales, or as an outlet for local rivalries, as in the bloodthirsty football matches between villages. All display a pre-industrial sense of time. Events are dated by references to the ecclesiastical calendar. Festivals occur at the slack periods of the agrarian year, wakes and ales drag on for days or even weeks.[11]

There are however significant differences. One is the sharp decline of religion and the church as the focus for popular recreation and celebration and the other is the dwindling importance of kinship. Much of the religious significance of popular festivities had been destroyed in the sixteenth and seventeenth centuries; whereas in Catholic Europe the direction of reform had been to do away with what was pagan in the holiday calendar, in England its aim was to divorce religion from 'Popish superstitions' and much of the Church's old intimacy with the festivals and customs of the agricultural cycle disappeared.

The very high geographical mobility of English society from at least the late sixteenth century makes it impossible to regard village society as characterised by strong kinship ties. The work of Peter Laslett and other members of the Cambridge Group for the History of Population and Social Structure has exploded many myths which, nevertheless, still permeate much work on popular culture.[12] We now know just how mobile the pre-industrial population was. We also know that in England and indeed in North-western Europe the extended or multiple family has throughout the modern period been a rarity. Studies of individual villages demonstrate that over half the population died in a different parish from that in which they were born and in one Worcestershire village 80 per cent of the 75 surnames disappeared from the parish records between 1666 and 1750.[13] Much of this mobility was over comparatively short distances but it was sufficient in an age of slow transport to render inaccurate any model of village life as a web of kinship.

A strong sense of community is not necessarily dependent upon kinship nor even upon a hereditary association of the community's members with the locality, but an association of nuclear families, many of them recent arrivals, suggests a different type of community from the village with strong kinship ties so often put forward as the basis of traditional society. Community without the dominance of kinship and made up of a group of individuals many of whom were newcomers, is inevitably a more self-conscious association than that made up of kin with a long standing relationship with land and locality. Neighbourliness is prized, work and play in association with others can create strong bonds and collective identity be acquired, but such an association is qualitatively different from that of kinship.

Our knowledge of the private and intimate life of the mass of the population in this period is necessarily limited and yet obviously central to popular culture. It is from the home that the individual goes to the fairground and the alehouse, and to the home, however uncomfortable, that he returns. There is a paucity of diaries and memoirs by labourers, artisans and shopkeepers and inevitably doubts as to the typicality of those which do exist, so our information as to the private leisure activities and the attitudes towards courtship, marriage and children of such social groups is thin. It does not, however, follow that the public and collective activities were all-important.

The restrictions upon what we would regard as normal family life are obvious: a low life expectancy limited the duration of most marriages; it was necessary for children to leave home and go into service at an early age; and the comforts of home were by subsequent standards almost non-existent. In these circumstances opportunities for privacy were necessarily limited, although this does not entitle us to conclude that it was not desired. Other factors may, however, have caused historians to overemphasise the communal and public aspects of the life of the pre-industrial labouring poor and to undervalue domestic intimacy. Many historians have a vested ideological interest in emphasising the influence of community, custom and public leisure and in seeing the nuclear family with its private interests as the product of post-industrial 'bourgeois' society. In addition modern attitudes towards child-rearing are so removed from those of the eighteenth century poor as to cause some historians of the family to see the treatment of children by labourers and artisans as cruel, callous and uncaring.[14]

Public leisure pursuits were characteristic of all sectors of eighteenth century society, with the exception of elements of the upper middle ranks. For the lower orders the attractions of the alehouse or of the fair, of the street or of the village green were reinforced by limited domestic comfort. Lack of evidence of private leisure activities and the nature of family life does not, however, entitle us to dismiss the former as unimportant nor marriages as not companionate. Rising living standards and greater longevity were over the next two centuries gradually to change the ratio between private and public leisure in working-class life, but there is little justification for believing that because homes were less comfortable, marriages more brief and childhood terminated earlier the collective culture of community was the only way in which the individual could express his tastes or enjoy his leisure. As Ferdinand Mount has argued:

> Of course, in all rural societies up to and including the present, we can find examples of village festivals, of village solidarity and of village moral and social pressures upon young people; picturesque ceremonies such as the charivari and dancing round the maypole delight folklorists and anthropologists. But to represent these ceremonies, important though they may be in the life of the village, as either essential to or the most important thing in the life of the individual is mere fantasy.[15]

A recent work on popular recreations has seen their decline in the late eighteenth and early nineteenth century, as '. . . intimately associated with the gradual breakdown of what we now call "traditional society". With the rise of the market economy, and the accompanying development of new normative standards and material conditions for the conduct of social relations, the foundations of many traditional practices were relentlessly swept away, leaving a vacuum which would be only gradually re-occupied, and then of necessity by novel or radically revamped forms of diversion'.[16] But by the late eighteenth century the English economy had been characterised by market relations for a very long time indeed. What perhaps needs to be explained is why so many of these traditional practices survived the destruction of their 'foundations'.

By the late seventeenth century, and many would argue much earlier, England was a highly developed capitalist economy and most of the impediments to a free market had been swept away. Nor was this economy confined to manufacturers or to the towns where the guild system had long fallen into desuetude. English agriculture had solved the problem of feeding the country's increased population, by economic individualism and by riding roughshod over traditional communal rights. Some three-quarters of English enclosure was complete by 1700 and the agricultural revolution of the seventeenth century had led to greatly increased production geared to the market.[17]

The structure of English villages had been considerably altered. In 1552 only about one village in ten had a resident squire, whereas by 1690 such a squire was to be found in over two-thirds of villages.[18] In addition village elites made up of farmers, tradesmen and artisans seem from the early seventeenth century to have been concerned to distance themselves from the poor and from their noisy and vulgar celebrations and pastimes. Such elites, subordinate rulers of parishes under the gentry, filled the posts of constables and churchwardens and comprised village vestries; they were generally more concerned than the gentry to control alehouses,[19] discourage idleness and present sinners to church courts. They were the most immediate and considerable threat to traditional customs and rituals.

Why then did so many of the old customs and rituals, the traditional celebrations and holidays and the same games and sports continue in the eighteenth century countryside, when most villages were more tightly supervised, most workers were now wage labourers, kinship no longer defined most communities and the Reformation and Puritanism had led the church to withdraw its patronage?

Much of the culture still made sense because it remained attuned to work: the holidays either still fell in the pauses between work or were celebrations of its completion; many fairs either marked such holidays or accompanied hirings; and blood sports were the natural focus for the energies of rural people. We must remember also that superstition continued to be at least as important as organised religion for the labouring poor and that the symbolism of rural rituals accommodated such beliefs rather better than did the dignified services of the established church. In addition the poor still had a very real interest in the success of their labour; Plough Mondays and harvest suppers were not just good excuses for drinking and eating well and relaxing, though they were that. Most agricultural workers lived in a limited wage economy: much of their wages were still in kind and depended like their masters' incomes on a successful harvest.

It may well be also that one result of Puritanism, the Civil War and the Restoration was the strengthening of support for holidays, customs and rituals. From early in the post-Reformation period they had been under attack for both religious and secular reasons, because they were fleshly and because they promoted idleness. A growing sense of the importance of labour and the merits of hard work seems to have resulted in a constant worry that the poor were altogether too ready to neglect their labours. The renewed prohibition of suicide is perhaps an extreme instance; an attempt to safeguard work by preventing the worker seeking refuge in eternity. The seventeenth century saw a series of measures aimed at curbing the pastimes and recreations with which the poor passed their idle time. The associ-

27

ation of these attacks with Puritanism, however, discredited them for some time after the Restoration.

The societies for the reformation of manners which inveighed against the gambling, drinking and whoring which they claimed was turning England into another Sodom and Gomorrah, were strongly opposed to traditional holidays and recreations, which were often accompanied by heavy drinking, involved the association of the sexes in the free and easy atmosphere of the fair, and encouraged gambling. They could make little headway in the atmosphere of the early eighteenth century, where magistrates were reluctant to prosecute against those accused of breaking moral laws and where traditional pursuits were defended in political and religious terms. A traditionalist defence of the Book of Sports argued that from the death of Charles I:

> . . . we have been loaded with the pretended statutes of Reformation; Laws which if they were to be strictly executed, a Man must not be allow'd to drink a Pot of Ale, or take a Walk in the Fields, or play at Cudgels, or go to the Morrice Dancers, or any such things on the Sabbath Day. But, Thanks be to God, the Awe of those things, which by the Policy of our Puritanical Invaders, was impressed on the Minds of Our People, begins to wear off again . . . [20]

Others were less nostalgic but would probably have despised the enthusiasm of the societies and felt that popular recreations were, on the whole, harmless enough.

Much of traditional popular culture did then survive into the eighteenth century, fiercely clung to by the labouring poor as their right by custom, a heritage, even though much of the superstructure of rite and ritual was anachronistic (a word only coined in the late seventeenth century). Nor was it vital only in the countryside. Even in London and the big towns leisure and recreation appear to have shared many of the characteristics of rural culture. There was no sharp division between the culture of town and country. After all, the country came literally into the middle of towns, with dairy herds being pastured within their ambit, and town life continued to be influenced by the rhythms of the agricultural year; townspeople enjoyed the same physical activities and blood sports and their fairs and wakes differed more in size than essential characteristics.

There are, however, significant qualifications that have to be made to this image of a popular culture of wakes, ales and bloodsports. There is in the first place the nature of the source material. We have ample evidence that the recreational calendar was indeed as has been described and that blood sports and football were important recreations. Much of the detailed evidence comes, however, from gentlemen mediators, some of whom were concerned to point to the social and economic disadvantages of such festivals and recreations, some to defend them as part of the Englishman's heritage and others – for antiquarianism had now arrived on the scene – to seize upon their traditional and picturesque features.[21] There is then the question of how accurate a picture of any culture we get from concentrating upon major festivals and sporting events – a depiction of contemporary popular culture which concentrated upon holidays, cup finals and pop concerts would tell us something but by no means everything about it. How people dressed, what possessions, however meagre, they valued and what they read or had read to them could be as important to any investigation of a culture. Above all a concentration upon such cultural forms can result in an oversimplification of eighteenth century society and culture and the ignoring of important social strata and cultural phenomena. A new, more commercialised culture was in the making.

A two-tier model of high culture and low or popular culture works best with societies which have little in the way of middle strata. The two traditions co-exist but nevertheless impinge upon each other. Although it is only the elite who participate in both cultures there is a two-way traffic in the adaptation by one culture of forms originally developed by the other. There is both 'sinking' and 'rising'. Dances, for instance, were usually developed within peasant society but were then taken up and adapted by the upper orders, while styles of architecture tended to descend the social scale as did much elite poetry and drama, often ending up in modified form in popular song or with village players. The play within the play in Shakespeare's *Midsummer Night's Dream* is an example of a parody of the end result of such a process. The romances of chivalry began at court but were long preserved in popular culture.

In a society with many and various middle strata, stretching with scarcely perceptible gradations from ranks of society adjacent to the labouring poor to those mixing and inter-marrying with the gentry and aristocracy, a two-tier model works less perfectly and the charting of cultural tides becomes more complex. Eighteenth century England was such a society. Although some fifty per cent of the population would be classified as labouring poor with – by some calculations – insufficient income for survival but for poor relief, charity or dishonest gains, and although enormous wealth and power was possessed by the less than two per cent of the population who made up the largely landowning upper orders, there was a very large middle to society. Even if we consign artisans and poorer alehouse keepers to the lower orders (and such people did at least own modest property even if only the tools of their trade), the middle ranks were a substantial group making up over thirty per cent of the population and in receipt of more than fifty per cent of the total national income.[22] They were seen by contemporaries as ranging from very small farmers, shopkeepers and tailors to more prosperous figures like doctors, lawyers and substantial farmers, finally reaching upper levels where rich bankers and merchants were demarcated from gentry and aristocracy more by the source of their wealth than the amount of it.

It would be convenient and tidy to move to a three-tier model and to identify a homogeneous culture of the middle ranks, but their culture was as diverse as their means. At the top it overlapped with the culture of the landowning upper orders and at the bottom it was often indistinguishable from that of the labouring poor. In places it could appear to be a distinct culture of its own, often synonymous with the culture of dissent or of the godly, and opposed both to the worldly and pleasure loving aspects of high culture and to the lewd and fleshly pursuits of the poor. But dissent, even after the expansion of Methodism, never accounted for more than a minority within the middle ranks and found its mass following among the lower orders. The effect of the middle ranks of society was to accelerate the process of cultural transmission, to modify or adapt aspects of high culture and, most fittingly, to commercialise culture into a marketable commodity.

Eighteenth century English society was hierarchical and status-conscious. It shared this characteristic with other European countries. It was not, however, a caste society with status determined purely by birth and with legal barriers determining who should do different sorts of work. It was an achieving society in which status and honours generally followed, at least in the long run, the acquisition of wealth. It was also characterised by the spirit of emulation. Upward social mobility can be measured by the numbers of people achieving a station in life superior to that in which they were born, but the desire for such mobility is evidenced by the degree to which those who remain within a given strata nevertheless emulate the life style of that immediately above them.

The history of fashion is an important guide to social and cultural attitudes. Jonathan Swift described 'Opinions like Fashions' as 'always descending from those of Quality to the Middle Sort, and thence to the Vulgar, where at length they are dropt and vanish'. But fashions only really did this in England. Fashion itself was common to all European countries but it was largely an upper class phenomenon and for the most part the fashion cycle reached no further down the social scale. In England the fashions of aristocracy and gentry were copied by merchants and farmers and their wives, taken up by servants and often ended up with labourers. The custom of revealing one's place and station in life by one's dress was thus partially eroded in England, itself suggesting that the sense of corporate identity within orders and trades was similarly in decline. Servants seem to have led the way amongst the lower ranks of society in the emulation of the fashions of the elite; they were in a good position to observe fashion's nuances and to obtain the cast-offs of their masters and mistresses. Most significantly there was no national costume or peasant dress in England save for the smock-frock which continued to be worn by agricultural labourers in the south.

Nor was it simply in dress that greater prosperity, combined with cheaper manufacturing processes and new marketing techniques, was enabling each stratum of society to emulate the one above it. People increasingly aspired to housing, domestic furnishings and ornaments, and to food and drink, which would previously have been out of reach to persons of their rank and station. Coaches became the prized possessions of the professional classes, tenant farmers purchased clocks and silverware and later in the century Wedgwood pottery, while even the lower orders down to the labouring poor were to benefit from cotton goods and to change their dietary habits, insisting on wheaten bread and mass-produced porter. Those in superior social positions have never taken kindly to evidence of the increased prosperity of those in inferior stations and their aspirations to comforts and refinements. Singing and piano lessons for tenant farmers' daughters in the eighteenth century, and holidays abroad for the working classes in the late twentieth, have similarly been received with sarcasm mingled with outrage. There was an unceasing flood of tracts bewailing the spread of luxury, pride and vanity among the middle and lower ranks. One moralist argued that it should be an offence to dress in the manner peculiar to a gentleman if one was not such by birth and fortune. Others raged against the aspirations of tradesmen to gentility, while servants who wore velvet breeches and shopkeepers who wore wigs, and even swords, were a constant target.

The increasing availability of the printed word and one of the highest literacy rates in Europe fed upon each other to produce a publishing revolution. Much of high culture became available to those with rudimentary education. Here one might toy with the notion of a scale of accessibility of high cultures; as J.H. Plumb has pointed out the mandarin culture of China was very inaccessible because of the difficulty of learning the written language with its thousands of characters, while the Western alphabet made learning to read easy.[23] The culture of the upper orders in much of early modern Europe, however, remained comparatively inaccessible, given the importance of Latin and the degree to which in many areas the everyday language of the elite was not the same as that of the lower orders; but much, though not all, of the literary culture of eighteenth century England was within the reach of a person with some education.

But a wider reading public did not simply facilitate the transmission of the literary culture which already existed. It also resulted in the emergence of new forms of literature — the novel and the periodical essay — and the development of newspapers. One effect of what one author has called a '. . . change in the centre of gravity of the reading public' was the rise of easier forms of literary entertainment than classical literature or poetry.[24]

The novel fulfilled such a demand and provided readers from among the middle ranks of society – especially the growing numbers of educated and leisured women – with a literary form suited to their tastes. The novels of the period placed an emphasis upon originality in their plots and upon the individual experiences of central characters. They were more realistic than previous literary genres, increasingly giving their characters ordinary rather than symbolic names and paying attention to accuracy and verisimilitude in their descriptions of environment, especially of interiors. The novel, because it developed in the context of a widening readership and appealed to the tastes and aspirations of that readership, has often been seen as a middle class art form. It is important to distinguish here, however, between form and ideological content. W.A. Speck has written:

> The early novel . . . displays surprisingly genteel values.
> After many vicissitudes their heroines must end happily

married to a country gentleman if not to peers, while their heroes must finish up as landed gentry in charge of broad acres, which they have either been fraudulently denied or have earned through their superior merits. These are scarcely bourgeois aspirations.[25]

Or are they? Perhaps the essence of bourgeois culture, at any rate in England, has been to aspire to the status of the gentleman, especially the landed gentleman, with the proviso that the worthy man can attain what others inherit.

Rather than being a middle class art form, the novel testified to the increasing homogeneity of the wealthier merchants and bankers with the gentry: their similar attitudes to individual liberties and property rights and the ease of cultural and social connections between them. There emerged in the novel and in the *Spectator* and the *Tatler* a literature for the Quality. Ian Watt has described such literature as a '. . . compromise, between the wits and the less educated, between the belles lettres and religious instruction'.[26] The new periodicals offered a secular puritanism as an entry to the world of letters. One could be a gentleman and a member of polite society while being critical of the loose morals and hedonism of the sophisticated world.

With the growth of the reading public and the decline of patronage by court and nobility a publishing industry emerged. Commercial considerations became more important. The author's patron was now the publisher and bookseller and the readership or the market the determinant of success. The inevitable result was a tendency to seek a wider market in the lower echelons of the reading public. Larger sales and cheaper paper could bring books, periodicals and newspapers within the reach of such a market. The *Gentleman's Magazine*, far more successful in its sales than the *Tatler* and *Spectator*, was a sign of such a tendency. The name is itself significant, for those secure in the status of gentleman would not need to be so flattered.

The expansion of the press in the first half of the century was also considerable. The first daily newspaper started in 1702 and by 1760 there were four daily London papers and six which appeared thrice weekly while by the latter date there were also 35 provincial papers. Such expansion was achieved despite the imposition of a tax on sales in 1712 and its successive increases thereafter.

Differing estimates of the size of the reading public and its composition have been made and obviously the answers to such questions as how many people may have read a single copy of a paper or book are conjectural. It seems certain however that it extended as far down the social scale as craftsmen and tradesmen, that it included increasing numbers of women and that it was more numerous in towns and most heavily concentrated in London.

The lower fringes of the reading public were where popular culture and modified high culture met. The ballads and chapbooks which were sold for as little as a half-penny or a penny contained much of the traditional material of oral popular culture: chivalric tales, legends, accounts of extraordinary events and, of course, accounts of both executions and the last words of the executed. Peculiar to England were tales of commercial achievement, the rise to fame or fortune of such entrepreneurs as Dick Whittington, Jack of Newbury and Simon Eyre. At the same time, however, novels, often in abbreviated form, were made available to this class of readership via serialisation in newspapers and in chapbooks. The practice of publishing ever cheaper editions, often in several volumes (*Clarissa* appeared in eight volumes, *Tom Jones* in six), increased the accessibility of novels, while the circulating libraries and private subscription libraries which expanded rapidly around mid-century made both fiction and non-fiction available at the cost of half a guinea per annum or a few pence a time.

The explosion in publishing was just the most spectacular example of the development of a commercialised leisure and entertainment industry in the eighteenth century, but it also facilitated the commercialisation of many leisure pursuits. As newspapers started to carry more advertisements so musical concerts, dramas, circuses, cricket matches and boxing contests were publicised and popularised by them. By the middle of the century an entertainment industry existed with the potential for vast growth. Much of it was evolved for the Quality, helping to create the world of spas and resorts, assembly rooms, theatres and public concerts which transformed the social life of 'society'. J.H. Plumb has argued:

> Theatre, music, dancing, sport – these were the cultural pastimes for which the prosperous gentry and the new leisured middle class hungered. But their houses were not large enough for private theatres, for private orchestras and private concerts, nor had they the money to lavish on such conspicuous aristocratic consumption as a string of race-horses.[27]

The transition from private to public entertainment is a profoundly important step even if the aim is, via high prices and the insistence on a certain mode of dress, to keep the audience exclusive. It opens entertainment to the man who can pay the price and at the same time creates the entrepreneur or impresario who may well feel that profits can be increased by a lower price and a larger audience. The nineteenth century was to see a continual conflict at the race course, at the theatre and at the seaside between those who wished to retain exclusivity and those who wished to exploit wider markets.

Almost as important as publishing for its impact on the commercialisation of leisure was the public house, which was to become the principal centre for entrepreneurs of entertainment for the working classes. The term 'public house' or 'inn' could, of course, embrace the entire social spectrum from the meanest unlicensed alehouse to the most sumptuous of coaching inns or those taverns in market towns where gentry, farmers and merchants transacted the business of the day.

With the progressive withdrawal of the church from popular recreations in the sixteenth and seventeenth centuries the alehouse appears to have occupied an increasingly central place in village life. The impact of Puritanism was to erode alternative recreational facilities; church and churchyard ceased to be the focus for festivities while clergy and magistrates condemned disorderly public sports. The alehouse became a haven for traditional recreations, the place where births, marriages and funerals were saluted by ritual drinking and even the centre for the charity of communal self-help where 'bidales' (drinking parties to raise money for a needy neighbour) were held.

Despite the restrictions placed upon it by the Justices, the attacks of Puritans and its increased supervision by village elites, the alehouse survived into the eighteenth century with many of its ancillary functions intact. It may well be that in villages controlled by a single landlord the conduct of alehouses was closely supervised by squire or steward, and that in many others village elites concerned with work discipline and sobriety cut down the number of alehouses and enforced notions of orderliness, but the alehouse remained the centre of warmth, conviviality and the place to sing, play the fiddle or dance.

In towns, inns and alehouses served even more varied functions. They were often specialised in terms of their clientele, not merely stratified in serving different ranks of society but specifically catering for particular occupations and trades. They were where men were paid as well as where they spent some of their wages; and they served as employment exchanges, meeting places for trade associations and

35

friendly societies as well as centres for such varied leisure activities as skittles, cock-fighting or improving lectures.

Inns provided a ladder of opportunity for the efficient and imaginative publican who could at once dispense cheer and ale, keep order and preside over the many activities which took place on his premises. In Northampton, we are told, the landlords of the three inns at the top of the scale, able to accommodate some eighty travellers and a large number of horses, had usually graduated from smaller establishments in the area and when one died 'a general post ensued in half the inns of the town'.[28]

Inns, taverns and alehouses thus offered many services to the different ranks of society. They provided comfort for the gentleman traveller, such as that which impressed an early nineteenth century visitor to England:

> In the country, even in small villages, you find them equally neat and well attended. Cleanliness, great convenience, and even elegance, are always combined in them; and a stranger is never invited to eat, sit and sleep in the same room, as in the German inns. . . . The table service generally consists of silver and porcelain: the furniture is well contrived; the beds are always excellent; and the friendly, flickering fire never fails to greet you.[29]

They were often places where much business was conducted, especially trade in agricultural products. For artisans and labourers they were meeting places, reading rooms and sports pavilions. They did much more than dispense drink for, just as drink was an inseparable accompaniment to so much of life, entertainment, like work, was closely attached to the inn. Landlords were already entrepreneurs of leisure in the eighteenth century, marketing their commodity with increasing zest and well placed to exploit an expanding market in the nineteenth.

Another institution which, like the inn, was to display a great capacity for survival in its own right and also act as the nursery bed for the growth of more specialised forms of entertainment, was the fair. The fair was both a traditional institution, firmly rooted in the old religious and economic calendars, and one able to adapt to new environments. Fairs had combined a number of functions: the celebration of religious festivals, the furtherance of trade, the hiring of labour and an opportunity for pleasure and recreation. By the eighteenth century the religious purpose was long forgotten and many of the larger fairs, especially those held in or adjacent to large towns, had lost their trading or hiring functions and become purely pleasure-orientated.

Eighteenth century fairs formed the nucleus of a highly commercialised leisure and entertainments industry. The commercial character was hardly new. Why else, save in the pursuit of a living, had men traversed the country in the company of other travelling players or with attendant dancing bears, dwarves or bearded ladies in previous centuries? But a new professionalism was creeping in; the most prominent showmen at the bigger fairs presented ambitious programmes with elaborate wardrobes and numerous actors, clowns and acrobats; the owners of menageries and freak shows vied with each other to present greater variety and offer yet more wondrous marvels to their customers. Long before the coming of the railways, improvements in roads made it possible for the better organised and more affluent showmen to move around regional circuits appearing at all the principal fairs. Advertising by means of hand-bills supplemented older forms of publicity, such as the processional advance of the company to the fair-ground and the drumming-up of an audience from the platform outside the theatrical booth.

The world of the fair is a rich quarry for those historians who wish to portray the survival of a society in which custom and community were supreme. Many fairs retained their trading and hiring functions and for many towns and villages the coming of the fair marked the time of annual holiday. They were seen as the signal for the release of high spirits and the temporary suspension of authority, and many local customs and rituals were associated with them. There was certainly a saturnalian aspect to them and often the Lord of Misrule was present. In the streets around Smithfield, the beginning of St Bartholomew Fair in 1785

> ... was according to annual custom, ushered in by Lady Holland's Mob, accompanied with a charming band of music, consisting of marrow bones and cleavers tin kettles etc., etc.[30]

The parading by the youth of the town of Sherborne in Dorset before the opening of the Pack Monday Fair, with their rough music, continued according to one authority until 1964.[31] Many of the traditional ingredients of customary holidays are associated with fairs: a considerable degree of license, the reversal of sexual roles, special ceremonies for declaring them open like that at Croydon

37

where the key to the fair was paraded through the town, and the
consumption of special food, pork in some instances, roast goose in
others. One cannot, however, ignore the pronounced commercial
individualism of the showmen and their capacity to speculate, inno-
vate and diversify. Merchants and manufacturers might well be
foremost in attempting to suppress fairs as unconducive to public order
and decency and as impediments to work discipline – what they failed
to realise was that these colourful and to them disreputable fellows
were brothers under the skin, entrepreneurs of leisure and as much part
of the dynamism of a capitalist economy as any iron master.

The entertainment available at fairs was bewildering in its variety.
At the bigger fairs there were booths offering drama, sometimes
classical themes, occasionally abbreviated Shakespeare but more often
melodramas, supplemented and interpolated by other divisions. At St
Bartholomew's Fair in 1747 the manager Hussey presented *Tamerlane
the Great* with singing and 'several curious equilibres on the slack rope
by Mahomet Achmed Vizaro Mussalmo a Turk just arrived from
Constantinople, who not only balances without a pole, but also plays a
variety of excellent airs on the violin when on the slack pole. . . .' A rival
booth offered the *Siege of Troy*, and an entertainment of singing and
dancing, while another proffered a pantomime entertainment called
Frolicsome Lasses with singing and dancing between the acts and a
fireworks display at the end.[32] Fairground booths were no place for the
serious or the squeamish. The English appetite for freaks and mon-
strosities, which still exists and is given vicarious satisfaction by the
Guinness Book of Records, was lavishly provided for. A succession of
dwarfs was paraded before the public of which the most famous was
probably Maria Teresa, the Corsican fairy, who was thirty-four inches
high and weighed twenty-six pounds. Giants, usually Scottish or Irish,
appear to have been equally popular, as were bearded women, wild
black women and the spectacularly fat such as William Whitehead the
twenty-two stone boy. Good sized fairs generally included menageries
and waxworks and few were without booths exhibiting such delights as
mermaids, seven-legged mares and cannibals' heads. Educated
animals were a perennial attraction and throughout the century a
succession of intelligent horses and pigs, the latter usually called Toby
in memory of an outstanding porcine intellectual, amazed audiences.

For much of the eighteenth century there were close links between
the theatrical booths at the principal London fairs and the established
theatre. Well known actors and actresses from Drury Lane or Covent
Garden would appear at St Bartholomew's or Southwark Fair; Henry

Fielding promoted plays and operas at those fairs and with a partner was instrumental in getting much of the company of the Haymarket Theatre to take part in a production of *The Beggar's Opera* at Southwark. The limitation of St Bartholomew's Fair to three days and the suppression of Southwark Fair in 1760 put an end to the easy exchange of personnel between the fairs and the London stage but the theatre of the fairs remained a valuable training ground for actors and actresses who were later to become famous in established theatres. More importantly fairs nurtured whole genres of entertainment, such as the pantomime, the menagerie and the circus, which were to develop independently, and were also to prove themselves a fecund influence on the nineteenth century theatre and music hall.

Historians have discerned two broad and contradictory currents of change modifying the cultural map of pre-industrial English society. The first was the erosion and decay of an old popular culture as the upper orders ceased to participate and then withdrew their patronage, and as burgeoning industrialisation destroyed the social and economic framework which gave it expression; it is also held that such erosion was materially assisted by the attack upon the more public manifestations of such a culture by a combination of religious evangelicism and a secular desire to promote work discipline. The second was the development of a more commercialised culture: this is most clearly discernible within the middle strata of society and involved a modification of both the content and the transmission of high culture in the interests of polite society; but popular cultural products such as circuses, cock-fights, and prize-fights were also seen as marketable commodities as entrepreneurs discovered the potential of a wider clientele.

These two currents of change should not be regarded as separate, one culture dying while another grew up in its stead. The old culture was not the folk culture many have perceived it to be. In the early nineteenth century much of the superstructure of custom and ritual was shed but this had in many ways already become cut off from its socio-economic roots. More importantly, as the economy changed with industrialisation and as the country became more urbanised, popular culture gradually ceased to move to the rhythms of agriculture and responded instead to the mechanical beat of the factory; this was to affect holidays, their number and duration, and in the long run to make blood sports less important for the majority of artisans and labourers. But much of the old culture fulfilled important needs, whether in country or in town, and as such was infinitely adaptable.

39

The most obvious instance of adaptability is the inn or alehouse which was as capable of providing the main community centre for an urban working class as of continuing as a centre for village life; it was to be the power house for the development of a great deal of nineteenth-century popular culture. Much of the culture of the urban nineteenth-century working class was thus to be a modification and commercialisation of aspects of the old popular culture.

Perhaps the most important development was the increase in communication between the two cultural tiers. Peter Burke has commented:

> The paradox remains that the more communication takes place between the two tiers, the less useful is the concept of two tiers; yet there is no other way of talking about that interaction.[33]

The importance and the size of the middle ranks of society increased such communication and, indeed, they may be seen as acting as a transmission belt between the tiers. The mobility and tendency to emulation of English society increased the speed and the depth of the 'sinking' process from high to low culture. But 'rising' was also a feature of the new society; it would not be long before Queen Victoria patronised the circus and the public schools took up football. Just at the moment when, it is alleged, the upper orders finally gave up their participation in and patronage of the old popular culture a reshaping of the entire field of cultural relationships was taking place.

TWO

Popular culture and its enemies

'The present age was not improved in anything so much as in their puppet-shows; which, by throwing out Punch and his wife Joan, and such idle trumpery, were at last brought to be a rational entertainment. I remember', said he, 'when I first took to the business, there was a great deal of low stuff that did very well to make folks laugh; but was never calculated to improve the morals of young people, which certainly ought to be principally aimed at in every puppet show: for why may not good and instructive lessons be conveyed this way, as well as any other? My figures are as big as the life, and they represent the life in every particular; and I question not but people rise from my little drama as much improved as they do from the great.' 'I would by no means degrade the ingenuity of your profession', answered Jones; 'but I should have been glad to have seen my old acquaintance Master Punch, for all that; and so far from improving, I think, by leaving out him and his merry wife Joan, you have spoiled your puppet-show.

Henry Fielding, Tom Jones, 1748

There can be little doubt that there has been, during what we conventionally regard as the modern period, a pronounced tendency for some – and they have often been the most vocal – of the educated to regard popular culture as a problem and as a subject for reform. This chapter is concerned with the attacks upon popular culture in the eighteenth and early nineteenth centuries, but later chapters will suggest that critics of the attitudes, values, recreations and customs of the mass of the population in the later nineteenth and in the twentieth centuries, whether conservatives or socialists, rational recreationalists or Workers' Educational Association tutors, shared a common lineage of distrust and contempt for the popular culture of their day.

The attack upon the life-styles and the recreations of the common people and the attempt to reform them is usually seen to have gathered impetus in the sixteenth century and with the Reformation. Its major thrusts, which many have seen as inextricably linked, were a religious concern that much of popular culture was irreligious, immoral and profane and a secular perception that it was detrimental to economic efficiency and social order.

It would, of course, be naive to assume that a distaste for aspects of the leisure habits of the mass of the population and a concern for their beliefs and superstitions was not to be found in medieval society. It is unlikely that clerics never bewailed the lewdness and drunkenness of their parishioners, that lord or knight never wished the agricultural workforce produced more or tradesmen never expressed the hope that apprentices be less idle. Indeed, we know that from the time of St Augustine and before, a succession of churchmen attacked the pastimes and festivities of the populace. There does, however, appear to have been a significant change in attitude towards popular recreations in England during and after the sixteenth century, as indeed there was in early modern Europe as a whole. Sporadic criticisms and efforts at reform were replaced by a more concerted attack. As one authority has commented:

> There were more frequent attacks on traditional popular culture and there were more systematic attempts to purge it of both its 'paganism' and its 'licence'. This movement has, of course, a good deal to do with the Protestant and Catholic reformations, for the reform of the church, as it was understood at the time, necessarily involved the reform of what we call popular culture.[1]

Both the Reformation and the Counter-Reformation saw a determined effort to purify religious observance by ridding it of its pagan and superstitious elements. Protestant reformers were also concerned to stamp out Catholic practices and beliefs. Thus Catholics and Protestants alike attacked festivals such as Carnival and popular religious drama while Protestants also attacked the cults of saints and the celebration of their days. Religious reformers objected to much of popular culture, too, on moral grounds in that it encouraged drunkenness and sexual immorality and that many festivals were occasions for violence and disorder.

The religious attack upon popular culture must not be seen, even in secular terms, as purely negative. In some ways the Reformation and, to a lesser extent, the Counter-Reformation can be considered as movements with a pronounced democratic streak, emphasising as they did the equality of individual souls. The ways in which the common people worshipped, thought and played were seen to matter and reform was thought necessary for the salvation of souls. A religion contaminated by paganism and superstition, and a way of life in which religious observance alternated with fleshly and lewd pursuits were not good enough for even the craftsman or peasant. Religious reformers sought not just to eradicate what was pagan and immoral from popular culture but to replace that culture by one deeply permeated by religion and characterised by piety, sobriety and abstinence which would express itself through prayer, devotional books and psalms.

Paralleling and interacting with the attack by religious reformers on the life-styles, recreations and festivals of the poor was a new stress upon the importance and duty of every man to work and a consequential attack upon the idleness of labourers. There seems little reason to doubt that the new emphasis upon work that historians have detected in the sixteenth century was connected with, not the emergence, but the increasing ubiquity of commercial considerations and individual economic ambitions in agriculture and manufacturing alike. That most men prefer leisure to work appears an unexceptionable enough proposition. It is probable, however, that it is only in certain sorts of societies and economies that this propensity produces severe problems.

We are told by anthropologists that in primitive societies there is no real division between work and leisure and the individual is unconscious as to whether he is at one or the other.[2] Historians of the Middle Ages have impressed upon us the close relationship between work and leisure in medieval society; both were communal activities and the rituals and timetable of the latter were set by the former. Certainly in a peasant society, where work is largely to obtain the means of subsistence for the family unit, it is likely that men will work hard enough to fulfil that simple aim; in so far as late medieval England was a peasant society – and as we have seen, doubts have been expressed about this – the problem of idleness may have been minimised. Conversely, in a developed consumer economy, where not only is there plenty to spend one's wages on, but new needs are perpetually invented, then both stick and carrot operate in favour of work. It is in the half-way house between the peasant and the fully developed market economy and, *mutatis mutandis*, in some present day socialist societies, that idleness and the pull of leisure away from work become a major problem.

The incentive to work harder was lacking for many of the labouring poor in early modern England. Many agricultural workers lived in a partial wage economy, being paid partly and sometimes largely in kind. There were, to be sure, several sticks that could be wielded to force men to do the minimum amount of work but the carrots to persuade them to work harder were singularly lacking. Employers strove to impose greater discipline and regular hours upon the labour force but their methods were largely to attempt to increase working hours, and consequently cut down the time available for leisure, and to keep wages as low as possible on the grounds that any reward above that required for bare subsistence would merely encourage idleness. No doubt they were right, at least in the short-term. Higher wages would probably have simply increased the propensity of workers in manufacturing to make St Monday stretch into Tuesday and Wednesday as well while, his basic needs satisfied, the farmworker would simply have spent more time in the alehouse. In the long run, however, it was to be not low wages, legislation, the influence of religion or changes in the administration of the Poor Law but the growth of new patterns of leisure and consumption, pump-primed by limited wage increases, that was to lead to a more positive attitude to work.

The desire of religious reformers to transform men into pious, chaste, sober and godly citizens and of economic reformers to make them equally chaste and sober in the interests of economic efficiency and social discipline achieved a dominant intellectual position and maximum political leverage in the mid-seventeenth and again in the early nineteenth centuries. In both periods the temporary ascendancy of puritan religiosity, sexual repression and patriarchal authoritarian attitudes both within the family and towards the labour force can be partly explained by a sense of social and political crisis. Rapid social and economic change, an expanding population and the desuetude of older forms of social control led to the maximum influence of those who called for moral regeneration and stricter disciplining of the lives of the lower orders.

The Restoration saw a reaction to the attacks on popular culture of the Puritan period, which lasted well into the eighteenth century. Not only did the recreations and institutions which had been suppressed –theatre, gambling, maypoles, cock-fighting and brothels – make a considerable come-back but country gentlemen as Justices of the Peace showed little enthusiasm for the role of moral policemen. To a considerable extent the paths of sexual morality and the law went separate ways as the powers of Church courts declined and the number of cases brought before them dropped sharply. Justices and parish vestries remained concerned about the consequences of fornication, in the shape of illegitimate births, but it is difficult not to believe that the concern was more economic – a desire to keep down the poor rates – than moral.

Concern about the moral standards, the thriftlessness and hedonism of the lower orders, and the encouragement to these qualities given by festivals, fairs and holidays continued to be a contrapuntal theme accompanying the more relaxed and permissive attitude that characterised the early eighteenth century. Christopher Hill has argued that 'Much of the social content of puritan doctrine was ultimately accepted outside the ranks of the nonconformists and even by the apparently triumphant Church of England'.[3] Lawrence Stone has perceived such doctrine as being preserved intact by some sections of the middle ranks who had since the sixteenth century been particularly attracted by 'reticence, sobriety and thrift, punctuality, self-discipline and industry, chastity, prudery and piety'.[4] It was only, however, in the later decades of the century that such doctrine again found impetus and was able to make substantial headway in a renewed call for moral regeneration and social discipline.

Historians have found some foundation for the reformers' belief that the labouring classes were slipping from the control of respectable society, that their sexual attitudes were permissive, that popular culture was hedonistic and bawdy and that public festivals and recreations were generally accompanied by heavy drinking and often ended in violence and sometimes riot.

The statistics carefully gleaned from parish records do suggest that pre-nuptial conceptions rose as high as forty per cent and that there was a considerable increase in the illegitimacy rate during the eighteenth century. Such figures contrast with the exceptionally low levels for both rates found in the mid-seventeenth century. Lawrence Stone points to a significant change having taken place in plebeian sexual behaviour, sexual relations before marriage becoming the norm amongst the labouring poor and to some extent among artisans and small tradesmen as well.[5] Edward Shorter has argued that there was a sexual revolution borne of modernisation and involving the dissolution of traditional cultural patterns and the growth of individual self-expression.[6]

Important qualifications must however, be made to this broad picture of increasing extra-marital sexual activity. In the first place the mid-seventeenth century trough followed on an early seventeenth century peak. Secondly, although it appears likely that the picture of extraordinary sexual probity which emerges for the mid-seventeenth century reflects the success of Puritanism in both proselytising its mores and policing its parishes, other factors may have exaggerated this picture: the unreliability of registration in a time of war and disorder and the degree to which the consequences of extra-marital sexual activity were successfully concealed.

What appears to have happened is that the age at time of marriage, although it remained high by modern standards, decreased during the eighteenth century. It was not a consistent trend for, as Wrigley and Schofield have shown, it was sensitive to the economic climate, declining after a period of low food prices and rising again after a period of high prices,[7] a development which one historian has termed Malthusianism 'unencumbered by the strictures of learned gentlemen'.[8] The illegitimacy rate, which continued to be a low proportion (some two per cent throughout the country) of recorded births, rose in line with the lower rate of marriage.

The control of the church and established authority over the courtship and marital customs of the common people had never been absolutely secure and there had usually been some tacit compromise between the rules and ceremonies of the church and those of popular belief and custom. The social control exercised by these latter could, however, be as effective as the former. The post-Restoration church never re-established intimate contact with or control over plebeian society but the evidence that its mores were disregarded aroused consternation. Much of that consternation was based upon a misunderstanding of popular attitudes towards marriage and upon a failure to recognise that what could appear libertine and permissive to an outsider, was in fact a parallel moral order.

Popular opinion continued, with some basis in law, to adhere to an older tradition that marriage was essentially a private affair and that espousals constituted a marriage. Partly for reasons of privacy and partly to avoid expense, many couples preferred to be married in districts immune from superior ecclesiastical supervision, such as the Fleet or St Pancras, rather than in the parish church, and in many communities it was usual to recognise consensual unions as *de facto* marriages. It is instructive, however, to note that many considered the performance of the ceremony by a clergyman, however decayed or corrupt, important while those in consensual unions were normally anxious for some public recognition of their 'marriage'. Espousals were widely regarded as important and to be as binding as the marriage itself:

> A contract publicly entered into before witnesses and marked by two overt actions, the kissing of the woman by the man and the presentation of gifts – often a gold ring, or, oddly enough half a gold ring – constituted a binding marriage, provided only that the couple then proceeded to sexual intercourse.[9]

'Pre-nuptial fornication' might be an offence punishable in the Archdeacon's court but, provided it took place after espousal, it was approved by popular opinion.

The Marriage Act of 1753 cleared up the question of what was and what was not a legal marriage; from then on only properly conducted church weddings were to count. One effect of the act may have been to push up the illegitimacy rate, in that parish clerks were far less likely to consider consensual unions as legal. It seems clear, however, that such unions continued to be prevalent and that espousals also continued to be regarded as tantamount to marriage. That many of the lower orders considered church weddings dispensable is demonstrated by the fact that where an alternative continued to exist in parishes adjacent to the Scottish border it was widely made use of.

The attitudes towards courtship and marriage of labouring people, far from suggesting a casual approach towards sex and marriage, point to a general belief in the importance of stable unions and of fatherhood and to the ability of public opinion to command obedience to the community's values. It may well have been that there was a weakening of some of the unofficial parental and community controls – fondling and petting giving way to full intercourse long before formal espousals, and an increase in the propensity of the fathers of illegitimate children to make off – while the existence of a sub-society of the bastardy-prone has been suggested by recent studies, but there are few reasons for believing a moral revolution to have taken place.

The existence of an unofficial system of divorce also testifies to the importance attached to marriage. In the absence of the possibility of divorce, bigamy on the part of deserted husbands and wives was one solution while the custom of ritual 'wife-sale' was another. This practice appears to have had a medieval origin but was much reported in newspapers in the late eighteenth century. The best known example is of course fictional, the selling of Susan by Michael

Henchard in Hardy's *The Mayor of Casterbridge.* Far from the drunken, spur of the moment affair depicted in that novel, however, wife selling was a ritualised ceremony regarded by popular opinion as a perfectly legitimate form of divorce. It generally took place at markets where a halter was put round the woman's neck, she was led around and then sold to the highest bidder. Usually the bargain was pre-arranged and the successful bidder was the wife's lover who would often then 'marry her'. Prices could vary from sixpence to as much as six guineas. Where ritual was neglected there could be an attempt to use the processes of law to underwrite an agreement the law itself would not have recognised as legitimate, as with the blacksmith from Cliffe near Leeds, who, 'sold his wife, a smart young woman, with a child, to one of his journeymen, for two guineas, agreeably to an engagement drawn up by an attorney'.[10]

 Such a practice was probably not very widespread and the attention devoted to it by newspapers is largely explained by its sensational and scandalous nature, but it does illustrate the gulf between respectable and popular opinion. In their sexual behaviour, in their approach to courtship and marriage and in much else, the customs of the labouring poor were an affront to respectable society. If the manner in which many of the lower orders entered the world was often unlicensed, the somewhat ribald accompaniment to their manner of leaving it could also be a subject for criticism. Henry Bourne, Curate of All Saints Chapel in Newcastle upon Tyne, complained of the, 'Sport, and Drinking and Lewdness' which accompanied wakes for the dead. 'How unchristian, instead of becoming sorrow and decent Gravity, to put on an unbecoming Joy and undecent Pastime.'[11] John Brand, similarly a Newcastle clergyman but more of a rationalist and a cynic, who took over and extended Bourne's work later in the century, wrote rather facetiously about such wakes, where the corpse too often ended up as the centre-piece of a drunken party:

> They still continue to resemble too much the ancient Bacchanalian orgies. – An instance of depravity that highly disgraces human nature! It would be treating the serious Subject with too much levity, to say, that if the inconsiderate Wretches, who abuse such solemn Meetings, think at all, they think with Epicurean licentiousness, that since Life is so uncertain, no opportunity should be neglected of transmitting it; and that the Loss, by the Death of one relation, should be made up as soon as possible by the Birth of another.'[12]

Drink was notoriously cheap during the eighteenth century, especially during the so-called 'gin period' when London appeared to many to be drowning in a sea of gin. The early seventeen-thirties were somewhat exceptional, one of those peaks of heavy drinking when higher wages combined with the low price of alcohol to alter the regular pattern of consumption, but, even after the passing of the Gin Act of 1751 drink, and plenty of it, continued to be a facet of the life style of the lower orders as, indeed, it was of the upper ranks. Beer was the companion of work as well as leisure and was commonly regarded as a source of health and strength. To a degree this was true as, especially in the towns, it was a far safer drink than either water or milk. Francis Place's remark that for the urban poor in the late eighteenth century sex and drinking were the only pleasures in life and of the two '. . . drunkenness is by the far most desired',[13] is well known. Those who, like Place, have dragged themselves up from humble beginnings are, especially when writing in old age, wont to exaggerate the bleakness of their early life, but it seems certain that drink did play an enormously important part in the lives of the poor. To respectable society labouring people seemed only too ready to overindulge whenever they had money in their pockets; this was at the same time a sign of their indolence and want of thrift, a spur to their sexual immorality and a constant threat to public order.

Many historians have seen the propensity of the lower orders to riot as being not so much a danger to social stability but a necessary and inevitable ingredient in the maintenance of basic stability. The mock riot that was Carnival or the Feast of Fools and which allowed the social order to be overturned for the day in the interests of its long term reinforcement, the bread riot that was almost a market force for negotiating a 'fair price', or the frequent riots when the polls were declared at elections can all be interpreted as part of the functioning of a social system. Fairs, football matches and executions were frequently the scene of riots and the mock battles around the maypole between the forces of 'winter' and 'summer' could become very real. Whether riots were more frequent or more serious in the eighteenth century than previously or whether respectable society was simply more worried by them and less patient of them is debatable. Possibly in towns with an expanding population, many of whom did not have roots where they resided, the unofficial controls which kept boisterous occasions within bounds may have been breaking down, while the forces available to magistrates or corporations were inadequate to deal with bread riots or anti-Popery disturbances which got out of

49

hand. Certainly it was found necessary to pass the Riot Act in 1715 and an event like the invasion and looting of the Newcastle Guildhall in 1740 can hardly be regarded as an example of the successful functioning of the system. The Gordon Riots which brought chaos, death and injury to London for a week brought home to authority and respectable society just how paper-thin even rudimentary law and order could be.

 Sexual permissiveness, drink and riot were all associated with popular festivals, fairs and recreations, and an attack upon these was a central part of the attempt to reform the manners and morals of the lower orders. In 1738 a Society for the Reformation of Manners was formed and although it collapsed a renewed effort was made to attack current manners and morals in 1757, when a second Society was set up. As might be expected, organised religion was the spearhead of the attack. Clergymen, indeed, are the source for many of the verbal onslaughts on popular culture; they are also often the mediators between us and the opinions and customs of the populace (so many of them were folklorists). Eighteenth century clerical attitudes could however be diverse indeed. Henry Bourne, for instance, viewed popular opinions and customs with mingled fascination and horror and, writing in 1725, sought either to regulate or abolish them. Mumming, for instance, in which men and women exchanged clothes and visited each other's houses at New Year was '. . . the occasion of much uncleanness and debauchery, and directly opposite to the word of God. *The woman shall not wear that which pertaineth unto a man, neither shall a man put on a woman's garment* (Deuteronomy xxii)'. May Day and in particular the custom of going to the woods the night before also incurred his wrath, '. . . because also so much wickedness and debauchery are committed that night, to the scandal of whole families, and the dishonour of religion . . . .'[14] Brand, writing in 1776, was much more the enthusiastic antiquarian folklorist than the moralising clergyman; he bewailed the demise of many popular pastimes:

> The common people, confined by daily labour, seem to require their proper intervals of relaxation; perhaps it is of the highest political utility to encourage innocent sports and games among them. The revival of many of these would, I think, be highly pertinent at this particular season, when the general spread of luxury and dissipation threatens more than at any preceding period to extinguish the character of our

boasted national bravery. For the observation of an honest old writer Stow (who tells us speaking of the May-games, Mid-summer-eve rejoicings, etc. anciently used in the streets of London, 'which *open* pastimes in my youth being now supprest, worse practices *within* doors are to be feared') may be with singular propriety adopted on the most transient survey of our present popular manners.[15]

Brand's tolerance of the profane and fascination by old customs was not, however, to be the dominant religious voice for the next century or so. Rather, the Evangelicals and the Methodists were to assail popular culture with an enthusiasm and vigilance which would have been admired by many a seventeenth century Puritan.

Evangelicalism was not, of course, concerned only with reforming the morals, customs and recreations of the lower orders. In many ways, its greatest success was to be in extracting acquiescence, at least publicly, to its central tenets from a broad section of the upper ranks. The Evangelical ethic diffused itself through all sections of society but it is still hard to escape the conclusion that, from its inception and throughout its period of influence, it was most naturally the ethic of elements of the mercantile, manufacturing and professional strata. It might win aristocrats, tailors and stocking weavers to its standard but it was most at home beneath the roof of the town house of the successful merchant or manufacturer or within the humbler edifice of the shopkeeper. G.M. Young pointed to this in a celebrated passage:

> Nor could it escape the notice of a converted man, whose calling brought him into frequent contact with the world, that the virtues of a Christian after the Evangelical model were easily exchangeable with the virtues of a successful merchant or a rising manufacturer, and that a more than casual analogy could be established between Grace and Corruption and the Respectable and the Low. To be serious, to redeem the time, to abstain from gambling, to remember the Sabbath day to keep it holy, to limit the gratification of the senses to the pleasures of a table lawfully earned and the embraces of a wife lawfully wedded, are virtues for which the reward is not laid up in heaven only. The world is very evil.[16]

To Evangelicalism, at least in its pristine phase, the problem of recreation was not so much which recreations should be considered sinful but whether any at all were permissible. The ways of the world were a snare and a temptation; even when apparently innocent they took men's minds off the real business of life, which was salvation. Time should not be spent in the pursuit of pleasure but rather in the contemplation of the contrary states of those who followed the world's path and were condemned to darkness, and those who had heard the call and came to Christ. The belief that every act and every desire would one day be weighed in the judgment was not conducive to recreation. Though Evangelicalism placed a stress upon public duty it disavowed public pleasure. What recreation, if any, was permissible should take place within the family and the home and should dovetail with piety and prayer. If withdrawal from the world, save as the dictates of duty and business required, was a marked feature of the movement, its corollary was an emphasis upon the private world of the family in which a patriarchal God had his earthly representative in a stern and authoritarian father.

The Evangelicals set out to reform the morals of the rich as well as the poor and they did succeed in converting many of the upper class to their viewpoint. Their influence upon the great, upon the aristocracy and society, developed slowly in the last decades of the century and suffered something of a set-back during the Regency, but it was on the whole successful in creating a climate in which there was an outward conformity to their notions of conduct. If the plain living family life beloved of George III was an early pointer and was to be challenged by the more gamey tastes of his sons, the ascendant ethos was in the long run to make the conspicuous parading of mistresses and public displays of dissipation no longer fashionable. There is much truth, however, in Sydney Smith's aphorism that the Society for the Suppression of Vice would have been more properly entitled 'a Society for suppressing the vices of persons whose income does not exceed £500 a year'.[17] The rich could only be reached by persuasion but it was tempting to consider legislation as a means of abolishing the vices of the poor or, at any rate, the public exhibition of such vices. The value which Evangelicals placed on privacy, family and home made them especially suspicious of public gatherings of pleasure seekers. Fairs, football matches and such annual celebrations as bull-runnings and parish feasts were particularly criticised; they were also vulnerable as they needed space and the consent of the authorities to use it. From the seventies onwards Evangelicalism within and without the established church sought to destroy a hedonistic popular culture, both in its older and in its more innovative forms, and to reform the morals and recreations of the lower orders.

Like seventeenth century Puritanism before it, it found a natural ally in the concern of employers that the morals and customs of the people were an impediment to economic progress.

As we have seen, it was widely assumed, and probably rightly, that workers had a high leisure preference and that higher wages would simply result in more leisure, not more work. If the carrot was not to be used and wages were to be kept low then more work would be extracted from the workforce only by making the hours of work as long as possible and by inculcating more disciplined work practices. Popular culture was seen as an impediment to such a development. Frequent holidays held up work, heavy drinking interfered with the worker's effectiveness, while sports and gambling distracted him.

Those who advocated measures to change the leisure habits of the poor met with only limited success. It was probably industrial rather than agricultural or commercial employers who felt the need to impose work discipline most urgently. Inuring urban workers to regular hours and steady production was an increasing problem in the eighteenth century. But most industrial workers still had considerable control over when and how they should work. Employers who put out work to labourers and their families in their own cottages could control wage rates but had only an indirect influence on working hours, while workers in small workshops clung fiercely to tradition and St Monday. Only the minority of employers who directly controlled a substantial number of employees could hope to impose regular and standardised work discipline. Some progress was made in abolishing official holidays and cutting down the number of fairs but workers were quite likely simply to take more unofficial holidays of the St Monday type to make up for them.

There was, of course, a contradiction in the attitudes of many of those who called for draconian legislation to abolish holidays, do away with fairs and regulate public houses, for they were often those most opposed to state regulation in other spheres, especially the remaining Elizabethan statutes which sought to regulate wages and the duration of apprenticeships. Josiah Tucker – who suggested that taxes be levied on:

> all places of public Resort and Diversion, such as Public Rooms, Music-Gardens, Play Houses, etc. also on Booths and Stands for Country Wakes, Cricket Matches, and Horse Racing, Stages for Mountebanks, Cudgel Playing, etc. moreover on Fires Places.[18]

53

–was not a man who normally approved of new or increased taxes.

Those who relied upon the discipline of low wages – like William Temple who wrote, 'The only way to make them temperate and industrious is to lay them under a necessity of labouring all the time they can spare from means and sleep'[19] – did not have it all their own way, however. Wages had in fact been rising since the late seventeenth century and, in the late eighteenth, English earners were the most prosperous in Europe.

Not all eighteenth century thinkers neglected the importance of demand as a positive aspect of the economy. Although a majority of writers appear to have been horrified at the growth of what they saw as luxurious tastes among sectors of society previously not known for their conspicuous consumption, and to have railed against the pride, vanity and emulation of their betters that lay behind this, Bernard Mandeville argued in the *Fable of the Bees* that consumer demand for luxuries was an important stimulant to economic growth.[20] He did not, however, consider that the labouring poor could ever fulfil such a function and considered that they were destined to remain producers. Like Gregory King he considered that the mass of the people were destined to decrease the total wealth of the population as their earnings were always likely to be insufficient for their essential needs. Rising expectations or the merest taste of frivolity among the labouring poor would merely increase the degree to which they were a drain on the nation's, and more particularly the parish's, resources. In the later eighteenth century economic thinkers were to take Mandeville's point as to the importance of consumer demand much further and consider that high wages for labour might be a positive good. To Adam Smith the high price of labour was the very basis of public opulence.

If the attack on popular culture by the Evangelicals and by employers and some economists can be seen as something of a replay of the attack mounted in the seventeenth century, there was a new element in the criticisms of certain aspects of popular recreation, which had not been present before. This was an essentially secular distaste for the irrational nature of much popular amusement and a queasiness about the amount of gratuitous cruelty to animals involved in many of the recreations of the poor. The secular, humanitarian nature of Enlightenment thought had far-reaching implications. Essentially it proposed that the poverty, drunkenness, cruelty and promiscuity of the lower orders were not God-given but were

54

rather the result of human error in the ordering of society. Problems were soluble if man and government would only apply reason. The thrust of the strain of thought emanating from the Enlightenment was profoundly radical but anything but populist. Thus, while it threatened the most basic institutions and hallowed traditions of established government and religion, it had little time for the crude and atavistic recreations and customs of the common man. It set itself against the humiliating treatment often meted out to women, against cruelty to children and, more germane to popular recreations, against cruelty to animals. A growing chorus of criticism against cock-throwing, bear-baiting, badger-baiting, cock-fighting and bull-baiting and running is discernible in the late eighteenth century.

Thus Henry Brand describes cock-throwing as 'a barbarous custom ... which we hope will soon be forgotten amongst us. It is an amusement fit only for the bloodiest savages, and not for humanized men, much less for Christians!', and cock-fighting as 'an heathenish mode of diversion from the first, and at this day ought certainly to be confined to barbarous nations'.[21]

It is often pointed out that in the long war against blood sports it was the most plebeian activities, first cock-throwing and then bull-baiting, which were the first to go under and that those sports with gentry and upper class support survived. It would be more correct to say that it was the most pointless and purely cruel pastimes which went first, followed by those which involved contests and were a focus for gambling, like cock-fighting and dog-fighting, while those which could be defended as an entertaining way of killing edible species or keeping down the voracious but uneatable have survived into modern times. Campaigns in this war were waged from the mid-eighteenth century onwards by individual reformers, municipalities and, after 1824, by the Society for the Prevention of Cruelty to Animals and other animal protection societies.

Robert Malcolmson has described the demise of one such blood sport, the Stamford bull-running, in considerable detail[22] and it is clear that it, like many similar events, did not die out without considerable popular opposition. There was undoubtedly a clash between two cultures and an effort to impose the standards of one upon the other. It was not only the cruelty of blood sports that many reformers found distasteful; they could also be seen as turbulent, worldly and associated with public disorder.

Much has been written about the withdrawal of the aristocracy and gentry from participation in the celebrations, festivals and exuberant physical recreations of the labouring poor, and consequently from their role of champions of popular culture against urban and middle class reformers. As with so much else which concerns the cultural world of pre-industrial England, this has very often been distorted by the myth of a pre-lapsarian 'Merrie', England. Both Leavisites and cruder Marxists, who owe perhaps more to Engels than to Marx himself, have seen social relations between high and low as having been far more intimate, and the change in such relations as more sudden and general, than in fact they were. Although he thought in terms of a rise rather than a fall, that greatest of optimistic historians, Macaulay, early exaggerated the intimacy of social relations and the extent of change during the eighteenth century:

> The heir of an estate often passed his boyhood and youth at the seat of his family with no better tutor than grooms and gamekeepers, and scarce attained learning enough to sign his name to a Mittimus. If he went to school and college, he generally returned before he was twenty to the seclusion of the old hall, and there, unless his mind was very happily constituted by nature, soon forgot his academical pursuits in rural business and pleasure.[23]

Most historians would now find Macaulay's picture of the lack of refinement and the degree of rural isolation of the gentry in 1685 overdrawn.

The history of architecture gives us iconographical evidence of the slow but steady change in attitudes of the aristocracy and gentry towards tenantry and farmworkers and towards domestic servants. Over several centuries the layout of country houses and their gardens testified to a move towards domestic privacy, to a withdrawal from the surrounding countryside, to an emphasis upon the entertainment of equals rather than the dispensing of hospitality to dependents and inferiors. Signifying these developments were the demise of the great hall, the introduction of corridors and drawing rooms and the retreat behind walled gardens and enclosed paths. By the nineteenth century servants were, when not waiting upon the owners, confined to their own world behind green baize doors; tenants were still entertained but normally at special tenant dinners; and although the custom of giving sustenance to ordinary farmworkers and villagers continued, it was, save on special occasions such as a marriage or the birth of an heir, more likely to be in the form of distributions of food and drink than of sit down dinners in the house.

Developments in the eighteenth century marked a stage in the gradual modification of the life style of aristocracy and gentry rather than a sharp break with tradition. Certainly such a life as that described by Macaulay would have been regarded as eccentric for any substantial landowner. No doubt Sir Roger de Coverleys did exist, for there is usually some substance to lampoons and many Tory squires did eschew London and even county towns in the twenties and thirties, but the propensity of the gentry to spend more time in town and to emulate the aristocracy by maintaining houses there generally increased. Richer gentry went to London for the season, visited spas and travelled abroad; those of more modest means, in conjunction with merchants and bankers and provincial polite society, made towns like Newcastle, York, Norwich or Exeter cultural centres providing assembly rooms, baths, concerts and literary and philosophical societies.

Aristocracy and gentry might still continue to patronise local festivities and recreations but they did so on the whole with detachment. Of course, devotees of sport and gambling from among the upper orders were still to be found at cock-fights and boxing matches and the Regency period was to see something of a fashion for such louche behaviour, but those who rubbed shoulders or even exchanged blows with prize fighters and chatted amiably and knowledgeably with horse dealers were well aware that they were 'slumming'. More traditional squires would still approve of May Day, and give their servants time off to attend local fairs, donate prizes for pedestrian races and give a guinea to mummers, but such patronage was less commonly seen as a general and necessary tradition.

Perhaps more important for the demise of many popular customs and recreations was the disposition of many of those below the quality to cut themselves off from the lives of the poor. The tendency for small merchants and tradesmen in towns to find the working habits of apprentices and artisans insufficiently disciplined, their frequent holidays an irritant and their sports a threat to social order has been well documented. Village elites made up of farmers, traders and better-off artisans increasingly held themselves aloof from the more gross and antic of popular celebrations. They were often pre-occupied with discouraging idleness and with keeping down the poor rate and the ale house; rural sports and customary holidays came to be seen by them as wasteful distractions from work.

It was at this level of society, among the lower strata of the middling sort of people, that we can detect two contrary dispositions both of which were antipathetic to much of popular culture. The first was simply a quickening of social ambition and the emulation of life styles of superior strata made possible by rising incomes, better transport and new patterns of communication. It was only negatively injurious to the older popular culture, in the sense that it left it behind and looked down on it. Those farmers with parlours, mahogany tables, carpets and decanters, their sons and daughters turned into mock gentlefolks, that Cobbett railed against, were part of this disposition. So too were the wives of urban tradesmen in provincial towns who eagerly awaited the arrival of the newest fashions, aped London manners, and were able to see performances of the latest plays rushed from the metropolis by enterprising impresarios. Such tendencies removed a layer of leadership and support from many of the older popular customs and recreations but were an essential part of the new, more commercial and national, culture that was developing. The other disposition rejected most of the expressions of popular culture, whether old or new, and expressed itself in two dissenting sub-cultures, the one religious and the other political. Finding their leadership among small merchants, shopkeepers and artisans they generated a mass following among sections of the labouring classes.

Old Dissent had grown prosperous and quietist by the early eighteenth century. Its members remained godly and abstinent but were little disposed to proselytise; numbers fell as the richer and more worldly of the flock departed 'on their second horse' for the Church of England. It was Methodism, beginning as a popular manifestation of Evangelicalism within the Anglican Church and only leaving that fold after its founder's death, which re-established vital religion among sections of the lower classes and re-invigorated the older dissenting sects by its example. Methodism provided a community and a culture for its members, for one could live out one's non-working life entirely within its ambit; the life of the chapel could absorb administrative energies and provide a social life while worship and preaching, psalm and hymn were vehicles for cultural expression. It was at the same time *of* popular culture and opposed to it. From the beginning Wesley assaulted worldly and impious recreations as the work of the devil and urged the faithful to turn aside from the fair, dancing and the tavern. The more populist tendency within Method-ism, which broke away to form Primitive Methodism, was even more active in its condemnation of popular culture: 'No person shall be continued a member of our society who visits public or worldly amusements; nor those who waste their time at public houses'.[24] Yet it was Methodism's ability to express itself in popular language and its appreciation of the importance of music, spectacle and drama which enabled it to win and retain its converts. William Cobbett was no friend of Methodism but he could see the attraction of its services:

> The *singing* makes a great part of what passes in these meeting-houses. A number of women and girls singing together make very *sweet sounds*. Few men there are who have not felt *the power* of sounds of this sort. Men are sometimes pretty nearly bewitched, without knowing how. *Eyes* do a good deal, but *tongues* do more. We may talk of sparkling eyes and snowy bosoms as long as we please; but what are these with a *croaking, masculine* voice? The parson seemed to be fully aware of this part of the '*service*'. The subject of his hymn was something about *love*: Christian love; love of Jesus; but, still it was about *love*; and the parson read, or gave out, the verses, in a singularly *soft* and *sighing* voice, with his head on one side, and giving it rather a swing. I am satisfied that the singing forms great part of the *attraction*.[25]

Methodist services were indeed emotional and provided spectacle and drama as well as singing. Salvation was especially high drama, climaxing in the moment of redemption: the sinner saved, the parting of the ways, the coming to Christ and the acclamation of the congregation. They were certainly occasions for emotional release and it is tempting for post-Freudian eyes to single out the sexual element they contained, the images of blood and fertility, of union, consummation and regeneration, fundamental to the rites and festivals of rural culture. But the sense of community which Methodism gave its followers, a common fellowship of the saved, was probably more important to its appeal than love feasts and orgasmic release. To be among the saved can be accounted perhaps the ultimate in respectability and the certainty of salvation came as much from the common fellowship of those who eschewed worldly vices and the public recreations of the ungodly, and in the steady pursuit of a sober way of life, as in the high moments of what has been termed 'psychic masturbation'.

Although Methodism's numbers remained modest at the end of the eighteenth century (only some 77,000 by 1796) it was to expand rapidly in the early nineteenth century. Non-conformity as a whole came to form a powerful and influential sub-culture for most of the nineteenth century. Primitive Methodism took over whole communities, for example mining villages in Cornwall, the Pennines and

North-East England, but such successes were exceptional. In general the world of chapel was one of a powerful minority of both the middle and working classes, characterised by a leadership drawn from the middle classes and superior artisanate, and a wider working class membership. There was some correspondence between social stratum and church, sect or chapel. Unitarianism for instance attracted wealthy and influential congregations, while Primitive Methodism was at the other extreme, being far more working class, with lay preachers drawn from artisans and small shopkeepers. Nonconformity was to mount an incessant critique of the worldliness and sensuality of popular culture and to attack not only the fairs, cock-fighting and wakes of the old rural culture but the Sunday newspapers, pantomimes and 'free and easies' of the emergent popular culture. Its distaste for the 'live for today' hedonism that characterised so much of popular culture was to be paralleled by that of the other important sub-culture, secular radicalism.

The paradox of the secular radical culture which developed in the late eighteenth and early nineteenth centuries was that much of the ideology espoused by radical leaders was at variance with the beliefs and emotions that provided the impetus for radical discontent among broad sections of the population. The basis for such discontent was essentially populist and reactionary: it drew on opposition to economic change and to the overriding of custom and tradition, and on a consciousness of declining standards of living. Its wider following was composed of those dispossessed or distressed by legal and economic change: artisans, domestic outworkers and agricultural labourers threatened by the disregarding of Elizabethan statutes, technological development and the final phase of enclosures. Many historians have perceived it as an attempt to retain an older moral economy as against the economy of the free market; it was, rather, an attempt to preserve a previous economy, itself the product of a free market, against the economic changes which were dislocating it. England was not, as we have seen, a peasant society faced with the rise of capitalist individualism but instead a well-established capitalist economy and a highly individualist society accelerating towards a more sophisticated level of development. This did not stop those sections of society whose economic and social position was in decline from perceiving their previous position as 'traditional' and the economic relations which had underpinned it as somehow 'moral'. In modern English history the moral economy is yesterday's economy, whether those who lay claim to it are the handloom weavers of the late eighteenth century or shipyard workers in the twentieth. As Craig Calhoun has written in a recent work:

> The conception of a moral economy to which somewhat differently focused appeals were made did not come directly from any prior state of virtuous relations among men. Rather, it was the result of integrating the different kinds of disruptive pressures which faced the members of rural and craft communities during the industrial revolution. From trying to make common sense of their communal experiences, they created their idealised version of the moral past. It is because tradition was shaped in this way, by present experience as well as 'real' history, that populations of workers whose prosperity was of recent origin and dependent on industrialisation and/or intensified capitalist commercialisation could interpret their grievances in terms of the disruption of a traditional way of life.[26]

The radical leadership, however, drew not upon opposition to the dominant tenets of Enlightenment liberalism, itself at one with the changes opposed by the mass following, but simply altered the emphasis and extrapolated from middle class liberal interpretations of them. It stressed reason and the rights of the individual rather than custom and community.

The attitude of the articulate spokesmen of radical discontent towards much of popular culture is significant. It might have been expected that a movement whose mass following was populist and plebeian and relied upon notions of custom, the moral economy, traditional rights and status would have defended traditional recreations and the customary pleasures of the people. But they were literate working men who differed in skill, income and outlook from the less skilled majority, and the officers of the movement were small shopkeepers, masters, superior artisans and even professional men. Their outlook was characterised by an emphasis upon reason, education and independence. In so far as they drew upon an older intellectual tradition, it was that of the puritan radicalism of the seventeenth century which was antipathetic to popular culture, as was the contemporary influence of Enlightenment liberalism. If the older popular culture appeared to such men as atavistic, undignified and closely linked with Old Corruption, the developing commercial culture seemed a snare and a distraction. Among the leading figures of popular radicalism only the Tory, Cobbett, expressed the inchoate desire of the mass following to return to old ways and customs. He gave expression to the ordinary Englishman's prejudices and feelings with his dislike of education, Scotsmen, dissenters and canals and his belief that, if only stock-jobbers, taxes and paper money could be swept away, a return to an older England giving a simple but sufficient life to all could be achieved. The leaders of secular radicalism stressed moral and intellectual self-improvement, which meant books, lectures and debating societies, not bear-baiting, bull-runnings, races or circuses. If respectability, to rising men in the middle orders of society, meant a demarcation of themselves from the crude, bawdy and often callous world of the lower orders, secular radicals sought to redefine it for the independent artisan or labourer as a self-sufficient, non-deferential and plebeian respectability. Popular culture was flawed by the venality and crudity of fallen men, and secular radicalism no less than Methodism sought to redeem the populace, but by reason rather than through Christ.

Poor popular culture, poor Punch, beset on all sides by enemies and deserted by erstwhile protectors; and yet he thrived, managed to leer and mock at Methodists and radicals alike, to slip through the nets cast by societies for the suppression of innumerable vices, to escape the best laid programmes for his reform and to acquire new tastes and take up new fashions. He was to become less of an old Tory and to embrace free trade in pleasure. He would no longer be content to turn society upside down on the high days and holidays decreed by those above him; for his deferential aspect was fading fast, and in the freer towns, with their lighted streets and numerous palaces of entertainment, he would demand – and get, for he was a paying customer – the satisfaction of his venal, bawdy and amoral appetites as often as he had money in his pocket.

THREE

Continuity and change in popular culture

The streets [of London] remained busy until midnight: nay, I even saw a boy of eight years old at the utmost, perfectly alone in a little child's carriage drawn by a large dog, driving along full trot, and without the slightest fear, among the latest carriages and stage-coaches. Such a thing can be seen only in England where children are independent at eight and hanged at twelve.

A Regency Visitor. The English Tour of Prince
Pückler-Mushau, 1826–28

Salient features of English society in the early nineteenth century were its disorderly and undisciplined nature and the self-assertiveness of people from all social strata. It was a lightly policed and little regulated society in which, as Professor Gash has written, 'People were free to behave as they thought fit, subject to the uncertain and tardy consequences of the law should they be identified, caught and proved in a court of law to have broken it.'[1] A major theme of the nineteenth century was to be the taming of English society and, when we consider the callous and brutal nature of much of life at the beginning of the century, the easy resort to fists and cudgels and the almost automatic or absent-minded cruelty to the weak, neither a romantic conception of the colour and vitality of the Regency, nor a retrospective solidarity with 'the working class' against new mechanisms of social control should make us regret this. But it *was* a very free society.

Freedom was at the heart of the changes in popular culture. In the cities and larger towns especially, the individual, free from the suffocating embrace and the unofficial pressures of small communities, had not yet to contend with the many formal regulations and controls which were to be found necessary for orderly life in the developing urban environment. The withering of custom released men from a bondage which dictated the form and occasion of their pleasures and imposed a rhythm and meaning on their lives. It was the positive appeal of the towns which attracted their growing populations. The prospect of higher wages was important but so were the bustle of the streets, the plethora of entertainment and the freedom of choice. However long the hours of work and however exacting the discipline of the workplace a man could be much more his own master in his leisure time than had been possible for the vast majority of previous generations.

Individual freedom, the ubiquity of money wages and a commercial environment that catered for choice made possible a variety of life-styles and fuelled an explosion of leisure and entertainment. Of course, for many work still dominated leisure and men drank with their workmates and pursued other recreations along with them. Towns dominated by a single industry could have a social life permeated by the standards and ethics of the factory.[2] But especially in the cities, and above all in London, there were sufficient space and variety for the exercise of personal choice. Men could band together with others of similar inclination in 'taste publics' and publicans and other entrepreneurs were ready to satisfy their tastes. Aficionados of the turf or prize-fighting found pubs which were centres for their kind while race courses multiplied and increasing numbers of boxing and wrestling contests were promoted and advertised. Theatrical impresarios and diversifying publicans studied the popular appetite and sought to lead it; circuses became more elaborate, the hippodrama developed, the pantomime was created, the licensed theatres expanded, the unlicensed thrived, pleasure gardens multiplied and the 'free and easy' nourished an embryonic music-hall. For some there were other choices, the self-contained world of the chapel or of secular radicalism with its debating, literary and corresponding societies. These latter, however, were for the minority; for the majority a leisure culture which was hedonistic, ribald and sensational beckoned.

Great divides, moments when the process of change appears to crystallise, are a constant attraction to historians and some have discerned a pattern in the popular culture and leisure of this period in which, as a phenomenon of the industrialisation and/or modernisation process, a definite break with past traditions occurred. An older popular culture – customary, collective, and in which work and popular amusements dovetailed with each other – decayed and modern leisure emerged, commercial and individualist.[3] It has even been alleged that there was probably no real leisure for the majority before this period but rather a sociability dependent upon the obligation to work, and on family, religion and society.[4] Such interpretations neglect continuity and the considerable degree to which the emergent culture drew upon tradition; they also ignore the commercial element in pre-industrial culture. There was, rather, a change of emphasis consequent upon greater individual autonomy, the growth of a wider market and the prospect of higher profits.

Major characteristics of the popular culture of Regency England were that it was predominantly a public and gregarious culture, that it was largely masculine, that it involved excitement and gambling and that it had an undercurrent of disorder and violence. It was much like the preferred cuisine of the population, great helpings of meat and plum pudding, cooked plainly and washed down with ale or claret according to status; it was robust, satisfying and indelicate. People took their pleasures in great gulps and were addicted to excitement and spectacle. Despite the efforts of reformers, of Evangelicals, of Sabbatarians and humanitarians, the popular culture of the period flourished luxuriantly in a society which had still to will the means of effectively implementing curbs on popular behaviour. Indeed, among the governors, there was little haste to impose such curbs. The governing classes were well aware of the excesses of the populace, of their taste for violence and unbridled appetite for spectacle, and of the frequency of public disorders, but were on the whole tolerant. There was, albeit temporarily, something of a reversal of that tendency of the upper orders to withdraw themselves from popular pastimes, and the great age of the horse and of the 'fancy' brought the extremes of society into intimate contact. Had government desired to legislate effectively against brutal pastimes, against fights between men or animals, to supervise closely what was performed on the stage or in the fairground booth or even to limit the turbulence and disorder on the streets of great cities, it would have had to provide effective policing. This it was not yet prepared to do. Parliamentary and popular opinion was at one in considering an effective police as a foreign institution and incompatible with the Englishman's liberty.

Foreign visitors to England were often horrified by the English addiction to violence and were frequently made uneasy by the licence of the lower orders. Some marvelled at the country's prosperity: the neatness of the countryside with its sleek fat cattle and solid farmhouses and the burgeoning economic miracle of Manchester and the cotton industry. All commented on the bewildering size of London, the numbers of its population and the incessant traffic of the streets. One visitor, Prince Pückler-Mushau, tasted the variety of entertainment that was on offer in the capital during the eighteen twenties. He went to the opera and the pantomime, saw productions of Shakespeare, watched street players and was delighted by Punch and Judy. His catholic tastes enabled him to see the funny side of the impudent swindles perpetrated by the lowliest showmen:

> On my way home [from a visit to the West India Docks] I passed a booth where a man was calling out that here were the famous German dwarf and his three dwarf children; the living skeleton; and to conclude, the fattest girl that was ever seen. I paid my shilling and went in. After waiting a quarter of an hour, till five other spectators arrived, the curtain was drawn up, and the most impertinent 'charlatancrie' exhibited that ever I witnessed. The living skeleton was a very ordinary sized man, not much thinner than I. As an excuse for our disappointment, we were assured that when he arrived from France he was a skeleton, but that since he had eaten good English beef steaks, it had been found impossible to curb his tendency to corpulence.[5]

The fattest woman and the dwarf family proved equally disappointing and Pückler-Mushau found the exhibition 'an English hoax which no Frenchman could have executed with more effrontery'.

He went to see Mozart's *Figaro* at Drury Lane and was disgusted at the treatment of the work of his fellow-countryman by an English producer. Popularising influences were at work modifying the art form of opera in an attempt to make it acceptable to unsophisticated tastes. Mere actors took the principal parts and the songs were sung by others. Popular songs of the day were fitted in to suit Mozart's music, 'just as pitch-plaster would suit the face of the Venus de Medici'. The opera had been 'adapted to English ears by means of the most tasteless and shocking alterations'.[6]

He had kinder words for English drama, thinking much of Charles Kemble, 'a man of the best education, and has always lived in good society'. Kemble's performance as Falstaff was, however, immediately followed by a melodrama in which a large Newfoundland dog, 'really acted admirably; he defended a banner for a long time, pursued the enemy, and afterwards came on the stage wounded, lame, and bleeding, and died in the most masterly manner, with a last wag of the tail that was really full of genius'.[7]

Along with Punch and Judy which he termed a 'genuine national comedy', pantomime received his highest praise. He described thus a Christmas Pantomime, *Mother Goose* at Covent Garden:

> At the rising of the curtain a thick mist covers the stage and gradually rolls off. This is remarkably well managed by means of fine gauze. In the dim light you distinguish a little cottage, the dwelling of a sorceress; in the background a lake surrounded by mountains, some of whose peaks are clothed with snow. All as yet is misty and indistinct; – the sun then rises triumphantly, chases the morning dews, and the hut, with the village in the distance, now appear in perfect outline. And now you behold upon the roof a large cock, who flaps his wings, plumes himself, stretches his neck, and greets the sun with several very natural Kikerikis [German equivalent of Cock-a-doodle-doo]. A magpie near him begins to chatter and to strut about, and to peck at a gigantic tom-cat . . . this tom-cat is acted with great 'virtuosité' by an actor who is afterwards transformed into Harlequin . . . Meanwhile the door opens, and Mother Skipton, a frightful old witch, enters with a son very like herself. The household animals, to whom is added an enormous duck, pay their morning court to the best of their ability. But the witch is in a bad humour, utters a curse upon them all, and changes them upon the spot into the persons of the Italian comedy, who, like the rest of the world, persecute each other without rest, till at last the most cunning conquers. The web of the story is then spun on through a thousand transformations and extravagances, without any particular connexion, but with occasional good hits at the incidents of the day; and above all, with admirable decoration, and great wit on the part of the machinist.[8]

The world our German visitor was describing was one in which the divisions between high and popular art, between opera and drama on the one hand and spectacle, circus and showmanship on the other had broken down. The fairground barker, the showman, the ringmaster and the clown reached up and influenced even the licensed

London theatres. Excitement, novelty and spectacle became all important. Commercial forces did not replace either the elite or the popular traditions in dramatic entertainment; rather, they mixed them up with a magnificent unconcern for past distinctions and niceties, with the overriding aim of exciting, titillating and enthralling the audience. Shakespeare, melodramas and performing animals did not merely co-exist but intermingled. Patent theatres sought to retain their privileged position behind protective legislation but were forced to adapt, to anglicise and plebeianise their opera, to set Shakespeare amidst spectacular stage sets and follow him with performing dogs. Unlicensed theatres mounted their challenge to the monopoly of drama held by the licensed, a battle they were not to win until 1843 but in which they were to be successful in skirmish after skirmish.

A major development was the spreading of much of the culture of the pleasure fairs. Fairs showed a considerable ability to survive in their own right but much of their content found its way to more permanent homes exemplifying the way in which older forms of cultural expression continued autonomously, and simultaneously provided the basis for cultural expression in new milieux.

The attack upon fairs by influential sections of opinion resulted in the suppression and demise of some, but many more were to continue into the late nineteenth and the twentieth centuries. In the industrial towns of the north-west, for instance, Wakes Week remained an annual holiday since it was convenient to halt mills and factories for the servicing and renovation of machinery during a common week; it was only the advent of the seaside holiday which diminished the importance of the fairground. In metropolitan areas, however, fairs, though they often survived, were in the long run to decline in importance because of the very expansion of the leisure industry they did so much to create. Entertainment ceased to be located on particular days and in a temporary encampment but was instead available throughout the year in more specialist permanent locations.

In the short run, however, the fairs in and around London, despite losing the patronage of the Quality, enjoyed something of an Indian summer in the early nineteenth century. Richardson, Gyngell, Samwell and Scowton provided the public with melodramas and pantomimes and with new generations of dwarves, giants and such curiosities: Josephine Girardelli, the Female Salamander; O'Brien, the Irish Giant; Simon Paap, the Dutch Dwarf; and Madame Gobert, the French Female Hercules.

The menageries which were a feature of most large fairs were presented on a grander scale and with consummate showmanship. Wombwell's was the most famous but was for long engaged in rivalry with Atkins's. This rivalry provided a magnificent example of the showman's ability to turn disaster into success. When Wombwell's elephant died at St Bartholomew's Fair, Atkins advertised that his menagerie had the only live elephant in the fair – only to find that the crowds deserted him to see the attraction advertised by Wombwell, 'The only dead elephant in the fair'.[9]

Circuses did begin to appear at fairs in the early nineteenth century but, whether on permanent sites or travelling with tents, they have generally been separate from but closely associated with the world of the fair. The emphasis of the circus was upon equestrianism but circuses also included clowns and acrobats and, later, wild animals and thus overlapped with the booths and menageries of the fairground. The open-air equestrian performances of Prince and Sampson may have been the technical beginning of circuses but it was Philip Astley, who opened a permanent amphitheatre in 1780, who was the real founder of the circus, which soon became a popular form of entertainment both at permanent and temporary sites. The circus, under the leadership of Astley and of the great equestrian and entrepreneur Andrew Ducrow, rapidly became established throughout the country, most large provincial towns having permanent amphitheatres. It also proved capable of upward mobility, attracting more well-to-do audiences and achieving royal patronage as early as 1828.

The relationship between high and popular art forms is to a considerable extent one of interdependence, and the one is continually reinforced by the other. Cut off from the vigour and vitality of the popular, high art can ossify into a rigid Alexandrianism while, unrestrained by law, conventions and the influence of higher art forms, the popular has an innate tendency towards mere spectacle and sensationalism. The theatre in the early nineteenth century received considerable infusions of innovation and vigour from popular art forms, especially those whose erstwhile home was the fairground. The mainstream of dramatic history has tended to see the English theatre as in decline during this period, swamped by melodrama, lavish stage sets and performing animals. Although a fashionable anti-elitism is now reassessing these criticisms and is finding virtues in melodrama, neither drama nor opera appear to have been produced with a cultivated and informed audience in mind. The audience for theatre expanded enormously; Covent

Garden, Drury Lane and Sadler's Wells were extensively rebuilt, while other theatres, not only in the West End but south of the river and in the East End – the Lyceum, the Haymarket, the Coburg, the Surrey and the Pavilion – could hold vast audiences. Such expansion was based on a decline in the social status of audiences; managers and producers had at all costs to keep their rowdy and potentially turbulent audiences entertained.

> The most striking thing to a foreigner in English theatre is the unheard-of coarseness and brutality of the audience. The consequence of this is that the higher and more civilised classes go only to the Italian Opera, and very rarely visit their national theatre . . . English freedom here degenerates into the rudest licence, and it is not uncommon in the midst of the most affecting part of a tragedy, or the most charming 'cadenza' of a singer, to hear some coarse expression shouted from the galleries in a stentor voice. This is followed, according to the taste of the bystanders, either by loud laughter or approbation or by the castigation and expulsion of the offender . . . And such things happen not once, but sometimes, twenty times, in the course of a performance, and amuse many of the audience more than that does. It is also no rarity for someone to throw the fragments of his 'goûte', which do not always consist of orange-peels alone, without the smallest ceremony on the heads of the people in the pit, or to hail them with singular dexterity into the boxes; while others hang their coats and waistcoats over the railings of the gallery, and sit in their shirt-sleeves. . .[10]

Managers and actors bored such an audience at their peril!

 The input from the fairground to the theatre took place in the context of this change in the composition of theatrical audiences. Many of the customers of the fair were now also the audience at the Surrey or even at Drury Lane. If the great actors of the day no longer appeared at St Bartholomew's or Greenwich Fair, the theatrical booths still produced much of the talent later to be found at the principal theatres. Richardson was proud of the fact that James Wallach, Oxberry, Saville Faucit and, most importantly, Edmund Kean, the great tragedian, had first appeared at his booths. But it was with new forms of entertainment rather than with individual actors that the fairs made their great contribution. Richardson's productions often presented melodrama and pantomime together –

following melodramas such as *The Children of the Desert*, *The Roman Wife* or *Wandering Outlaw* with pantomimes like *Harlequin in the Deep* or *Harlequin and the Devil*.[11] In 1802 melodrama was launched on the legitimate stage with Thomas Holcroft's *A Tale of Mystery*, presented at Covent Garden. The entrepreneurs of the fairground had already made significant alterations to the Italian treatment of Harlequin and Colombine. The traditional Harlequinade at the end of the entertainment had become more and more important and Harlequin himself increasingly a clown. On the London stage more drastic changes were to follow as Dubois, an ex-circus clown, and then Grimaldi gave their own interpretations to the Harlequinade. By the twenties the modern pantomime had largely evolved: a basic and usually traditional storyline was interpolated with scenes and performances which were largely autonomous, transformations and elaborate stage settings became obligatory and jokes and squibs on matters of the day came to the lips of Mother Goose or Baron Munchausen. It was not exclusively or even predominantly an entertainment for children but it did remain, like the fairground which nurtured it, an entertainment for high days and holidays: after Christmas, at Easter or Whit or at the summer theatre.

Some have detected a radical audience in the pantomime in particular, and in the theatre generally, while one recent essayist has fantasised about dispossessed villagers, vicariously overthrowing authority as they watched pantomime, or symbolically reclaiming lost commons as they participated in the 1809 Old Price Riot at Covent Garden and knocked down the boxes.[12] The audience was populist in its tastes and sympathies rather than radical and so were its entertainers. Thomas Frost was right to term entertainers, '. . . as a class, loyal, under whatever dynasty or form of government they live, providing that it does not interfere with the exercise of their profession'.[13] There is, of course, always an element of the Lord of Misrule in popular culture, and pantomime certainly incorporated it. It is significant, however, that the humbling of the mighty and the elevation of the clown is in pantomime, as in carnival and other traditional festivals, a temporary affair that emphasises rather than questions the normal order of things; in both pantomime and much of melodrama it is not authority *per se* which is derided but the *wicked* squire, the *pompous* mayor or the lord who in the final scene turns out to have no right to his title and estate and has to hand them back to the rightful owner, the hitherto humble hero.

The audience at the theatre in Regency England was certainly rowdy and at times riotous, it enjoyed caricature and delighted in seeing

71

royalty, the rich and famous, and politicians satirised, while its sympathies could be easily enlisted for a cause and could as easily wane. Much of it was drawn from the same crowd that supported Queen Caroline and greeted George IV with rough music. It enjoyed at the theatre the same themes and heroes and villains as had long been presented in chapbooks and broadsheets; sometimes we can discern the moral economy: virtuous cottagers persecuted by wicked landowners, valuable animals swindled away from the poor and heirs denied their rightful estate; but the entrepreneurial ethic is also represented as the industrious apprentice proceeds to fame, fortune and his master's daughter.

The London theatre was thus still close to the world of the great pleasure fairs and embodied many of the staple themes of popular reading matter, yet it was highly innovative and fiercely commercial. It was also very conscious of stardom, its actors and actresses highly paid and much feted, while the attention which the theatrical critics paid to Madame Vestris's celebrated legs strikes a very modern note. Provincial theatre incorporated not only the Theatre Royals which so many towns had proudly acquired in the course of the eighteenth century and which made haste to emulate the productions of Covent Garden or Drury Lane, but the much more vernacular world of the travelling troupes who made their circuits of parish feasts and race meetings.

As in London, theatre in the provinces tended to become decidedly less respectable during the early nineteenth century. Although the influence of Evangelicalism may have accounted for some of the decline in theatre going among the middle ranks of provincial society it is probable that, as in the metropolis, a rougher audience frightened away more affluent customers. Provincial theatre became less prosperous after 1820. There may well have been more of it, however, as previously itinerant showmen found it convenient to set up elaborate booths on urban sites for longer and longer periods.

A general development, even at the lowest level of the theatrical profession, was an increase in professionalism. Even itinerant troupes of entertainers started to advertise their coming and their programme in advance by posters and handbills. The stage journal *The Era* made its appearance and players could scan its pages for vacancies. Organisation and a bit of capital became more important to showmen. There was a chorus of complaint from those squeezed out by such developments, from those less talented and less perceptive of changing tastes who could not keep up with the new professionalism.

The career of Billy Purvis demonstrates this development but also points to the versatility, the range of repertoire and adaptability required of one who was to begin his professional life in pubs, the drawing rooms of the gentry and local fairs and then make the transition to semi-permanent sites in the centre of Newcastle.[14] Purvis did not become a full-time showman until he was 32, when he began touring Northern England and the Scottish borders performing in the open air at village feasts, race courses, hiring fairs and hoppings, from spring to autumn, and hiring rooms in assembly halls or inns. His range was considerable: he was a clown, an occasional actor, a tight-rope walker; he played the Northumbrian pipes and the fiddle, conjured, read minds and manipulated puppets. By 1819 he had acquired a booth and demonstrated that he had talents as a barker, drumming up an audience and enticing them into his booth by his wit; he was now a manager and impresario in charge of his own company and hired horses to transport his equipment from place to place. After 1827 he acquired increasingly impressive booths, with both a pit and a gallery, the most famous of which was his Victoria theatre named in honour of the new queen in 1837. He also hired permanent theatres at Whitehaven, Carlisle and Greenock. Gradually, however, his theatre came to be in the centre of Newcastle for lengthy periods at a time, an accepted part of the city's entertainment and a rival to the patent theatre, the Theatre Royal.

Purvis's two great fortes were his ability as a showman-entrepreneur and his skill as a clown or comic. In the former role he followed much the same path as his contemporaries in other regions, Prince Miller in Scotland or Hurd in the South-West, but in his performance as a comic he was a seminal influence on what was to become the North-East music-hall. His technique was a combination of the old pantomime tradition and the dialect story. His most famous sketch was 'stealing the bundle' in which gesture and mime were interpolated with soliloquies in broad dialect as the would-be thief wrestled with his conscience. He was, perhaps, the first stage 'Geordie' evolving that almost narcissistic love affair with the slightly gullible yet streetwise regional ethos. He combined a tolerance of, indeed almost a pride in, drunkenness and the surrender to temptation with an antipathy to any affectation of superiority, especially when it came from the South.

The development of sport in the Regency period exhibited many of the same features as the changes in entertainment. The sports were not new and indeed, even the crudest of blood sports showed a considerable capacity to survive in the face of the hostility of authority and legal curbs, but many sports became more public and more governed by commercial factors.

Despite the attempts of the leisured classes to keep their sports exclusive, shooting alone remained the private pastime of the gentleman. It too became much more organised, with its hierarchies of gamekeepers and underkeepers and armies of beaters making possible the 'battue', the killing of hundreds of birds and animals on a single day. But the right to shoot depended on the ownership of land and the law rigidly and strenuously underwrote the monopoly held by country landowners. Until 1831 shooting was legally restricted to owners of land worth at least £100. Even after that date the sport remained both private and class specific.

If shooting demonstrated a horizontal cleavage in rural society, dividing landowners from even the more prosperous tenant farmers, and a source of animosity and even bloodshed between gamekeepers and agricultural labourers, fox-hunting contrived, as it still does today, to bond together the strata of rural society. As F.M.L. Thompson has concluded, '. . . fox-hunting engaged the passions . . . of a cross section of the whole rural community'.[15] It was of course led and dominated by aristocrats and country gentlemen but farmers and professional men could join in as well. Despite discouragement the poorer sections of the community showed a disposition to follow on foot and the appearance of the hunt was a welcome distraction to the labourers in the fields. As E.W. Bovill has remarked, fox-hunting at the time of Waterloo was 'little more than a private pastime of sporting squires'.[16] The subsequent decades saw important innovations in hunting which made it substantially the sport it is today. It became highly organised, evolved conventions, a mystique and elaborate codes of dress and behaviour. The countryside became divided up into regular hunts; as the last phase of enclosures produced more hedges and fences, clearing such obstacles became the mark of the intrepid; foxes were conserved; and faster hounds were bred. There were 69 packs of hounds in Britain in 1812 and 91 in 1825. Although some hunts remained the property of single great landowners, even ducal incomes could find their maintenance a strain and subscription hunts became more common. The period has been termed the golden age of hunting, the time of the Great Masters such as Ralph Lambton of the Durham and George Osbaldeston of the Quorn. Hunting became popular enough to win the attention of the expanding sporting press. *Sporting Magazine* paid large sums of money to enable Charles James Apperley to tour with an entourage of horses, coaches and servants, hunting in all parts of the country and writing as 'Nimrod' on his experiences. Robert Smith Surtees also wrote on hunting for *Sporting Magazine* and *Bell's Life in London* before helping to found *New Sporting Magazine*.

Hunting remained relatively exclusive. It did not require large numbers of participants; the subscription hunt opened the sport to urban gentry and professionals as well as to the middle ranks of the countryside but such numbers as these provided were sufficient for its health. Some sports are in any case destined to be the pursuits of minorities because of the expense of the necessary equipment – for example, yachting in the late nineteenth century and, of course, polo – and the purchase and upkeep of a decent hunter was an expensive business. That other great horsey pastime, racing, became, however, the sport not merely of aristocrats and gentlemen but of large numbers of the lower orders. The attempt to maintain exclusivity ended in failure although the impact on it of a mass public was softened by the internal demarcation between classes imposed by the differential prices charged for the stands, the paddock and the ordinary enclosure. By the end of the Napoleonic Wars, the classics – the Derby, the Oaks , the One Thousand and Two Thousand Guineas, the St Leger and the Ascot Gold Cup – were all established, and by the beginning of Victoria's reign there were to be some 150 places in Britain where race meetings were held.

Horse racing combined two English obsessions, love of horses and a delight in gambling. At all levels of society, but especially at the top and the bottom, it was smart to know about horses, and the attraction of combining knowledge of past performances and present form with betting was a potent one. Betting was more important than prize-money to the sport from the beginning. Professional bookmakers appeared in the early years of the century. They were known as 'betters-round' as they would take bets on all horses in the field. Previously sportsmen had wagered amongst themselves on single horses. By mid-century off-course betting had become well-established and those who vicariously experienced the thrills of the race course vastly outnumbered those who attended in person.

Despite the popularity of racing the organisation of the sport remained somewhat loose and the layout of the courses themselves somewhat basic and unstandardised. Even at so prestigious a venue as Newmarket, only the end of the course was enclosed with ropes and the judges sat in a wooden hut on wheels which was moved, as the course was lengthened or shortened, opposite to the winning post, by which they determined which horse's nose or neck was in the lead. The dominance of betting led to numerous shady practices creeping into racing: favourites could be restrained from winning in a number of ways – jockeys could be bribed and horses nobbled. As Professor Gash has commented:

> . . . until Lord George Bentinck and his almost equally autocratic successor Admiral Rous came to preside over the Jockey Club in the middle decades of the century, aristocratic owners themselves habitually indulged in practices for which they would have been warned off the turf a generation later. The main sporting object of Englishmen of all kinds was to win and make money; they were not too particular how they did it.[17]

If horse-racing can be seen as a pastime of the aristocracy and gentry that, as it became more organised and public, attracted a wider audience which it eventually came to rely on, pugilism began as a sport of the lower orders and in the late eighteenth and early nineteenth century attracted aristocratic patronage. Many supporters of prize-fighting argued that it was an intrinsically English activity reflecting the sturdiness, the courage and the manliness of the race. It was immensely popular with working men, and the great fighters of the day – Tom Crib, Molyneux, Tom Spring and Dutch Sam – were popular heroes who were the focus of fierce regional loyalties. It was the increasing commercialisation of the sport and the fact that these heroes were full-time professionals that made for its growing popularity. Sporting journalists built up interest in the leading fighters, describing their skills and past achievements. A champion could make a very good living, not simply from the purses he fought for and the rewards of his backers, but by setting up a gymnasium and instructing the rich in the noble art or science of self-defence. Daniel Mendoza achieved the greatest fame, a fame which was exploited and extended by a minor industry producing Mendoza mugs, plaques and instruction books; he himself wrote *The Art of Boxing*. The least a successful pugilist could expect, if he survived the considerable dangers and rigours of his profession, was to retire as the owner of a public house frequented by supporters of 'the fancy'. As with horse-racing, prize-fighting was inseparable from betting and huge sums of money, made up of the shillings of working men and the thousands of pounds of aristocratic punters, were placed on bouts. It became part of the code of young aristocrats that the most indolent dandy, should he take his coat off, should be capable of mixing it with a coal-heaver. Noted patrons of the sport were Captain Barclay and the indefatigable Squire Osbaldeston. Even the occasional clergyman was an enthusiast, like Thackeray's Reverend Bute Crawley who had 'thrashed all the best bruisers in town'.[18]

There were marked similarities in the ethos and style of horse-racing and prize-fighting, and the supporters of the turf and the fancy overlapped considerably. Both sports evoked an atmosphere redolent of an older, half-imaginary England where sporting squires and sturdy labourers rubbed shoulders in common appreciation of physical prowess, whether of man or animal. Yet both sports flourished as industry and towns expanded, and themselves consti-tuted a new industry with full-time professionals and specialist newspapers.

The upper classes remained loyal to the turf but after the twenties their patronage of prize-fighting was less in evidence. Yet there was always a section of the well-born who supported it and when pugilism, its violence codified and limited, found a new incarnation as boxing, its birth and development were presided over by Marquises and Earls. The general decline of prize-fighting must not, in any case, be exaggerated or ante-dated for it remained enormously popular with working men. As Hugh Cunningham has pointed out:

> Harassed by the magistrates and the police, condemned by the respectable, prize-fighting remained a popular sport which, like the horse-racing in the environs of London, may well prove to have been growing. The decline came after not before the Sayers v Heenan fight [of 1860].[19]

Majority taste among the educated classes was, however, becoming more squeamish. In 1831 the prospectus of Surtees's *New Sporting Magazine* announced that its pages would be closed to prize-fighting, bull-baiting and cock-fighting which were 'low and demoralising pursuits'.[20] The influence of reformers, of Evangelicals, humanitarians and those proponents of public order who argued that demotic blood sports gathered together criminal elements and occasioned riotous behaviour, was growing. The Justices of the Peace had the power to restrain prize-fighting on the grounds of breach of the peace and unlawful assembly, but the enforcement of such restraint was a continuing problem as fights were arranged with secrecy, venues selected on the borders of counties and the constables often insufficient in number to disperse the crowds. In 1829 the Lord Lieutenant of Nottinghamshire, the fourth Duke of Newcastle, received information that people were travelling from as far afield as London to witness a fight in the county. His attempts to stop it were unsuccessful and it was reported that 4,000 spectators witnessed the fight.[21] Prize-fighting retained its popularity especially in certain parts of the country. In the coal mining districts of Warwickshire in the 1840s it was reported that 'when there is such a matter of universal interest as a prize-fight all must go to see it, and it is a day's play. Upon the average there may be five or six such occasions in the course of the summer.'[22] Wrestling, too, was popular both in the north-west and south-west of the country. Even in the furthest Methodist mining communities of Cornwall, where preachers inveighed against the sport, wrestling matches, often promoted by local publicans, survived.[23]

Blood sports could also be dealt with by magistrates if they were prepared to consider them as a common nuisance, but there was no parliamentary legislation forbidding them. Several bills were brought before parliament either to ban particular sports such as bull or bear-baiting or to prevent cruelty to animals in general. Many of them were brought in by Richard Martin, M P for Galway, who earned himself the nickname of 'Humanity Dick'. A majority of parliamentary opinion continued, however, to defend the sports as the traditional recreations of the people, and while Sir Robert Peel was at the Home Office he resolutely opposed legislation on blood sports. Most members of the House of Commons came from landed families and were themselves enthusiasts for field sports; many of them were conscious that it would be unfair to restrict the amusements of the poor while permitting those of the rich. The campaign against cruel sports was nevertheless becoming more organised and influential. Societies such as the Society for the Prevention of Cruelty to Animals, the Association for Promoting Rational Humanity Towards the Animal Creation and the Animals' Friend Society were founded in the twenties and early thirties and produced a stream of tracts and pamphlets. Parliament after 1832 may have been more sensitive to urban and middle class opinion, provided it did not interfere with a gentleman's sport. The time was approaching when, as Surtees's Jorrocks put it, 'Humanity is all the h'order of the day – folks protect other people's donkeys and let their own relatives starve'. The campaign against cruel sports was substantially won in parliament in 1835 when a Cruelty to Animals Act made all sports illegal which involved the baiting of animals, while an act of 1845 forbade cock-fighting. The suppression of the sports in practice was less easily achieved although as police forces were adopted, first in boroughs then in counties, a more effective means of control was at hand. Nevertheless these sports continued. *The Morning Chronicle* reported in 1851 that in Birmingham and the manufacturing districts of Staffordshire both 'bull-baits and cock-fights . . . are still indulged in on the sly, by workmen of the old school.'[24] Twenty-six years later another newspaper, the *Oldham Chronicle*, was claiming that blood sports, including cock-fighting, 'are no doubt practised to an alarming extent at the present day, but it is done under cover.'[25] Indeed, many sports such as dog-fighting, badger-baiting and cock-fighting were never to be completely eradicated but were to have a subterranean existence which continues up to the present day.

Other sports of the time, such as cricket, pedestrianism and rowing shared certain common characteristics with horse-racing and prize-fighting. They all became more organised, more dependent upon attracting spectators, and all were accompanied by heavy gambling. Regency England had an inordinate desire to wager, whether in the gilded surroundings of London clubs like Almack's or Whites, at the after-dinner card tables of genteel society or in the lowest of pubs or beer-houses. Cricket provided almost infinite possibilities for betting: how many runs an individual player would make or how many wickets he would take as well as which team would win the match. Bookmakers were present at all big matches and the teams themselves competed for high stakes.

Cricket was already being seen by contemporaries, as it has been perceived by historians, as a great harmoniser of class differences. G.M. Trevelyan was perhaps an extreme proponent of this viewpoint, writing:

> Squire, farmer, blacksmith and labourer, with their women and children came to see the fun, were at ease together and happy all the summer afternoon. If the French *noblesse* had been capable of playing cricket with their peasants, their chateaux would never have been burnt.[26]

It is undoubtedly true that from the mid-eighteenth century onwards there was a considerable mingling of the classes at cricket matches. Cricket originated as a game of the common people in the south of England, most notably in Kent and Hampshire, and was then taken up by the Quality. In the north and especially in Yorkshire it was introduced by the gentry who had learned to play at school and university, but it rapidly acquired a popular following. The different origins of the game in the south and north were to set their stamp upon it. It is conventional to regard southern cricket as having the more gentlemanly ethos and to see the game in the north as more dour and plebeian. In fact it is because the game was introduced to the north by the upper classes, at a time when both rules and technique were well developed, that it was from the beginning treated as a serious business; aristocrats and gentry in Georgian and Regency England set out to win, and the notion that the true gentleman is a good loser more interested in playing the game than winning is a late Victorian innovation. Village cricket in the south, with its festive atmosphere and greater conviviality, was closer to the game's popular origins. Whether in north or south, whether promoted by publicans or the owners of country houses, cricket increased rapidly in popularity. Matches between county teams attracted thousands of spectators and there were already professional players. The game was taking on much of its modern aspect: the M.C.C. had been founded in 1787 at Lord's in Marylebone; there were now three wickets, straight bats and a leg before wicket rule.

Pedestrianism and rowing were both to move up the social scale later in the nineteenth century but for the moment both remained essentially plebeian diversions. Running usually took place on public highways and when it attracted crowds of spectators could be seen as a public nuisance. Races were generally organised by publicans and the purses competed for were sufficient to create groups of part-time professionals. Rowing, especially on the Thames, was a popular spectator sport at the beginning of the century. Its heyday was to be in the middle decades of the century when it became a major sport and its most successful exponents popular heroes.

The leisure culture of early nineteenth century England was vigorous and varied. Whether in the heartlands of the industrial revolution or in the most isolated rural village the notion of a vacuum, as a traditional culture withered and an urban culture waited in the wings, is mythical.

Many traditional customs, even those which contained the potential for violence and which from time to time came under attack, continued for most of the century. New Year's mumming festivities were observed in the north at least until the 1870s and the outward form hardly changed at all.[27] The same can be said for the celebration of Guy Fawkes Night. It remained one of the most important dates in the calendar year throughout the nineteenth century, especially in the south of the country. Although the links of the festival with popular radicalism had been severed very early in the nineteenth century, there were still many objections to the celebrations on the grounds that there was a strong likelihood of fires breaking out and also that the burning of effigies, especially when they represented local dignitaries, was not to be encouraged. In some places, as in Guildford in the 1820s, there was a concerted effort on the part of the magistrates to suppress the Guy Fawkes activities, but the celebrations continued, sometimes passing off peaceably and at other times, especially in the 1850s and 60s, with a considerable amount of disorder and damage to property. In Exeter the authorities attempted to reduce rowdyism and possible violence on the 5th November by holding an official event which involved the ringing of churchbells, processions and sermons, and the illumination of some of the municipal premises. Despite this, they were unable to eliminate the traditional elements, a large group gathered in the cathedral yard, and bonfires and effigies were burnt amid noisy and boisterous celebrations. But, as with attitudes towards so many leisure activities, opinions for and against the celebration of Guy Fawkes could not be accounted for merely along class lines. Crowds on Guy Fawkes night were not always just composed of artisans and labourers. On the other hand, some of the fiercest critics of the festival were 'Chartists, trade unionists and self-improving workmen.'[28]

Even in the cotton areas of industrial Lancashire, which were the first parts of the country to undergo intensive mechanisation and where the need for a new factory discipline was, quite understandably, strongest, changes to traditional customs were not easily enforced. Although the 1833 Factory Act designated only Christmas Day and Good Friday, together with eight half days as holidays, some workers insisted on continuing to take the traditional days of New Year and Easter Monday instead. It was also difficult to restrict the workers to taking just these holidays. In the 1840s the Factory Commissioners reported occasions when extra holidays were given by employers, 'not due to liberality on the part of the masters, but to custom.'[29]

These concessions to the traditional wakes weeks which were the most important event in the recreational year in most parts of Lancashire (as well as many other parts of the country), were forced from the millowners rather than freely given. Admittedly some owners, especially those from landed backgrounds and who worked small or medium-sized firms, still maintained a fairly paternalistic approach towards their workers and were prepared to be tolerant, at least to some extent, about these customs and holidays[30]; but most were deeply concerned with maintaining production and this required strict factory discipline. Nevertheless, they were often powerless to prevent their workers from absenting themselves from the factory during the wakes. One thing in the workers' favour was that they were often all recruited from nearby parishes and so the workers in particular mills often had the same attachment to particular wakes. In this sense there was strength in numbers and when mill workers voted with their feet at the time of important festivals mill owners could do very little. For example, when it was announced at Padiham Fair that Monseigneur Signor de la Unsinque would walk on the river and be drawn in a chariot by geese, many workpeople from Colne and Bacup attended the fair and several of the mills in Burnley were closed for the day.[31] In any case, it is important even in Lancashire not to overemphasize the importance of the mills in the community at this period. Although factory work was the norm among young people, most of them did not spend their whole working lives in the mills but went on to other jobs such as labouring, building and handicrafts which were not so intensively mechanised and where a more casual approach to the working day still existed.

Of course, wakes and fairs did not come under attack just from employers. Moral reformers, the magistracy and police were all anxious about occasions which were liable to attract disreputable characters such as pickpockets, thieves, street traders and whores, and where drunkenness, turbulent behaviour and even violence was likely to occur. Too much external interference in the wakes, however, met with opposition from various quarters. When the police made a number of arrests at Oldham wakes in 1864 they were not only resisted by the merrymakers but were also criticised by the *Oldham Chronicle* for their petty behaviour.[32] Indeed, one reason why the wakes continued was that the respectable elements in the towns were far from unanimous in condemning them and very often disagreed about what action should be taken. At times the police were reluctant to interfere, despite the urgings of the magistracy and reformers, on the grounds that activities at fairs and wakes were invariably harmless and could easily be kept under control. Consequently, they argued that it was preferable to maintain these gatherings rather than take drastic action which might result in them having to cope with unsupervised, unorganised and potentially mischievous assemblies.[33] Wakes, in fact, had many powerful defenders. In Stockport, for instance, although the Corporation consistently attempted to abolish the street stalls and alter the timing of the wakes, they were opposed successfully for many years by the local publicans and tradespeople.[34]

There was no sharp break with the past in the leisure activities of the majority of the population, for the essentials of most sports and entertainments were already well established. Rather, there was an acceleration of the pre-existing tendency towards a widening of the market for a commercial leisure industry. The entrepreneurs of that industry were small-scale capitalists, often publicans, and its economy paralleled, was fuelled by and itself contributed to, the manufacturing and commercial economy. So while many fairs and wakes maintained their traditional elements, all of them made adaptations and innovations. Leisure activities were re-packaged, marketed more professionally and adapted to larger numbers and to urban environments.

The popular culture of Regency England was highly gregarious and was intimately connected with the sale of alcohol and the provision of opportunities for betting. It put a high premium on sensation and could at times be both macabre and callous. If actors and prize-fighters were its everyday heroes, the murderer or celebrated criminal were regarded with an ambiguity which made them at least anti-heroes. There was a considerable interest in the careers of famous villains, an appetite which was catered for by a mini-industry producing ballads, broadsheets and pamphlets giving accounts of murders and the murderers' confessions. Such prurience was no last kick of a dying pre-industrial culture, for it was to become a central feature of the new Sunday press and to live on into our own time. The abolition of public executions was to be one of the most unpopular acts of Lord Russell's second administration and until then executions were something of a carnival. In 1807 a crowd of 45,000 gathered to see two men hanged, and 27 spectators died in the crush. Forty years later J. Ewing Ritchie described the crowd that gathered to watch the execution of the murderer Marley:

> We have seen every execution for the last ten years, and boast how on one day we saw one man hung at Newgate, and took a cab and got to Horsemonger-lane in time to see another.[35]

Interest was not confined to plebeian circles for, when the trial of William Corder, perhaps the most celebrated murderer of the early nineteenth century, took place at Bury St Edmunds, the court was unable to accommodate the crowds of well-to-do people who flocked from London to witness it.

The sensational and violent nature of much of popular culture and the ubiquity of drinking and gambling were nothing new but were more noticeable and threatening in a more urban, crowded and complex society. They threatened and troubled those especially whose tastes and sensibilities had been changed and refined by religious revival or humanitarianism. Evangelicalism and Methodism provided the impetus for an attempt to reform the manners and morals of the lower orders, while the rational humanitarian spirit inspired confidence that enquiry and wise legislation could engineer improvement.

It is above all with the middle orders of society, or the middle classes as they were soon to be called, that we associate opposition to much of popular culture. The terms 'middle class' or 'the middle classes' encompass, however, a heterogeneous assortment of people: the barber, the manufacturer, the shopkeeper, the farmer, doctor or clerk. Many of them were religious, earnest and sober while others were self-consciously respectable and concerned to distance themselves from that which was immediately below them. A considerable number of them were, of course, neither earnest nor respectable, save in their economic position; they drank, gambled, attended race-meetings and cared not one whit for improving their morals and habits nor anyone else's. There is, however, truth in the notion that parts of the middle sections of society tended to be particularly susceptible, for moral, intellectual and economic reasons, to the desire to improve the manners and morals of society and of the lower classes in particular. Religious revival transcended class but evangelical religion, which put a premium upon family piety and restrained and disciplined living, made a special appeal to those whose economic position rested upon the same virtues. An outward conformity to the standards of the day is in any case thrust upon certain sections of society; a gambling aristocrat or a drunken coalheaver has less pressure upon him to hide his proclivities than a gambling bank manager or drunken doctor. The economic case for reforming the habits of the workforce made an obvious appeal to those who themselves employed labour and felt their profits imperilled by drink in the workshop, the working week cut short by St Monday or the day taken off for a prize-fight. Above all, the less prosperous and secure or those who had most recently and with exertion pulled themselves out of the ranks of the lower orders were most conscious of, because they were closest to, the sheer brutality of much of popular life.

The contrast between the dominant intellectual movements of the day – religious revival and rational liberalism – and the cruel, rough and vicious nature of much of everyday life, resulted in a self-conscious cultivation of respectability on the part of those of all classes who wished to emphasise their social superiority, and produced much of the impetus for reform.

Industrialisation and urbanisation were bound to require both an increase in the power and activity of government and changes in the nature of social discipline. The attempt to reform popular culture by legislation and proselytisation from above can be seen to be at one with the reform of the institutions of government and administration, as society struggled to come to terms with unexpected and unplanned demographic and economic changes. From George III's Proclamation against Vice of 1787, in which he urged his subjects to help suppress 'excessive drinking, blasphemy, profane swearing and cursing, profanation of the Lord's day, and other dissolute, immoral or disorderly practices' the campaign for reform had gained momentum. By the eighteen-thirties a formidable array of societies had been founded, all concerned to eradicate particular evils. There were, as we have seen, the societies concerned with preventing cruelty to animals but there were also the Lord's Day Observance Society, founded in 1831, and the British and Foreign Temperance Society. It was only after 1832 that such societies gained a purchase in parliament (and then only to a limited degree) and during the thirties that towns gained police forces which were supposedly capable of implementing legislation that was passed. Betting was, however, an early target for reform. The Select Committee on Lotteries of 1808 argued:

> Idleness, poverty, and dissipation are increased [by the State Lottery] . . . truth betrayed, domestic comfort destroyed, madness often created, crimes are committed and even suicide itself is produced . . . And this unseemly state of things is to continue, in order that the state may derive a certain annual sum from the partial encouragement of a Vice. . . .'[36]

However, acts making lotteries illegal were not passed until 1823 and 1825, and further measures to discourage gambling had to wait until the forties and fifties. In 1853 the working man's love of putting a few pence on a race horse was endangered when all off-course betting shops were declared illegal. But gambling was far too deeply ingrained to be ended by legislation and off-course betting was merely driven underground.

It is tempting to see the campaign to reform popular culture, and to develop in the working classes a frame of mind and attitude to leisure which would reinforce social discipline and make for a more diligent work-force, as emanating from changes in the means of production and as being in the interests solely of the owners of those means. Class was certainly an increasingly important factor in the developing industrial society but the essential beliefs of reformers were not the prerogative of any one class nor dictated by the interests of any class. They were, rather, a shared legacy from the Enlightenment and religious revivalism. As Brian Harrison has shown, Sabbatarianism, temperance and even the RSPCA cut across class divisions, finding considerable support among working men, and divided the working class internally 'between nonconformists and secularists, radicals and traditionalists, autodidacts and illiterates, puritans and *bon viveurs*'.[37]

The battle over popular culture was waged among the working classes themselves. In many working communities the effects of Evangelical missionaries were considerable. During a Primitive Methodist crusade in County Durham:

> The most impressive scenes were witnessed. Fallings were common, as many as fourteen being seen on the floor at once. At a lovefeast at Bishop Auckland the people fell in all directions, and there was a strange mingling of shouts groans and hallelujahs. During the revival at South Side, centres of gambling were broken up; confirmed gamblers burnt their dice, cards and books of enchantment; drunkards, hopeless incurable sots, were freed from the dread tyranny of fiery appetite; pugilists, practised and professional, and cock-fighters of terrible experience, turned from their brutalities.[38]

Nor, as we have seen, was working class radicalism well disposed towards popular culture. The class conflict between Owenism and Chartism on the one hand and middle-class liberalism on the other, which marked the eighteen thirties and forties, can easily obscure the intellectual tradition all had in common. All drew upon the tradition of the Enlightenment which provided the backbone for middle-class liberalism and working-class radicalism alike, although the former stressed individualism and the latter was more egalitarian. Both placed an enormous emphasis upon the capacity of the individual for self-improvement, which combined a reverence for reason with a distaste for sensual gratification owing more to Evangelicalism than to the Enlightenment. The fairground, the racecourse and the pantomime did not figure in radical utopias.

The popular culture which emerged in the first decades of the nineteenth century was assailed by middle-class reformers and working-class radicals and non-conformists alike. The combined influence of those forces, with their desire to make working men more rational, more sober and more far-sighted in their use of leisure time was slight. The male-orientated, drink and betting-based and gregarious popular culture that flourished in Regency England was to survive substantially unchanged until the middle decades of the century. Thereafter it did not disappear, though its cruder manifestations were trimmed, but it was balanced, and to some extent tamed, by a private and domestic culture when rises in real wages enabled home and family to become more of a centre and focus for leisure life.

FOUR

Improving and amusing recreations, 1820–60

London, July 29, 1841 . . . laudable efforts have been made to open institutions for workmen, citizens, mechanics and the lower classes in general, where they may receive instruction adapted to their condition, instead of squandering the time, when they are not at work, in mere indolence, or in sinful indulgences. Lectures and books, calculated to awaken their mental faculties, and to have a salutary influence on their ordinary occupations, were therefore provided. By this means, the influence of false teachers and false doctrines was to be combated, and the great danger to civil society, which has been so often mentioned, would be at the least diminished.

F. von Raumer, *England in 1841*

Britain in the first half of the nineteenth century was changing rapidly. The increase in the growth of population which had started earlier in the nineteenth century had gathered such a momentum that the population doubled in the period between 1801 and 1851. But not only was the population growing, it was moving, so that whereas at the time of the first census in 1801 the large majority lived in rural areas, by mid-century slightly more people lived in towns than in the countryside. The population of Manchester and its surrounding area increased nearly fivefold over this period from 75,000 to 339,000. The numbers living in Leeds shot up from 53,000 to 207,000 between 1801 and 1851 and similar increases took place in many other towns, especially in the midlands and the north of England. The problems caused by urbanisation together with those brought about by the rapid increase in the production of raw materials and the mechaniz-ation of certain industries – particularly those producing cotton products, where a factory based workforce grew from under 90,000 in

1800 to well over a quarter of a million by 1840 – were manifold and wide-ranging. For this transformation of the economy and society not only brought dislocation and hardships for large sections of the population: it also placed enormous strains upon the institutions of government and administration which were, to say the least, rudimentary and not designed for coping with an industrialising society. These problems were exacerbated by the political developments which were taking place both at home and abroad. There was an ever-present fear among the governing classes that the ideas of the French Revolution would spread and gain a hold in Britain. The wars with France which went on for 22 years brought their own strains, which were heightened after the peace in 1815 when Britain was thrown into a considerable post-war slump. The consequent unemployment, together with the effects of the high levels of indirect taxation which successive governments had been forced to levy, inevitably brought distress and discontent in the country. Indeed, there is no doubt that the first half of the nineteenth century was a period of considerable social and political unrest, which manifested itself in a variety of ways from inarticulate but violent reactions to food shortages and the introduction of machinery to coherent attempts to form trade unions and political pressure groups.

In this atmosphere it is understandable that local magistrates were extremely sensitive to possible threats to social order. They were especially concerned at times of public holidays when fairs, which attracted large numbers of people, occasionally erupted into disorder and sometimes riot. Whereas in the past these occurrences had been acceptable and, indeed, often regarded as a necessary safety valve, in the emerging urban industrial society where efficient police forces were only just developing, they were dreaded by many of the governing classes who were conscious of just how fragile and vulnerable was the social order of the country. At the same time many manufacturers, especially in those industries where mechanization was taking place, desired not only a more disciplined workforce but also more regulated working hours and a reduction of official and unofficial holidays. The attack on blood sports made by members of the growing Evangelical and humanitarian movements came together with these factors to make for an opposition to some aspects of demotic culture. Social historians aware of this attack have therefore concluded this was a period when popular pastimes virtually disappeared in the urban areas. But, as we have seen, this was not the case. Britain was not a country 'where leisure disappeared under an avalanche of work'.[1] Robert Malcolmson's conclusions that during this period 'the foundations of many traditional practices were relentlessly swept away, leaving a vacuum which would be only gradually reoccupied'[2] must be called into question. Even James Walvin's recent assertion that whereas 'In rural parts the old pastimes and customs died hard and could still be found in a thriving state towards the end of the nineteenth century', 'In the towns and cities of early Victorian England, however, there seemed no place for many of the traditional recreations,'[3] needs some modification. It does appear, for instance, that in the case of the wakes and fairs in Lancashire it was the rural, not the urban ones, which were the main casualties in these years and that many popular customs survived 'not only in spite of, but also because of, industrialisation.'[4]

Nevertheless there was a strong impression among some contemporaries that the attempt to abolish certain pastimes had done more harm than good because it had resulted in the labouring classes being left with very few outlets for leisure, other than those of the most debased kinds. Drunkenness, violence and fornication, it was claimed, were on the increase. Both Engels and de Tocqueville wrote of industrial Manchester in despairing tones, the latter describing the town as a place where 'civilised man is turned back almost into a savage.'[5] Another observer writing of Blackburn commented that there were 'few amusements . . . They run to foolish singing rooms . . . where depravity prevails and morality is at a low ebb; after which both parents and children retire to the beer shop and thus spend their hard-earned weekly wages. Their very bodies are poisoned with smoke and drink, ribaldry and obscenity.'[6] This alarm that moral standards were declining, combined with the fear that the social stability of the country was being undermined, was voiced by Robert Slaney MP who argued that it was the duty of those governing the working classes to provide suitable alternative recreations for these people who otherwise 'will fly to demagogues and dangerous causes.'[7]

It was not just the fear of an unregulated and potentially revolutionary workforce which prompted these concerns. By the 1820s and 1830s there was a growing sense, especially among reforming and Evangelical groups, that although the lower orders seemed to have an inbuilt disposition towards spending any free time they had in sexual excesses, gambling and drinking, the middle and upper classes were not entirely free from blame or responsibility for this state of affairs. There were a number of reasons for this very real feeling of guilt. First, urbanisation and enclosures, it was argued, had resulted in the loss of public open spaces and footpaths and hence restricted the scope of working class leisure time activities. Consequently, the lower orders had been driven from comparatively healthy outdoor activities towards the numerous temptations offered by the wide variety of drinking houses. Second, just as large sections of common land had been made private for the benefit of the middle and upper classes, so too nearly all the places of cultural improvement from which the working classes could benefit – art galleries, botanical gardens, libraries and museums – were denied to them, either because they could not afford the subscriptions or entrance fees or because they were, if not positively excluded, at least not welcomed. Third, the lower classes had been influenced and harmed by the lax manners and morals of their social superiors. It was the duty of the rich, so Hannah More and others claimed, to set a wholesome example to the poorer classes through their own behaviour and this was not being done. The life style of the gentry and aristocracy, who had plenty of leisure time and yet seemed to use it parasitically and to no real purpose, was one complained of by many reforming bodies. But blame was not reserved solely for the upper classes. The members of the Select Committee set up to investigate the extent of drunkenness among the labouring classes in 1834 concluded that one reason for its high incidence was that the 'humbler classes' had been influenced by 'the prevalence of intemperate habits and pernicious customs . . . among the middle and higher ranks.'[8] In the last resort, however, the problem was a much more fundamental one, which could not be resolved simply by blaming one particular social grouping or set of actions.

The early Victorians were genuinely concerned and bewildered about how leisure time should be used. For one thing leisure was often associated with idleness, so that while it was acknowledged that spare time could bring benefits it was also recognized that it had its dangers. In a society where the gospel of work was so deeply ingrained and its virtues so vigorously extolled, it was perhaps inevitable that leisure time should be regarded with suspicion. If work was a Christian virtue then leisure time was a potential temptation and man, being a fallible creature, could, if he had an excess of leisure, be easily and perhaps inevitably led towards delinquency or idleness. This view was expressed very early on in the century by that prophet of doom and despair, Thomas Malthus. 'Leisure is, without doubt, highly valuable to man but, taking man as he is, the probability seems to be that in the greater number of instances it will produce evil rather than good.'[9]

If Malthus was correct, the only sure way of avoiding the dangers inherent in leisure time was to restrict it to a minimum. In the short term, in the early decades of the nineteenth century, there probably was a contraction of such time among many of the industrial workers. The only other alternative was for religious, humanitarian and educational bodies to confront and provide the labouring classes with as many acceptable and improving activities as possible; these should cater for all age groups and be dispensed through a wide variety of agencies, from Sunday Schools to Mechanics' Institutes. It was only by this method, so reformers claimed, of providing 'improving' and 'rational' pastimes in place of debasing and degrading ones that the lower orders could be weaned away from drinking and gambling and other excesses and could develop as members of a culturally harmonious society. However, as the century progressed, it was increasingly recognised that by no means all working men wished to spend their leisure time in chapels, class rooms or reading rooms and that other more attractive alternatives needed to be provided which would combine both instruction and amusement. So what was meant by 'rational' changed during the century. By the 1850s and 1860s the educational content of many rational recreations had diminished and given way to activities which in the 1820s and 1830s would not have been acceptable.

Some writers have interpreted these developments of what has been called a 'cultural penetration of the poor' as a deliberate attempt on the part of the 'industrial bourgeoisie' to influence the cultural development of the working classes.[10] But this is far too simplistic and indeed it is misleading to conclude that the idea of rational recreations was merely an effort to impose 'bourgeois standards' of propriety on the working classes. In fact the desire for improvement and respectability came from a variety of sources and certainly was not pursued merely along class lines. It was not just radical MPs like William Ewart, Joseph Hume, Robert Slaney and Thomas Wyse who argued and strove for these ends. As we have already seen the battle over popular culture was waged among the working classes themselves, and temperance, decency and self-improvement were advocated just as strenuously by sections of the working classes as by the middle classes. The London Working Men's Association urged that radical leadership was needed just as much in relation to morality as it was in politics, and its secretary William Lovett, in presenting a petition in

1829 for the Sunday opening of museums, put forward an argument central to the beliefs of all rational recreationalists when he asserted that 'the best remedy for drunkenness is to divert and inform the mind.'[11]

Within the trade union and particularly the Chartist movements there were conscious and determined efforts not only to publish writings of a superior quality to the popular romantic and sensational novels but also to ensure that these works were of a quite separate nature from the writings produced by the upper and middle classes. Chartist writers attempted to inspire working men to improve their conditions by both political and educational means, but they also aimed to attack the sort of popular literature which was written *for* the poor and which invariably consisted of tales about the better-off, where the labouring classes were very often represented as good-natured but comic.

Although Chartist literature took various forms – essays, songs, short stories and novels, it was the Chartist poets who were the most well-known and most prolific. W.J. Linton, Ernest Jones, Gerald Massey and Thomas Cooper were all influenced by the Romantic poets, especially Wordsworth and Keats, but they attempted to adapt the Romantic style in such a way that they could incorporate their political viewpoints. To accomplish this task and, at the same time, to write poetry which was easily acceptable to working people was no easy task and it is perhaps not surprising that their audience was limited in number. Nevertheless, although the writers and readers of this literature were in the minority, the desire for self-improvement was something which is traceable in most towns and villages throughout the country. Joseph Lawson of Pudsey recalled how some of the young men in the town used to meet at 5 a.m. for an hour before work and again on certain nights of the week in order 'to read and converse on grammar, history, geography and theology.'[12] The hunger for knowledge and learning can also been seen in the development of many working men's mutual improvement societies and other similar bodies set up in the 1820s and 30s. A great many of the autobiographies of working men written in this period reveal a keen determination on the part of the writers to improve themselves. Nearly all of their leisure time, and some of their work time, was devoted to this end. On occasions these writers, although committed to improving the working and living conditions of their fellow working men, showed a scant regard for those colleagues who were not so single-minded. Thomas Dunning described a workman who had been arrested for trade union activities as a man who 'could read and write a little, but he was a lightminded, dancing, public house man.'[13] Christopher Thomson went even further and showed as much contempt for his fellow workers as any middle class gentleman might have for the unwashed poor. Thomson, describing how he started work as an apprentice in a shipwright's, recalled:

> My attention was turned to books, to drawing, to questions of political moment, to the theatres, but above all, to the flowery fields and the green country. Few of my pursuits found a response in the hearts of my every-day associates; their tastes were of the lowest grade; their conversations generally disgusting; their books, the obscene trash raked up from the pest-holes that unfortunately may be found in every town; their amusements being card-playing, tossing with halfpence, and other low modes of gambling, with drinking, smoking and chewing tobacco.[14]

If we consider the indigenously working class organisations dedicated to self-help and compare them with those launched with the assistance of upper or middle class patronage, we can find no clear dividing line between them. Certainly, Chartism and Owenism posited a working class radicalism with an emphasis upon collective help, in contrast to the stress placed by liberal radicals upon the lonely road to be followed by the sturdy individual as he strove for self-improvement. Yet working class radicalism, too, stressed self-improvement and accentuated the gap between the respectable and reasoning working man and his venal contemporary, while rational recreationalists saw voluntary organisations as necessary crucibles for individual improvement. In practice it was those working class organisations with ostensibly radical aims, such as the trade unions and co-operatives which thrived after mid-century, which most emphasised the distinction between the better-off working men and their fellows. Those co-operatives which followed on the foundation of the consumers' co-operative at Rochdale in 1844, although they retained a commitment to the wider aspirations of Owenite Co-operativism, limited, by their insistence on cash payment, their membership to the more prosperous sections of the working classes. The working men's self-help organisations which achieved by far the greatest and widest membership were the friendly benefit societies providing sickness and funeral benefits. They were more attuned to the requirements of a mass membership, and organisations like the Oddfellows, the Foresters and the Buffaloes, by centring a society social life around monthly meetings in pubs and annual feasts, were hugely successful.

Religious and temperance organisations, adult educationalists and rational recreationalists all proffered their own solutions for the best use of leisure time. At one extreme were those religious bodies which offered few alternatives other than a keen observance of the scriptures, and who issued dire warnings about the dangers of indulging in many of the popular pastimes. *The Baptist Children's Magazine* in October 1831, for example, asked the question 'Will you go to the Fair?' and then repeated the ominous story of

> Mary, who was going to the fair; she was just thirteen years old; another girl, older than herself, begged her not to go, but to go with her instead, to hear a sermon; at length she consented to go, and O! it was a happy choice for her, for the sermon she heard was blessed to the conversion of her soul. She returned home with different feelings than if she had gone to the fair; and it was well for her she was converted thus early, for she died while young. Ah! Think of her, dear children, if she had gone to the fair she might have become hardened in sin, and gone on from bad to worse, and think how different would have been her end; not happy and peaceful as it proved, but full of terror . . . [15]

Other religious bodies, while not propounding such a stern and unbending creed, argued that the best method of counteracting radical ideas as well as providing an alternative to the 'trashy' and 'immoral' literature which abounded was to produce their own improving and morally acceptable literature. The Religious Tract Society, founded in 1799, which served all denominations, was one of the first in the field. The Society for the Promotion of Christian Knowledge was another organization which concentrated on producing tracts and distributing them as widely as possible and particularly in the industrial areas. Many of their publications gave advice on how the working classes could improve their lives, the major solutions being to embrace God and to develop the principles of self-help. But religion, just like politics, could be socially divisive and therefore was a possible obstacle to producing cultural harmony. Consequently *Chambers Edinburgh Journal*, which first appeared in 1832 and which was primarily aimed at a working class readership, avoided both topics. *The Penny Magazine*, which undercut the *Edinburgh Journal* in price by a half-penny, went even further and also excluded all fiction, except poetry, on the grounds that it was not sufficiently educative. More informative and educational than the Chambers publication, *The Penny Magazine* was started by the members of the Society for the Diffusion of Useful Knowledge. Founded in 1827 by a group of middle class radicals, some of whom later became ministers in, or were closely connected with, the Whig ministries of the 1830s, the announced aim of the SDUK was 'to direct the powers of reading which they (the working classes) have acquired, to such employment of their leisure hours as may at once furnish amusement and instruction.'[16] The Society produced a variety of publications, including a manual on how to form and run Mechanics' Institutes. Although the circulation figures for *The Penny Magazine* reached 200,000 in 1833–4, it is impossible to assess just how many working class men were attracted to this sort of improving literature. It is hard to believe that, excluding fiction as it did, it would be read by those whose main literary diet was chap books and penny serials; this is probably one reason why circulation declined and the magazine stopped publication in 1846. Another criticism of *The Penny Magazine* and other improving publications came from working class radicals, who regarded them as 'that easy issue of Whig benevolence, all that kindly supply of juiceless chaff.'[17]

Similar criticisms were levelled at Mechanics' Institutes. First, it was said that they too often were merely middle class agencies and, although ostensibly intended for the working classes, depended too much upon the support and encouragement of the middle classes. In his evidence given to the Select Committee on Public Libraries in 1849, that major propagandist for the Victorian ideal of self-help, Samuel Smiles, bluntly asserted that these Institutes were 'not institutes for working people, but are principally supported by the middle classes, and by the higher order of skilled artisans; but the factory population, which constitutes the bulk of the population of the West Riding, do not belong to these mechanics' institutes, with a few rare exceptions.' Apart from the fact that for many working people 'their time is occupied for most of the day, and it is late evening before they get home' another major constraint upon working men becoming members was the fee, which was often prohibitive at 3d or 4d weekly.[18]

Mechanics' Institutes were first set up in the early 1820s with the specific aim of teaching science to working men. But as early as the end of that same decade it was becoming clear that these objectives were not being achieved. Instead, the Institutes provided literary and cultural programmes as well as a very large number of elementary education classes. By 1852, in the 59 Mechanics' Institutes in Yorkshire which provided education, four-fifths of the classes were concerned with elementary education. An even more interesting fact was that of the 11,813 members belonging to the 59 Institutes only 2,110 were attending any educational classes at all.[19] Increasingly they were becoming less specifically adult education establishments and much more places which provided a wide range of improving recreations. In the eyes of many rational recreationalists this was a development which was not necessarily disappointing. On the contrary, by providing acceptable recreations and amusements, it was hoped that the Institutes would provide a suitable milieu where people of all classes could meet. In this sense they were, it was hoped, ideal vehicles for promoting class harmony. The Annual Report of the Yorkshire Union of Mechanics' Institutes for 1861 claimed that they provided

> . . . an admirable common ground whereon the rich and the poor, the educated and the ignorant might meet, might learn to understand each other better, and perhaps to respect each other more. The greatest social evil of the present day is the isolation – between the employer and the employed. Indifference to each other's interests is the normal condition of their relation, and active hostility in the form of strikes has of late years become a painfully frequent feature of the time.[20]

There were those, however, who believed that the Institutes had moved too far towards providing recreations and had lost sight of their earlier educational aims. The *Banbury Guardian* in 1850 commented that it 'was most certainly high time' at least for the local branch of the Mechanics' Institute, 'to cease being a playroom and to become what it professes to be – an Institution for the promotion of arts and literature among the mechanics of Banbury.'[21]

Despite this plea it was becoming clearer as the century progressed that the only way the rational recreationalists would achieve their aims was to put a much greater emphasis on events in which the major ingredients were entertainment and amusement rather than education. Sir Benjamin Heywood appreciated this point: recognizing that Mechanics' Institutes were failing to attract working men in any large numbers, he attempted to provide an alternative institution in the form of Lyceums. The end results, he hoped, would be similar to those to which the Mechanics' Institutes aspired, and he too worked towards achieving a mixing together socially of employers and employed. So, at the Lyceums that he set up in Manchester and Salford in the late 1830s, he not only kept subscriptions low and encouraged the attendance of wives as well as husbands at meetings, but also provided programmes which were angled much more towards social evenings, sporting events and excursions than towards the formal lecture.

The various Temperance Societies which by the 1840s were perhaps the most important of the bodies providing rational re-creations, also found it much easier to attract large numbers to their recreational events than to their more formal and business meetings. Temperance Societies in particular took advantage of the low price railway excursions which became available in the 1840s. Railways were used increasingly for bringing together members of various branches to large rallies, as well as for annual and special outings or, as in the first rail trip organised by Thomas Cook in 1841, to take 3000 children from Leicester to Derby so that they would escape the evils of Leicester on horse race-day. This device of providing an alternative attraction to counter other local events was, of course, not new. Peter Bailey mentions how Sunday Schools of all denominations in the 1820s in Bolton 'instituted regular tea parties to keep their pupils from defection on race meeting day'; and how, in the same town in the 1840s, the traditional Whit walks were adapted by the Sunday Schools, whose members joined together with the young people in the Temperance movement to process through the streets of the town bearing flags and accompanied by bands.[22] But railway outings, especially at Whitsun, probably did more than anything else to alter the traditional nature of some of the old holidays. It has been argued that at first the fairs and wakes profited from the development of the railway system and that St Giles' fair in Oxford 'came of age with the excursion ticket' when a train brought 900 visitors from Banbury in 1850. Indeed, some came to Oxford fair from as far afield as Birmingham, Cardiff, Gloucester and London.[23] But gradually, as the varied alternatives that railway excursions provided grew in scope, so the fairs and wakes lost their primacy in the yearly calendar.

Many Mechanics' Institutes, benefit societies and a whole host of other organizations began, in the 1840s, to arrange railway outings at holiday time. But even where they did not, the activities of these societies, especially on special occasions like Whitsun, were affecting changes in leisure activities. Whitsun had always been an ideal time for annual club meetings and, perhaps understandably, events associated with benefit clubs or friendly societies were more well-ordered and less boisterous than many of the less organised activities which had taken place over the holiday earlier in the century.

The transformation of Whit-ales, wakes or feasts into a Whitsuntide celebration in which the focus of attention was upon village clubs or friendly societies is an important indicator of the changes that were taking place in rural life and culture. Such clubs, often branches of the Oddfellows or Foresters, would parade to church wearing ribbons and rosettes in the colours of their societies. Procession and church would be followed by a substantial meal, while side-shows and stalls provided entertainment and further refreshment, and the day would be concluded with dancing. Many clubs went to great lengths to ensure that their activities were peaceful and respectable. One of the rules of the Prince of Wales Club in Clanfield, Oxfordshire, laid down:

> That a feast shall be held on Whit Tuesday in every year, when the Society shall meet together by nine o'clock in the forenoon of the feast day, to go to church in a decent manner, walking two and two and returning in the same order, and if any member neglects going to Churh he shall pay sixpence to the funds of the Society. Every member shall, on feast day, pay three shillings and sixpence towards providing the feast. The feast to close the same night at 9.30 o'clock . . .

Nevertheless, however much care local organizations put into their preparations for Whit celebrations, on occasions old inter-village rivalries or the effects of drink still disrupted events. Much to the disappointment of the respectable sections of society, violence and idleness were still part of popular culture. So in Abingdon in 1832, where a sports day had been organised, it was sadly reported that 'Soon after the commencement of the proceedings several disgraceful fights occurred which at one time threatened to seriously prejudice the success of the sports.'[24]

Although such events gained the support and patronage of church and local gentry, we can distinguish in them the rural equivalent to the aspirations of urban working men to a margin of security and public acknowledgement of their respectability and independence. The development of these new Whitsuntide festivals can be said to come within the category of 'invented tradition' as opposed to custom[25] and, indeed, as custom withered and passed into desuetude new rural traditions, often in the guise of reformed custom, took its place. To say that the popular customary calendar was annexed by the Victorian middle class, purged of its disagreeable features and restored as a respectable medium for the suppression of social order within the village community[26], is both to overestimate the vitality and relevance of much of the old calendar and to give too passive a role to the rural workforce in the creation of the traditions of the new.

While opposition to rural customs among the upper orders of the countryside remained, it had never, as we have seen, been monolithic. The influence of the Romantic movement and the growing anti-quarian interests of country clergy and the more bookish squires, increasingly led to approval of what was considered traditional and customary, even if in practice such customs appeared decayed and inadequate as contrasted with their imagined heyday. Many rural festivals were ostensibly recreated or reformed but were in fact largely invented. It is easy to see the basis of such invention, in a dream of medieval harmony and order where the moral and social ideals owed more to Hannah More than to the middle ages. Even in the most 'closed' of parishes, however, the new festivals could only be successful in so far as they also met the aspirations and needs of the rural workforce. If village friendly societies and Whit walking most obviously manifested self-help and an independent respectability, which yet looked to big house and church for approval and legitimacy, the newly invented traditions which were gradually to be superimposed upon May Day fulfilled real needs as well. The ceremonies of May Day were indeed transformed 'to accord more with prevailing Victorian taste and ideas of social behaviour' but such taste and ideas were not the prerogative of any one class. A more caring, perhaps more sentimental, attitude towards children was to be found in many working class homes and found its public manifestation in the crowning of the Queen of the May and the carrying of garlands by her attendants.

It seems clear that the upper orders in the English countryside held to an ideal of social harmony in which older conceptions of paternalism and deference were reinterpreted, within a Victorian framework that drew a sharp distinction between the worthy and unworthy poor. It is also true that recreation, sport and village festivals were seen as crucial indicators of the health of the community, and that many older customs were bowdlerised and refurbished, with innovations such as village cricket made 'traditional' instantly. The labouring poor were, however, by no means passive in the face of such social engineering and even in the most 'closed' of villages, the 'traditional' rural community which had developed by the later decades of the century represented a synthesis between an upper class ideal of social order and harmony and a partial realisation of the changing ambitions and standards of labourers and their families. Such ambitions and standards were characterised by a more marked emphasis upon home and family, a desire for respectable status and for some recognition of a qualified independence. The authority of landowners and even of farmers was rarely questioned and the social position of parson was often accepted, even where his spiritual influence was negligible; authority was expected to subsidise and to legitimise the new institutions of village life, the reading rooms, the village halls and cricket fields which were provided from mid-century onwards; the organisation of village sewing circles by vicars' wives proved popular, while it was considered only proper that flower and vegetable shows and even self-help organisations such as friendly societies should receive gentry patronage. Officious interference, such as attempts to persuade village women to wear plain, sensible clothing rather than belatedly follow the urban fashions of the day before, prying into domestic budgets and family concerns, and the peremptory closure of public houses in the interests of either temperance or economic efficiency, was widely resented.

Older customs and festivals flourished and thrived where they still catered for real needs, whether economic or social. Thus the visit to a hiring fair was still the means of finding new employment for many country people and it was also the annual occasion on which they could participate in the bustle and excitement of a wider world. Other festivals were, as we have seen, reinterpreted and adorned with new traditions which reified community but also asserted the respectability of its members. Especially in open villages and some country towns, customs which temporarily overturned the whole social fabric, such as Guy Fawkes Night, defied both overt and covert efforts at control until well into the century; in the same way, charivari remained a means of enforcing unofficial local mores, and mumming and other means of gaining largesse retained some force as a tax on the well-to-do. But the general movement was one towards more orderly and organised celebrations, in which there was a greater role for women and children, and a compromise between the concepts of community and recreation held by the dominant sections of society and those which were developing within the lower classes. Even in the countryside, festivals and sports became more organised and limited to specific arenas – the rectory garden or squire's park loaned for the occasion or the cricket field, and later the football field, donated by a benefactor.

Although some farmers and landowners could be restrictive in their application of property rights, forbidding football or other pastimes on land which had once been common, and reluctant to make other land available, space for recreation was only rarely a problem in the countryside. In urban areas, however, it was the lack of common space which rational recreationalists believed was one of the major factors causing an increase in trespassing and damage to property, as well as excessive drinking among the poorer classes. In 1834 the Select Committee on drunkenness recommended as an immediate remedy: 'The establishment, by the joint aid of the Government and the local authorities and residents on the spot, of public walks, and gardens, or open spaces for athletic and healthy exercises in the open air, in the immediate vicinity of every town, of an extent and character adapted to its population.' In the previous year a Select Committee on Public Walks had come to similar conclusions for very much the same reasons. Public gardens and walks, it was suggested, would help wean the poorer classes 'from low and debasing pleasures. Great complaint is made of drinking-houses, dog-fights and boxing matches, yet, unless some opportunity for other recreations is afforded to workmen, they are driven to such pursuits. The spring to industry which occasional relaxation gives, seems quite as necessary to the poor as to the rich.'[27]

Successive governments in the 1830s were confronted not only by the argument that the provision of open spaces in urban areas would reduce crime, drunkenness and immorality, but also by current medical opinion, which held that infectious diseases were transmitted through pollution in the air and argued in favour of urban parks and gardens on the grounds that this was the only means by which these diseases could be checked. But although government legislation in the late 1830s laid down that within all future enclosure bills consideration must be given to providing sufficient open space for the use of local populations, the efforts of government to provide money for the purchase of parks and gardens were half-hearted and niggardly. In any case, most of the money provided by the government was spent on purchasing land in London. Primrose Hill was acquired in 1842 and Battersea Park in 1846. In the provincial cities the parks were provided either from private philanthropy or through public subscriptions. In a public meeting at Manchester in 1844 it was declared that it was necessary to provide parks in the town because they would 'contribute to the health, rational enjoyment, kindly intercourse and good morals of all classes of our industrious nation.'[28] As a result of public contributions, together with an exchequer grant, three parks covering a total of 92 acres were opened in Manchester in the 1840s.

Although many people acknowledged that there were benefits in making gardens and parks available to urban workers, there was also an inherent danger, as was noted when the Edgbaston Botanical Gardens were opened up to the working classes on Mondays for a payment of just one penny per person. Understandably, for some workers the gardens were a much more attractive proposition than the factory or workshop. This led to an increase in absenteeism and, as one writer noted, although the gardens fulfilled a great need, 'it encourages the working classes in the bad habit of keeping "St. Monday". . . . They are already well enough disposed to do so, and to waste a day that should be devoted to honest labour. They need no further inducement of this or any other kind.'[29]

While some advances were made in the provision of open spaces in the 1830s and 1840s, the authorities were very quick to lay down all kinds of rules and regulations relating to behaviour in the parks. Apart from walking and observing there were very few other diversions, especially on Sundays. To foreigners the British Sunday and British parks were both extremely dull. Frederick von Raumer writing in June 1835 described how,

> Yesterday I wandered into the Regent's Park and saw how the people amuse themselves on a Sunday. Of eating, drinking, singing, music, dancing, not a trace – they walk up and down and lie on the grass, which is now growing sear and yellow.[30]

Not until the opening of the Birkenhead and Manchester parks in the 1840s was serious consideration given to setting up places of amusement within the parks themselves, where the playing of games and sports could be permitted. It was only in the 1850s and 60s, and in some places the 70s, over twenty to thirty years after the recommendations of the Select Committee on Public Walks had been published, that municipal parks were established in most provincial towns and cities, either as a result of donations from local worthies or financed by the local authorities. Nevertheless, it has been argued that the provision of public parks was probably the greatest of the rational recreationalists' achievements. But their hopes of the 1830s, that a sizeable proportion of the land being enclosed would be made available for public use, did not materialise. Of the 614,000 acres of common land whose enclosure was sanctioned by Parliament in the period from 1845 to 1869, only 1,742 acres were set aside for recreation grounds.[31]

Perhaps surprisingly, in the same period a slightly higher proportion of enclosed land, some 2,200 acres, was set aside for garden allotments. Of course, gardening had long been a traditional pastime for many working men, and particular groups of workmen had reputations for particular interests in gardening. The weavers at Spitalfields were well known for the high standard of tulips that they produced. The weavers of Lancashire also had a reputation for their flower growing and so perhaps it was not surprising that some of the more philanthropic industrialists when setting up their factories provided opportunities for their workers to continue gardening. Samuel Greg allocated gardens on his industrial estate in Cheshire in the late 1830s and Samuel Oldknow left space for small gardens alongside the dwellings for his factory workers at Mellor. Arrowsmith and Slater at Bolton not only provided accommodation for their workers, but set aside an acre and a half of unfenced land for gardens, and encouraged their would-be gardeners by presenting annual prizes for the best flowers and vegetables produced on the plots. Gardening was certainly a socially acceptable pastime. Recreationalists saw it as an occupation which would instil within the working man a greater respect for property and a love for the home as well as being of some economic advantage. Enthusiasts like Samuel Broome emphasised to the Social Science Congress in 1858 just how valuable gardens were for the poorer sections of society:

> It is truly pleasing to see how much they seem to enjoy their bit of garden. They tell me it fills up all their leisure hours of a morning and evening; it keeps them from public houses in the evenings and visitors coming to see the flowers find the house and children clean when they call. The next neighbours copy their example and so it passes from one to another. I already belong to twelve floral societies, numbering from 50 to 100 members each and not one shabby man amongst them. Very rarely do you find a man who is fond of flowers taken up for a misdemeanour of any kind.[32]

Despite the popularity of gardening in some quarters and attempts in others to encourage it among the urban and rural working classes, there is no doubt that for town dwellers the possibilities for gardening decreased, at least in the first half of the century. Sometimes those workers who held gardens or allotments lost them as towns were developed. This is certainly the case in parts of London and Bolton as well as in Birmingham where the allotment holders or 'guinea gardeners' as they were called, lost their land as the pressure for building land intensified. Although some land was allocated for the use of allotments, by and large the government and local authorities showed scant interest and with the density of urban building which took place during these years, there was thus very little space available for this pastime. So 'attempts to make gardening the "rational recreation" of the urban masses were doomed to failure'. Indeed one writer has claimed that it was not merely in towns but in the countryside as well that gardening, as a recreational activity, was in the nineteenth century 'limited almost exclusively to the rural and urban elites.'[33] However, this statement is contradicted by a wealth of primary sources which attest to the importance of the cottage garden for the domestic economy and to the pride taken in growing for show as well as consumption.

Whereas most working men did not possess the luxury of a garden, music was something which, in one form or another, was available to all. Singing and the playing of instruments was indulged in by all sections of the population, whether literate or illiterate, both at home and in public. Songs and ballads had been passed on from generation to generation and an increasing number were being printed. In 1851 there were 700 publishers in the country producing street ballads. But once again, in the eyes of reformers and churchmen, there was both bad and good music. Many street ballads and songs sung in pubs and free-and-easies were regarded as risqué if not obscene, but some music, so it was believed, could be uplifting and improving and was therefore to be encouraged. One of the stated reasons for the formation of the Huddersfield Choral Society in 1836 was 'the improvement of the talent and taste of this town and neighbourhood in the performance of Sacred and Choral Music, Overtures etc.' Organ music in particular was regarded as acceptable and Birmingham Council in 1845 arranged that the Town Hall organ should be played once a week for the benefit of the labouring classes.[34] Temperance Societies and Mechanics' Institutes encouraged and organised music evenings. Mrs Gaskell's vision of the ideal self-improving working girl is personified in Mary Barton's blind friend Margaret who attends the Mechanics' Institute and helps a lecturer there by singing his songs. Religious bodies too encouraged the playing of and participation in the making of music. Many of the choral societies which were founded in the north of England in the first half of the century had close connections with Nonconformist chapels. The Church of England also put an increased emphasis on church music but in doing this they very often, especially in rural areas, lost rather than gained the support of working men and women. Improving the quality of church music was just one of the many reforms implemented by the church authorities at this time. But this involved doing away with the old church bands and, as J.A. La Trobe wrote in 1831, 'In place of boisterous anthems and fugues' the clergy should 'substitute simpler and more sober compositions.' In addition 'the bassoon must be dispensed with. . . . The fife may be easily put down.' It appears that these changes were implemented because by 1857, *The Church of England Quarterly Review* claimed, 'The days are happily numbered in which a fiddle and a bassoon were looked upon as the appropriate accompaniments to a church choir . . . Few churches are now not without an organ, and the wives and sisters of the clergy form an excellent staff of organists, where there are no funds to secure professional help.'[35] No doubt the quality of music was improved, but to the impoverishment of the labouring classes whose active participation in church services was greatly reduced.

It is difficult to assess just what percentage of working men and women wanted or were able to become members of the ever growing number of choirs. Many would have been excluded merely because of the relatively high membership fees and what evidence that does exist suggests that the membership of the large northern choirs consisted largely of the lower middle classes and skilled workmen. Of the 184 men in the Leeds Festival Chorus in 1895, 21 were factory workers, 49 tradesmen and shop assistants, 18 traders, 56 clerks and travellers and 40 shopkeepers or warehousemen. Less is known about the 161 women choir members: 47 were housewives, 25 teachers, 22 shop or factory girls and 67 had no designated occupation.[36]

Playing in brass bands was regarded primarily as an activity confined to working men. Of course, a whole range of bands – from military to church – had been popular for centuries. No local festival, procession or parliamentary election was without at least one band. But specifically brass bands were formed in the 1830s and 40s, when brass instruments were becoming cheaper. Again, encouragement came from churches, temperance societies and factory owners, some of whom helped with the buying of instruments and uniforms. The number of bands increased so rapidly that by 1887 it was estimated that there were over 40,000 throughout the country. Although, in general, brass bands were approved of by the rational recreationalists, they retained very close links with their working class backgrounds. Their associations with the local works, co-op, church or union and their increasing involvement in festivals and competitions meant that they played an important role in developing a local spirit, a role only paralleled in the last decades of the century by the growth of organised local cricket, football and other sporting clubs.

The growth in the number of choirs and brass bands in the nineteenth century was quite remarkable. Not only did numbers increase but standards improved. Joseph Lawson remarked that nothing in Pudsey had made so much progress during the last 60 years as the development of music. He pointed to the fact that whereas in the 1820s only one local chapel possessed an organ, now they were a common feature; and although there had been the Pudsey Old Reed Band and the Fartown Band, the standard of music performed earlier in the century was nothing compared with that produced by the present Pudsey Choral Union and the many local bands.[37] Music events were a major attraction. Admittedly some of the musical evenings organised by benevolent reformers specifically for working people were not always well-attended, but audiences for choral and brass band concerts were usually large and sometimes very partisan. In fact, music did have a justified claim to be the major organised leisure activity at this time. Well over a quarter of a million people, more than were attracted to any other event, attended the triennial Handel festivals held at the Crystal Palace during the period 1857–65.

There is no doubt that the staunch efforts of the rational recreationalists in the second quarter of the nineteenth century had some effect. At least they persuaded parliament to pass legislation which contained the potential for supporting and improving the cultural lives of the working classes. Both the Museums Act of 1845 and the Public Libraries Act of 1850 gave local authorities permission to build museums and libraries out of the public rates. In the case of libraries, consent from two-thirds of the ratepayers had to be achieved before building went ahead, and this was a potential deterrent for local authorities, but in any case they themselves were not immediately interested in spending their resources in this fashion. By 1860 only 28 library authorities had been set up. Nevertheless, the rational recreationalists could and did claim that the opportunities for improvement were now present. In addition, they argued that the working classes not only required these facilities but also now deserved them. George Dawson in his evidence before the Select

Committee on Public Libraries in 1849 believed there had been a great improvement in recent years in the character of the working class both 'in a moral and literacy point of view.' Samuel Smiles attested to the keen desire for improvement existing among at least the literate skilled artisans and workmen in the country. Working men's leaders, also, argued that the working classes were changing. William Lovett not only agreed with the Select Committee on Public Libraries that the working class had become 'a more reading and thinking class than they formerly were' but he also compared their leisure time behaviour favourably with that of the early 1820s:

> I may mention further, as regards the improvement of the working classes, that they are not so eager after brutal sports and pastimes as they were when I came to London. At that period you might see the working classes of London flocking out into the fields on a Sunday morning, or during a holiday in their dirt and deshabille, deciding their contests and challenges by pugilist contests. It was no uncommon thing, at that time, on taking a Sunday morning's walk, to see about twenty of such fights. Dog-fights and cock-fights were equally common at that time; and at that time what were called 'Cock-and-hen clubs' and 'free-and-easies' were very common among the working classes.[38]

Certainly changes were taking place and from the 1830s onwards, in some towns at least, there was an increasing number of organised recreations available to some sections of the working classes. The mid-1830s in Banbury witnessed the setting up of the Brass Band, the Mechanics' Institute, the Temperance Society, the Cricket Club and the Amateur Musical Society.[39] At the other end of the scale, however, was Bolton where the local newspaper in the mid-1850s was complaining angrily, 'Where is there a town which either in itself, its environment, or its public institutions, offers such scanty means of either physical or mental recreation to the workingman?'[40] But even in Banbury the rational recreationalists could not be too sanguine. Riotous behaviour and violence still occurred at the more popular and heavily-attended gatherings in the town. Within the space of a few months in 1843 a number of public events in Banbury were marred by violence. On July 6th a firework display was followed by a disturbance and a few days later a man was killed during a fight at Newland Wake. There were further disturbances during Banbury races in August and at the next race-meeting in October it was reported that 'working-class spectators became violent on the second day'.[41]

In towns and villages throughout the country it was the race meetings, wakes and fairs which drew the large crowds. Admittedly, the recreationalists claimed that on certain holidays the National Gallery in London attracted 10,000 visitors and on some Whit-Mondays the British Museum admitted over 32,000 visitors. But Mechanics' Institutes and Temperance Societies found that only very small groups of working men and women took advantage of the more informative lectures which they organised. In order to attract larger numbers it was necessary to provide, not education or information, but amusements. The various religious bodies were faced with the same problems and consequently, 'chapel celebrations began to display a surprising if bewildered worldliness.'[42] Even then chapels, Institutes and any other such bodies were not guaranteed success. In 1846 in Birmingham middle class reformers sponsored a threepenny Saturday evening concert at the People's Hall which was very badly attended. Their disappointed conclusion was that 'the working classes did not appreciate even such a cheap and rational amusement as that'.[43] But, quite understandably, many working class people did not appreciate the condescension and paternalism which was very often shown to them by their social superiors at these gatherings. They were suspicious of many of the activities and resented the rules and regulations very often laid down by the 'reformers'. Cleanliness, tidiness and respectability were often demanded by people who wished to improve the working classes. Although the firm of Stanfeld and Briggs near Huddersfield provided a clubroom, playground and gymnasium for their workers, admission to these amenities was dependent upon 'a respectable demeanour' and the workers' children could only attend if they had signed a Temperance pledge. Again, although an exhibition in Bury town hall was advertised as being free, admission was denied to those people wearing clogs.[44] To some organizations respectability meant not merely good manners, but a decent appearance and a temperance slip. The Huddersfield Choral Society would not accept as members those people who went to 'the "Hall of Science" or any of the "Socialist Meetings", nor shall the Librarian be allowed to lend any copies of music (knowingly) belonging to this Society, to any Socialist, upon a pain of expulsion'.[45]

When working men did become involved in improving activities some of them were a disappointment to the recreationalists because their interests often lay in radical politics and working class movements rather than in class conciliation and harmony. And even where working men did appear to adopt middle-class values, they did not imbue these values with the same meanings. This, in particular, became apparent in the second half of the century when the reformers turned to favour sport as an ideal medium for rational recreations. Although working men were quite prepared to accept the help of the upper classes in facilitating their playing of the game of football, they were not prepared to submit to their control or to their ideals. In any case, in the last resort the rational recreationalists met with little success because they were unable to convince the government and the local authorities that money should be spent on providing recreational facilities. In addition many of the new middle classes were far too concerned with making their own leisure pursuits more private and with moving out of industrial environments to live in more exclusive areas. The last thing they wanted was to share their pastimes with the labouring classes. So, despite all their efforts, the recreationalists were unable to develop a culture of self-improvement and rational recreations for the working man. What changes were made came through the efforts of the working men themselves and as a result of a number of major economic and social developments. A number of other factors were important in transforming popular culture from the 1840s on: the rapid development in that decade of a railway system which opened up a whole new range of recreational activities; the reduction of the working week from six days to five and a half which started in the 1850s and which gave working men a time for leisure which they had not been able to enjoy before, at least without undergoing a loss in earnings; a rise in real wages, especially in the last quarter of the century, which enabled working men to spend money on a wider range of goods and services than ever before; and accompanying these developments an increasing commercial influence in leisure, marked especially by the growth of the music hall, and of the popular press, professional sport and seaside holidays.

WHEREAS sundry persons, in violation of *His Majesty's Proclamation*, for the due observance of the *Lord's Day*, (and also of an Order issued by us to the same purport,) have practised *Playing at Ball* and other Games on the said Day, to the great annoyance of the Inhabitants;

Notice is hereby Given,

That if any person is hereafter found offending against the aforementioned *Proclamation of His Majesty*, they will be dealt with *according to Law*.

THOMAS SYMONDS, Minister.

RICHARD BOWERMAN, } Church-
SAMUAL DRUCE, } wardens.

JOSEPH FOSTER, } Constables.
WILLIAM BURCHELL, }

ENSHAM,
April 27, 1820.

J. AND T. BARTLETT, PRINTERS, OXFORD.

1. Proclamation preventing the playing of games on Sunday. Eynsham, Oxfordshire, 1820.

2. An improving and 'rational recreation'. Notice of a Penny Reading, Henley, 1864.

Henley Reading, Chess & Music Society.

The Committee beg to announce that the First

PENNY READING

FOR THIS SEASON, WILL TAKE PLACE

At St. MARY'S HALL, New St.

(*By kind permission of The Right Rev. The Bishop of Edinburgh, Co-adjutor.*)

On THURSDAY, OCT. 27th, 1864.

Programmes will be issued as early as possible.

THE CHAIR WILL BE TAKEN AT EIGHT O'CLOCK, BY

THE REV. C. WARNER.

ADMISSION ONE PENNY. **MEMBERS FREE.**

There will be reserved Seats at 6d. each, Tickets for which can be had at Kinch's Library, or of Mr. Palmer, Market Place.

BONNER EDMAN, Hon. Secretary.

E. Kinch, *Printer, Henley.*

ST. GILES' FAIR.

NOTICE.

City of Oxford to wit. ⟩ Numerous complaints having been made to the Justices of the Peace of this City of the Practice of using Squirts, Scratch-Backs, and other instruments of Personal Annoyance at this Fair, a SPECIAL MEETING of the Justices was held on the 1st September, 1876, and it was unanimously resolved to put an end to this objectionable practice, and to punish all offenders.

Notice is therefore given, that any person or persons who may be proved to have assaulted any other person or persons by means of a

SQUIRT,
SCRATCH-BACK,
CRACKER,
WHIP,
BRUSH,

or by RICE, FLOUR, MEAL, SAND, or any similar substance or article of an objectionable nature, will be liable to be convicted for an Assault, and to be IMPRISONED for TWO MONTHS or fined any sum not exceeding FIVE POUNDS.

And Notice is further given, that directions have been given to the Police to apprehend any person or persons who may be charged with the above or any other breaches of the Law.

JOHN H. SALTER,

Town Hall, 13th August, 1903.   MAYOR.

Printed by James Parker & Co., Crown Yard, Oxford.

3. Despite the efforts of the authorities, rowdiness and rough behaviour at fairs and wakes continued right up until the end of the period. Notice posted before the St Giles' Fair, Oxford, 1903.

BARRASFORD
ANNUAL PIC-NIC.

The Committee of the above Pic-Nic beg respectfully to inform the inhabitants of North Tyne and surrounding District that they intend holding their Annual

PIC-NIC

IN A FIELD ADJOINING

BARRASFORD,

Kindly granted for the occasion by P. C. J. Laws, Esq., on

SATURDAY, JULY 14, 1877.

THE
ACOMB BRASS BAND

Has been engaged for the occasion, and will discourse a choice Programme of popular Dance Music.

Tickets to the Field, 6d.; Tea and Field included, 1s.; may be had of the following Members of the Committee:—Messrs. William Prudhoe, John Barlow, John Welton, Robert Bell, Jacob Coulson, William Graham, R. Coulson, John Smith, Wm. Welton, N. Maughan, John Dodd, T. Jackson, John Charlton, A. Robson, Wm. Laidler, Js. Dodd, J. Taylor, H. Thomas, R. Dodd, J. Mattinson, A. Anderson, J. Dodd, R. Patterson, M. J. Welton, and R. Crisp.

Mr. JOSEPH CODLING, Treasurer.

Mr. FRED ATKINSON, Secretary.

Hexham: Printed at the Courant Office by J. Catherall & Co

4. New rural traditions. Annual picnics, such as the one advertised here for Barrasford in Northumberland, were organised by committees, had the support of the local gentry, and usually blended stalls, sports and the popular music of the day.

FIVE

Popular culture and the labouring classes

> 'You came by the railroad?', inquired Lord de Mowbray mournfully of Lady Marney.
> 'From Marham; about ten miles from us,' replied her ladyship.
> 'A great revolution!'
> 'Isn't it?'
> 'I fear it has a very dangerous tendency to equality,' said his lordship, shaking his head. . . .
>
> Benjamin Disraeli, *Sybil*, 1845

For those Victorians of a more optimistic nature than Disraeli's Lord de Mowbray, the railways were a symbol of progress. Their development was rapid: within the space of fifteen years the miles of track laid in England and Ireland increased nearly thirtyfold, from 471 miles in 1835 to well over 13,000 miles in 1850, and the economic and social consequences of this development were wide-ranging. Although the railway companies carefully classified their travellers so that the tendency towards equality which Lord de Mowbray feared so much would not be such that he actually had to travel in the same carriage as his social inferiors, there is no doubt that the railways gave the latter opportunities not only to travel but to develop a much wider range of recreational activities. Of course, many Victorians must have lived all their lives without ever travelling on the railways, but few would have been unaffected in some way or other by their development. To many working class Victorians, especially those whose standard of living was rising, the railways played a vital role in altering their cultural activities.

As we have seen, temperance societies, religious and adult education bodies and reformers all saw the railway excursion as a preferable alternative to many other popular activities. But their hopes that the majority of working men would see the advent of railways in this light were soon dashed. For at the same time that railways provided opportunities for passengers to visit the countryside and places of historic interest, they also enabled them to travel even further afield to race meetings, prize fights and other recreations so highly disapproved of by the reformers.

Once again a large section of the population was to show that it was not malleable to 'improvement', at least along middle class lines. No amount of exhortations or publicity could bring about such changes and this was seen time and time again. The religious census of 1851, in revealing that only 40% of the total population in England and Wales attended any form of divine service, made it clear that a very large section of the working population did not attend church or chapel. Despite the various efforts of religious bodies to rectify this state of affairs, including a great amount of church and chapel building, the working classes remained primarily secular in behaviour. In the large urban areas in particular church and chapel attendances were low. In 1881 it was estimated that in Nottingham only 24.2% of the population attended, and this was higher than Sheffield (23%) and Liverpool (19.9%). And again, despite all the efforts of temperance societies, and even many working men's groups, drink remained the great social problem of the nineteenth century. Of course it would be wrong to see intemperance as a class problem, since it affected all sectors of society. Nevertheless, and not without some justification, it was working class drinking habits which were most consistently criticised. Working class men spent a greater proportion of their incomes on drink than the middle and upper classes, and accounted for two-thirds to three-quarters of all the money in the country spent on beer and spirits.[1] There is plenty of evidence to show that many poor working class families suffered as wages were frittered away on drink and that very often drink was bought at the expense of essential foodstuffs. Towards the end of the century Charles Booth estimated that it was frequent for at least a quarter of working class incomes to be spent on drink and it has recently been suggested that, allowing for teetotal families, many working class families would have spent one third to one half of all their incomes on drink.[2]

Drunkenness was a major urban problem. In London alone arrests for this offence never fell below 17,000 per year in the 1860s and arrests throughout the country for drunkenness or being drunk and disorderly were far larger in number than for any other category of offences. Certainly, many observers believed that it was expenditure on 'intoxicating liquor' that was a major obstacle to many working class families obtaining respectability and maintaining a reasonable standard of living.

The consumption of drink throughout the country was high and increased through the century until it reached a peak around the mid-1870s. At that time about 1.3 gallons of spirits were drunk per person per year and beer consumption was over 34 gallons per person per year. Both beers and spirits were easy to obtain and there were very few restrictions on drinking in pubs. Opening hours in most places were, in theory, 24 hours per day and if there were local restrictions they related to Sunday opening hours. As late as 1914 pubs in London, apart from Sundays, had the right to be open from 5 a.m. until after midnight. Also, in urban areas at least, drink was available from a whole host of taverns, public houses, gin palaces and beer shops. But even in rural and nonconformist-dominated areas such as the mining districts of Cornwall, inns and beershops were an integral part of the community – the opening of a mine in a particular district would inevitably be followed by that of a beershop.[3] In towns and market towns the number of drinking establishments was high. In Banbury, for example, there was one drinking house for approximately every hundred of the population. In the same market town, alongside 34 bakers, 26 butchers and 13 milkmen existed 8 spirit merchants, 45 taverns and 38 beerhouses.[4] There was a similarly high proportion of drinking places in other parts of the country. In a suburb of Newcastle in 1854 there was one public house to every 22 families. A survey in West Bromwich made 11 years later[5] concluded that there were four liquor shops to every place of worship and school (including Sunday schools) and that there were two liquor sellers to every preacher and day school teacher in the town. A comparison was also made between the number of drinking places and other retailers. It produced some startling figures:

Public Houses	84	Grocers	140
Beerhouses	216	Butchers	55
Wine-selling grocers	19	Greengrocers	39
Dealers in drink not		Drapers	41
sold on premises	7	Bakers, Flour Dealers etc.	43
		Shoemakers	27
		Hatters	3
	326		348

The 1861 census revealed that in England and Wales there was one drinking place to every 186 inhabitants and in Scotland one to every 255.[6] Inevitably, therefore, drink and the drinking place were central to nineteenth century working men's culture. Of course they have a long tradition in British popular culture but they took on an additional importance in the nineteenth century, not just because of population growth and urbanisation but also because of certain legislative changes. The move towards free trade and the reduction of a wide range of duties, including those on spirits, in the 1820s led to a vast increase in the number of spirit sellers, a rapid growth in the number of gin palaces and, not surprisingly, a large increase in total spirit consumption. Alarmed at these developments, the government attempted to rectify the position by making beer, which was thought to be a much more beneficial drink than spirits, more readily available. Consequently, in 1830 a Beer Act was passed which ended the system whereby beer-sellers had to obtain a licence from a local magistrate; instead, as long as they paid the poor rates, they could, for just two guineas per year, obtain a beer-seller's licence from the excise department. This led to an immediate increase in the number of beer-drinking establishments so that by 1833 there were some 35,000 beershops in England and Wales.

No doubt this rapid increase in the availability of both beer and spirits led to an increase in drunkenness, but it would be erroneous to conclude, as many temperance reformers did, that the increased accessibility of drink inevitably entailed a corresponding increase in drunkenness. Men and women drank for a wide variety of reasons. True, drink represented an escape from a harsh and often boring working environment but it also asserted that there was more to life than just work. In addition there was a strong belief in the efficacy of drinking alcohol. It was not merely a pleasant drink, it was also much safer than many others. Safe drinking water was particularly hard to find. In the middle of the century only a small section of the better-off parts of the population received mains water supplies. In Bristol in 1845 only 5,000 out of 130,000 received a direct water supply, while in Birmingham the figure was one in five. In Manchester in 1847 only 23% of houses were connected to the mains. A further 28% were supplied by taps in the streets. This meant, of course, that virtually half the population, and mainly the poorer part, had to depend on the local pump and on rain water.[7] There were other alternatives to alcoholic drinks but some, such as milk which was easily adulterated, were distrusted and others were more expensive. Admittedly, the price of both tea and coffee fell during the first half of the century and the number of coffee houses in London soared in the 1840s to over 2,000. But while Londoners could buy coffee for 1½d per cup and tea for 2d per cup, porter was only 2½d per pint. Alcohol was looked upon not only as 'safe' but also beneficial. While spirits were regarded as important painkillers beer was looked upon as a drink which gave strength. In rural areas there was a tradition of the agricultural worker drinking much needed beer at harvest time and in the towns a similar tradition for workers in heavy industries.

Drinking was indeed a major leisure time activity. While it fulfilled all sorts of needs, as Francis Place pointed out in 1834 its major attraction for the poorer working classes was that it was 'the sole means such men have of getting away from themselves, and the pleasure of drinking to excess is beyond all comparison greater to such men than to any other class of persons'.[8] A similar viewpoint was expressed by Frederick von Raumer in the following year when he observed that most working people drank because they 'have generally no means of excitement or amusement at command during the week'.[9] In addition, at a time when working class housing was small, cramped, cold and uncomfortable, the pub provided warmth, lavatories and company as well as drink. Indeed, the pub was the centre of many working men's social life. It acted as both meeting place and recreation centre. It was the place where many of the old traditional pastimes were maintained and it was the breeding ground for many new activities. No doubt the major choice of leisure time activity for both rural and urban dwellers was between 'church, chapel and alehouse' but the view of Joseph Arch that 'The village lad has two kinds of recreation open to him, he could take his choice between lounging and boozing in the public house or playing bowls in the bowling alley. That was all',[10] ignores and unfairly downgrades the influence of the pub in the nineteenth century. The concept that 'there was *only* the pub to go to' completely understates the vital social role of the public house in working class lives.

There is a danger, of course, in romanticising the role of the pub in the popular culture of the nineteenth century. Some drinking establishments provided more entertainments and facilities and were regarded as more respectable than others. While some held prestigious meetings others were merely the haunts of thieves and prostitutes. In the countryside there was often a sharp distinction between the village inn, used by farmers, tradesmen and labourers alike (although there was sometimes a de facto demarcation between the bar and the tap room) and the more disreputable drinking places. Amongst the latter, beer shops, especially those on the edge of commons or in remote hamlets, were widely believed to be the haunts of poachers and other ne'er-do-wells. At the top of the respectability league were the inns which, especially before the development of the railways, were centres for transport connections and accommodated travellers. But many alehouses also offered accommodation and, what was more important, very often a large room which could be used for a wide variety of purposes, from political gatherings to amateur dramatics and small meetings of local organisations. Friendly societies invariably met in pubs, largely because there was no other place to go. That the conduct of their affairs in these surroundings did not always live up to the nobility of their aims is revealed by the experience of Thomas Wright. After deciding to make 'some provision out of the fruits of the good days, for the evil and unproductive days that would almost certainly come', he joined the Ancient Order of Good Fellows which met regularly in a public house. He found that despite the attempts at ceremony and the grand titles of the officials, the proceedings were drunken and unbusiness-like, and he concluded that 'The unrestricted drinking not only permitted, but in many cases practically enforced at the meetings of members of benefit societies, is at all times detrimental to the business interests of the societies. . .'[11]

There was a great shortage of rooms where groups could meet together for recreational, social or political purposes. This was especially so in the first half of the century, before the large public building programme got under way. The only alternative meeting places were schools, church rooms and chapels, and this accommodation was not always open to all groups, especially if these should contain radical or irreligious elements. Some publicans offered their rooms without charge in the hope of capturing extra custom at the bar and as they were often the only people in the town who had large rooms available, they had no difficulty in finding occupants. In some pubs much day-to-day business was transacted. Doctors used them for meeting patients; coroners held inquests there and often funds and savings were deposited with the publican for safe keeping. In many pubs newspapers and journals were kept and some even had libraries attached to them.

There was also a clear connection between leisure time activities in the pub and work. Not only were wages sometimes paid out in the pub but union meetings were also held there. There was a tendency for specific pubs to act as centres for particular groups of craftsmen and workmen who used the premises not merely for casual drinking but for celebrations, when promotions and other special events occurred. But perhaps above all, the pub was the major entertainment centre in the locality. The publican very often took on the responsibility of maintaining the old traditional blood sports of cockfighting and ratting as well as other less violent but just as traditional pastimes such as skittles, quoits and pitch and toss. In this respect the pub remained throughout the century the centre for gambling.

The pub, or at least the publican, also played a vital part in developing new activities. Many football and cricket clubs were based on the local pub which could at the very least provide a changing room and, of course, facilities for a drink afterwards. Also, the connections between the early music hall and the singing saloons and free-and-easies are well known. Taverns providing musical and other similar sorts of entertainments increased in numbers during the century. Licences could be obtained for music and dancing although tavern proprietors had to convince the magistrates that their entertainment would not be too unruly. Consequently, free-and-easies were usually well conducted establishments. One of the best descriptions of one is given by Disraeli in his novel *Sybil*. First published in 1845, it contains an episode where two of the main characters visit the Cat and Fiddle. They buy a couple of tickets at 3d each which are redeemable on the purchase of liquor, and are then permitted entrance to the 'Temple of the Muses':

> Gerard and Morley entered an apartment very long and sufficiently lofty, though rather narrow for such proportions. The ceiling was even richly decorated; the walls were painted, and by a brush of considerable power. . . . The room was very full; some three or four hundred persons were seated in different groups at different tables, eating, drinking, talking, laughing and even smoking, for, notwithstanding the pictures and the gilding, it was found impossible to forbid, though there were efforts to discourage, this practice, in the Temple of the Muses. Nothing, however, could be more decorous than the general conduct of the company, though they consisted principally of factory people. The waiters flew about with as much agility as if they were serving nobles. In general the noise was great, though not disagreeable; sometimes a bell rang, and there was a

comparative silence, while a curtain drew up at the farther
end of the room, opposite to the entrance, where there was a
theatre, the stage raised at a due elevation, and adorned with
side scenes, from which issued a lady in a fancy dress, who
sang a favourite ballad; or a gentleman elaborately habited
in a farmer's costume of the old comedy, a bod-wig, silver
buttons and buckles, with blue stockings, and who favoured
the company with that melancholy effusion called a comic
song. Some nights there was music on the stage; a young lady
in a white robe with a golden harp, and attended by a
gentleman in a black moustachios. This was when the
principal harpiste of the King of Saxony and his first fiddler
happened to be passing through Mowbray, merely by
accident, or on a tour of pleasure and instruction, to witness
the famous scenes of British industry. Otherwise the
audience of the Cat and Fiddle, we mean the Temple of the
Muses, were fain to be content with four Bohemian brothers,
or an equal number of Swiss sisters. The most popular
amusements however were the 'Thespian recitations'; by
amateurs, or novices who wished to become professional.
They tried their mettle on an audience which could be
critical.

The links between these free-and-easies and the early Music Hall
will be touched on again in chapter 7. Suffice it to conclude by
remarking that the role of the pub in developing working class
entertainment was considerable. Nevertheless, despite Disraeli's
description of an orderly gathering of factory workers at the Cat and
Fiddle, many 'respectable' Victorians regarded drinking places as
centres either for petty criminals, prostitutes and gambling, or as
meeting places for the socially and politically discontented elements
in society. Of course many such establishments did exist and they
were given a wide berth not only by law-abiding citizens but on
occasions also by the police. During the Chartist risings in Birmingham in July 1839, for example, although the army, police and special
constables regularly patrolled the streets during the height of the
troubles, they were specifically warned not to enter certain public
houses in case they were physically assaulted.[12]
What is perhaps surprising, considering the potential subversive-
ness of some pubs and the extent of drunkenness in the country, is that
compared with the attack on other working class pastimes in the early

nineteenth century, very little was done, at least until the 1860s and 70s, to reduce the number of drinking places and the hours of drinking. The reasons for this throw a good deal of light on the complexities of the changes that occurred in cultural relationships during the period. It would be totally wrong to depict the scene as one in which the upper and middle classes simply believed that drunkenness and drink consumption should be reduced. Many of the powerful landed interests opposed any attempt to limit drink and drinking places, partly because they objected to such government interference in principle and partly because they themselves were drinkers. But another weighty factor was that they relied heavily on the drink industry as a buyer and a market for their barley crops. Again, while certain industrialists did want a move towards temperance, others were much less eager because they looked to wealthy brewers as potential heavy investors of capital in their businesses. Indeed, the power and influence of those involved in the brewing industry must not be underestimated, and their numerous connections with other branches of industry and with retailers was such that perhaps a temperance speaker in Banbury was not far from the truth when he claimed in 1855 that one seventh of the inhabitants of the town were connected in one way or another with the drink trade.[13]

Obviously any anti-drink legislation was bound to alienate large sections of the dominant classes as well as many of the labouring class. Although Gladstone's contention, that the Liberal party had been borne down 'on a torrent of gin and beer' and he had lost the 1874 election primarily because of the general unpopularity of his 1872 Licensing Act, has now proved to be an exaggeration, nevertheless it was a vastly unpopular act which certainly breached many class divisions.

On the other hand, the numbers of people connected with temperance movements in the nineteenth century were considerable. Enrolments into temperance societies like the Good Templars and the Rechabites ran into hundreds of thousands and by the end of the century some 3 million children were members of the Band of Hope.[14] Despite these large numbers it is not easy to draw clear divisions between advocates of temperance and their opponents along either class or religious lines. Before the 1860s only two denominations, the Quakers and Primitive Methodists, barred their members from becoming innkeepers and in Banbury the owners of one of the largest breweries in the town were Calvinistic Baptists. Another prominent Banbury brewer was an Anglican and secretary to the local Bible

Society.[15] Nevertheless, generally speaking, temperance movements were strongest in the towns and industrial north, the areas where nonconformity tended to be most popular, and weakest in the rural areas, London and the Home Counties, where nonconformity was not such a powerful factor.

At first the various temperance societies which grew up in the late 1820s were devoted solely to opposing the drinking of spirits, but from the mid 1830s a wider teetotal movement developed which not only had the support of many working men and women but which grew partly because of their initiatives. Once again, however, divisions among the working people on the question of teetotalism were by no means clear cut. While some working men's leaders gave unqualified support to such extreme organisations as the United Kingdom Alliance, which demanded the prohibition of all trading in intoxicating liquors, others argued that self-reliance and the respectability of working men would be more honestly gained without resorting to signing the pledge. Even the radical Chartist movement was torn on the question of temperance and at the same time as many Chartist meetings were being held in pubs, a teetotal Chartist movement was developing in the 1840s.

Although one of the objections to the proposed licensing bills of 1871–2 was that it was 'class legislation' and although many working class radicals were suspicious of most temperance societies because of their religious connections, it would be wrong to see all the temperance societies as being dominated by the middle and upper classes. As we have seen, these sectors of society were just as divided as the working classes on this issue.

National spirit and beer consumption reached its peak in the 1870s. One persuasive explanation is that whereas there was a rise in real wages of something like 16% during the decade, this increase was not accompanied by an equivalent growth in the production of consumer products. Consequently, working men and women did not so much spend their money on drink at the expense of other goods; rather, what had happened was that 'purchasing power had temporarily outstripped the supply of consumer goods available.' After the 1870s, however, the price of alcohol remained fairly constant right up until the outbreak of the First World War, and the quantity of drink consumed per person began to fall as drink sellers faced much stiffer competition from an ever increasing range of consumer products coming on to the market. Smoking, both tobacco and cigarettes, but particularly the latter, became increasingly popular with all classes.

Expenditure on tobacco rose from some £3½ millions in 1870 to £42 millions in 1914, and what was most remarkable about these figures was that whereas in 1900 cigarettes only accounted for one-fifth of all expenditure on tobacco, by 1914 over half the total expenditure on tobacco came from the sale of cigarettes.[16]

Attitudes towards drink also changed towards the end of the century. It was less possible to talk about beer being an essential beverage as water supplies, and the quality and availability of milk, improved. The production of non-intoxicating cordials such as ginger beer, and the cheapness of tea and coffee compared with earlier in the century meant that there were many more drinks available as alternatives to beers and spirits. Even medical opinion, which had recognised the restorative qualities of beer, was now beginning to cast doubts on its efficacy.

Also, although the pub remained the most popular building within the community it did change in nature and lost its all-embracing importance as a social and meeting centre. It declined as a place of family recreation, especially when legislation preventing children under 16 from drinking spirits on the premises was introduced; in 1882 the presence of children in pubs was further reduced when it was forbidden to sell beer to those under the age of 13. Also, the growth of other entertainment industries, including the theatre and cinema, but especially the music hall, meant that the pub was by the end of the century only one of a number of centres of amusement. The same applied to its role as a meeting place. The growth in the number of town halls, libraries, museums, church halls and other places which provided accommodation for meetings of all sizes of groups meant that the pub was now often just one of a number of alternatives. Nevertheless, drink and the pub still played a leading role in popular culture. Drink remained one of the most important items of expenditure for many families and continued to be central to the economy of the country. The brewers retained and probably increased their power and wealth, as the statistics prove: between 1892 and 1912, nine brewers, two distillers, one maltster and one wine merchant died, all leaving more than £1 million each.[17]

If working class drinking habits were viewed with great concern it was, partly, because they were felt to impede the progress of working men towards making better use of their time. Paradoxically, however, the increase in literacy and spread of the reading habit which might have been considered evidence of such progress was seen by some as a threat to order and authority. The potential dangers of literacy and the fear that many would become dissatisfied and revolutionary through it haunted successive governments during the two decades following the Napoleonic Wars. While radical groups hoped this would indeed be the case, many Evangelical and other religious bodies argued in favour of the spread of literacy because they saw it as the best method by which the correct moral attitudes and values could be imbued in the mass of the population. But although the debate early on in the century was whether literacy would bring conflict or stability, by the second half of the century its direction had changed somewhat. This can be seen in the proceedings of the Select Committee on Public Libraries held in 1849. For though some witnesses were asked about the number of books dealing with the 'principles of socialism' which were circulating at the time, many more were questioned about the influence and extent of 'immoral' and 'trashy' literature. For example, Mr C. Corkram of Spitalfields was asked the following questions:

2691. Whence do the population derive their present supply of books? – I should say, from the small shop libraries, of which there is a very large number in the neighbourhood; and in some of the coffee-shops, a person who takes a cup of coffee may have a cheap novel or some work of fiction to read.

2692. What is the principal character of the books which they read? – The common popular cheap novel. I have been into one of those shops to-day for the purpose of satisfying myself on the point; and from the books which I see displayed in the shop windows, and what I found in the shop, I should say that is the general class.

2693. Are the novels of a superior or of an inferior character? – I should say of an inferior kind.

2694. Which might possibly pervert the mind, rather than give it a good direction? – Yes; such as the 'Mysteries of Paris', a well-known translation from the French, and books of that kind.

2695. Has there been a large circulation of translations of French novels among the reading classes of the working population of England? – I fear there has been.

2696. May not those books be held to contain some doctrines

of a doubtful social character, as well as other objectionable features? – I should say so.

2697. At least, may they not be considered as containing loose ideas on the subject of society, not proven, as the Scotch would say, by facts? – I should say they have a licentious tendency; they turn on love adventures painted in a very vivid kind of language, sufficient to excite evil passions, without expressing anything positively gross.

If the Committee members hoped that the setting up of public libraries would ensure that 'improving' literature would not only be made more easily accessible to the working classes but would also be read by them, they were, to quite a large extent, to be disappointed. For one thing, the growth of public libraries occurred only very slowly but, equally, all the evidence shows that novel reading was much more popular than what one writer called 'solid books'. Henry Maxwell writing in 1893 pointed out that in the annual report for the free libraries of Birmingham in 1891, of the 855,096 books issued in that year, 519,595 or over 60% of the issues were for novels and magazines. This was a particularly high figure in view of the fact that only 19% of the total stock held in the libraries was classified as prose fiction. Birmingham was no exception in this respect. In the same year four out of every five volumes taken out of the public libraries in Battersea were novels.[18]

The novel was regarded as an inferior sort of literature not only by most public library committees but also by preachers, teachers and organisers of Mechanics' Institutes, many of whom refused to stock novels in their libraries. Perhaps it is not surprising that working class radicals were very often the sternest critics of 'cheap' literature. Alexander Somerville bemoaned the fact that although a public library had been set up at his home in Innerwick, the greater number of books in the library 'were silly stories, of that silliest kind of literature – religious novels'[19]; and a reviewer in the Chartist *Northern Star* in 1843 stated that 'we think novel-reading, at its best, only an indifferent substitute for a worse occupation of time'.[20] But while novels were vilified poetry certainly was not. The Chartists produced a number of poets from within their ranks, all of whom attempted 'to create a new poetic tradition which embodied their political ideas'[21] and in the first half of the century virtually every newspaper, whether it was a radical one or not, contained a poetry column. The influence of the Romantic poets was considerable; many working class men belonged to poetry circles and attempted to write poetry, mainly in the Romantic style.

While many of the self-improving working class writers were dismissive in their attitude towards 'cheap' literature they also, quite innocently, presented a distorted picture of its popularity and availability. Christopher Thomson writing in 1847 reflected that when he was young he was too poor to buy most books 'and "cheap literature" was not then, as now, to be found in every out-o'-the-way nooking'. Again, James Watson, writing of his youth spent in the early years of the century commented that 'At that time there were no cheap books, no cheap newspapers or periodicals, no Mechanics' Institutions to facilitate the acquisition of knowledge'.[22] But by cheap literature these writers were referring to the availability of cheap copies of serious works. Certainly a 6d edition of Thomas Paine's *Rights of Man* was published in 1792, and Cobbett's *Political Register* appeared after the Wars priced at 2d, but for men like Thomson and Watson the sort of books they wished to read were scarce and very often out of their price range.

It would be quite wrong, however, to assume that there was a lack of cheap popular literature available either early in the century or, for that matter, in the preceding century. Chap books, almanacs, street ballads and broadsides had been popular reading since the sixteenth century and around 1800 they were sold in their thousands. Costing from ¼d to 1d they were hawked around the streets of every town in the land. In London alone at the start of the century there were 75 printers publishing ballads and broadsides. The most popular of this street literature dealt with romance, murders and other topical sensational and scandalous events but many also commented on current political issues, injustices and working conditions. The tradition of street ballads was a long-established one, and the nineteenth century brought no resounding changes. What did occur, however, was that some ballads were adapted to meet the conditions of growing urban industrial communities. Martha Vicinus in her book *The Industrial Muse* cites the example of a ballad called 'The Steam Loom Weaver' which appeared in the 1830s. Comic and full of sexual innuendoes, it reflects a developed industrial society where the lovers are an engine driver and a female steam loom weaver. However, this broadside was based on one which was first published in 1804 when the cotton industry was still largely a domestic one. In the earlier version, the girl was a weaver who worked in her own home and the man an itinerant worker who visited the weavers' homes to mend their looms.[23]

This literature was the major reading matter of the labouring classes both in town and country. At times the number of broadsheets published and sold seems to have been phenomenal. In 1828, 1,166,000 copies of James Catnach's account of the 'Last Dying Speech and Confession' of the murderer of Maria Marten were printed. Again, in 1849 something like 2,500,000 copies of a broadsheet describing the execution of F.G. Manning and his wife Maria, were sold.

Certainly the urban dweller was inundated with leaflets of one sort or another and surrounded by a variety of posters which were hung on any available wall space. It has been argued that because of the vast amount of posters and street literature which were easily available and short in length, and because the level of literacy required to read them was not high, they were all important elements in enabling many people to learn and practise reading skills. Whether this was the case or not literacy rates at the start of the century were much higher than was believed by many contemporary observers. It was assumed, quite incorrectly, that reading was alien to labouring class culture and something which only developed as the nineteenth century progressed. In 1832 a committee of the Society for the Promotion of Christian Knowledge was told that 'The population of this country (was) for the first time becoming a *reading* population, actuated by tastes and habits unknown to preceding generations'.[24] But there was a mass reading public long before this date and although it is extremely difficult to quantify the extent of literacy in the country, it has been estimated that by 1830 somewhere between two thirds to three quarters of the working classes had a minimal reading ability,[25] and figures taken from marriage registers show that the percentages of people able to sign their names were:[26]

	Men	Women	Total
1839	66.3%	50.5%	58.4%
1893	95.0%	94.3%	94.65%

Day schools, Ragged and Sunday schools and Mechanics' Institutes all played their part in developing literacy, so that long before the Education Act of 1870 a large proportion of the working classes had some ability both in reading and writing.

Contemporary evidence reveals that there was also a tradition in most working class homes, both urban and rural, of possessing at least a few books. The Central Society for Education in a survey made in the late 1830s concluded that among 65 families in five Norfolk parishes, only six possessed no books at all, while another three families owned only a hymn book, but that all the others possessed either a Bible, Testament and Prayer-Book, or at least two out of three of these books. Similar results were obtained from other rural counties in the south and south-east of England, although in their survey of the urban parish of Marylebone, the Society discovered that there was a much lower rate of ownership of Bibles than in the rural areas.[27]

Unfortunately the survey made no mention of any other kinds of book which may have been in the possession of these families and although a later survey made of poor working class parishes in London in 1848 concluded that the average number of books possessed by each household amounted to 11, this too did not include chapbooks or broadsheets, although there is clear evidence that despite being flimsy publications, they were very often kept in households for generations.[28] If these surveys can be believed it is interesting to note that the pattern of book ownership remained fairly similar throughout the century. Enquiries in a working class area in Lancashire in 1904 revealed that most households contained a small number of books of which most were of a religious nature.[29]

Of course, the possession of books did not necessarily mean that they were read and the CSE survey did show that out of the 50 families investigated in Kent, only two spent their evenings reading. This is not surprising. Reading at home in the evenings, especially in rural areas, was particularly difficult and uncomfortable. Windows in agricultural cottages were small and inadequate and as, until well into the second half of the century, artificial lighting was confined to candles and rushlights, opportunities for reading were limited. In towns matters were not much better. Long working hours meant that it was difficult to find time to read in the evenings. In addition, working class houses were small and there were few opportunities for reading at home to be done in any seclusion. No wonder then that reading, rather than being a solitary activity, was often a communal and social one. As we have seen, many pubs provided facilities for reading papers and magazines, so too did Mechanics' Institutes, but there was no public library system until after the passing of Ewart's Acts, in 1845 and 1850. Even then the provision of public libraries only spread very slowly so that by 1875 there were about 60 in the country.[30] In London, especially in the first half of the century, coffee houses played an important role in providing reading facilities. By the 1840s there were somewhere between 1,400 and 1,600 such houses where working men could take their own food and over a cup of coffee read periodicals and newspapers. Indeed about one in three of these shops had libraries attached to them. In the north of England, however, coffee shops were not popular and here the provision came mainly from penny reading rooms.

One reason why there was a large amount of cheap literature available at the start of the century was that printing was a comparatively cheap process. The iron press frame patented by Lord Stanhope in 1800 cost only £10 – £15 and in the 1820s printing costs were reduced still further with the introduction of Gamble's paper-making machine, which not only halved the cost of paper but also improved its quality. Not surprisingly, therefore, there were numerous small printing concerns in nearly every town in the country. In London in 1850 there were over 500, of which 80% employed less than three men.[31]. In these circumstances it was not difficult to set up a press and start a local newspaper – as Thomas Frost showed in the 1840s when, with just over £25, he was able to earn a living by founding and editing a local newspaper as well as contributing to other journals. Large sales figures were not essential for survival and Henry Hetherington estimated that by selling his paper *The Poor Man's Guardian* at a 1d per copy he could break even with a circulation of just 2,500.

These circumstances were ideal for the development of a radical press directed at the working classes. But this was viewed with suspicion and hostility by successive governments during and following the Napoleonic Wars. Their fear of the effect of the printed word and of the influence of radical ideas was such that a number of strategies were seized upon in an attempt to put radical newspaper owners out of business. There were many government prosecutions for libel and all newspapers were hit by a government imposed stamp duty (a duty on each newspaper copy) and an advertising duty (a tax on each advertisement placed in the newspaper). William Cobbett attempted to evade the Stamp Duty on his *Political Register* by excluding news and publishing only opinions. Others, like Henry Hetherington, deliberately faced prosecution by ignoring the duty. But those papers which did pay the duty were expensive. Thomas Dunning wrote of how, when he was a shoemaker at the time of the Reform agitation in 1832, he clubbed together with his mates to buy the radical *Weekly Despatch* at the high price of 8½d.

Not surprisingly, the lives of many radical newspapers were short-lived. Circulation figures fluctuated wildly but at the height of periods of agitation they were extremely high. In April 1839, for example, when the Chartist petition was being collected, the *Northern Star* claimed circulation figures of around 50,000.[32]

Towards the middle of the century there was a marked decline in the readership of the radical press. A number of writers have ascribed this decline to the government's reducing the stamp and advertising taxes on newspapers in the 1830s and then repealing them completely in the 1850s.

> The repeal of the duties enabled the capitalist press to reduce prices below the cost of production (largely because of the significantly increased advertising revenue it attracted) at a time when, as a result of technological developments, costs of production and capital requirements were rising way beyond the means of independent radical publishers. In the ensuing price war, the radical press was routed.[33]

The abolition of the stamp duty, the introduction of steam presses and other capital intensive processes and the possibilities (with the development of railways) of a fast country-wide distribution system, meant that there was a continued and marked shift in the control of newspaper ownership away from the small proprietor. By the end of the century, in the climate of a very competitive mass market, the capital required was such that only the very rich, or large consortia, could enter the national market. Whereas in 1844 the *Northern Star* needed a circulation of only some 6,200 to break even on its costs, in 1918 the *Sunday Express* was running at a loss although its circulation was estimated at 250,000.[34]

While these economic factors were important, the conclusion that the decline of the radical press in the 1850s is solely attributable to them would be much more convincing if there had not been a parallel decline of other radical and self-improving journals which were unaffected by stamp duties. The *Penny Magazine* was wound up in 1846 and two separate surveys of the literature circulating among the working classes in London, in 1840 and 1850, showed a remarkable swing towards fiction reading. Whereas in 1840 there were approximately 80 cheap 1d or 2d periodicals in circulation – of which 9 dealt with scientific concerns, 4 were political, 4 dealt with drama, 16 were biographies or memoirs, 5 were regarded as licentious and 22 dealt with romance and fiction – ten years later there were 100 similarly priced periodicals of which 60 were exclusively concerned with fiction.[35] In addition, it is important to remember that although the reduction of the stamp and advertising taxes may have played a part in the decline of the radical press, the gradual elimination of these taxes meant cheaper newspapers, coming within the price range of many more people in the country. This was a development which was not resented by many working class radicals. In fact, in 1849 William Lovett gave as the major reason why he thought the working classes were becoming 'a more reading and thinking class', 'the efforts that were made between the years 1830 and 1836 to remove the fourpenny stamp upon newspapers'.[36]

What does need to be taken into account when considering the decline of the radical press is that during the more prosperous 1850s and 1860s there was a marked reduction of working class radicalism. Although a Chartist movement continued into the 1850s it was nothing like the force it had been in the previous fifteen years. It was clear that the demands and needs of the labouring classes were, in the 1850s, different from what they had been when Chartism had been a movement of some consequence. In any case, although on occasions the circulation figures of radical papers had been high, these papers were only read by a small proportion of the population: as Raymond Williams has emphasised, the 'real history of the nineteenth century popular press has to be centred in the development of the *Sunday* paper'.[37]

Although the production of cheap daily papers, including the *Daily Telegraph*, increased in the 1850s, it was the Sundays with their concentrated mixture of crime and sensational stories which were growing most in popularity. *Lloyd's News*, for example, contained in one of its issues:

> The Emperor Napoleon on Assassination. Fearful stabbing case through jealousy. Terrible scene at an execution. Cannibalism at Liverpool. The Great Seizure of Indecent Prints. A man roasted to death. A cruel husband and an adulterous wife.[38]

The *News of the World*, which had been started in the 1820s and specialised in crime reporting, had by 1854 the largest circulation in the world, selling some 109,000 copies per week. These papers were beginning to win over the broadsheet reader. Indeed, the broadsides were being hit by competition on two fronts in the 1860s – from the Sundays and from the new 2d or 3d songbooks which included the latest music hall songs.

As the reading public grew so the number of books published annually increased. In the 1790s the annual average was 370. By the 1850s this figure had grown to 2,600, and by 1900 it was over 6,000.

There were large sums of money to be made in publishing, even for those publishers who around the middle of the century concentrated primarily on a working class readership. Edward Lloyd made a fortune by publishing wildly successful books like Thomas Prest's *Sweeney Todd* which was sold in 92 parts starting in 1850. The novel in weekly parts and sold at 1d a time, together with the 1d novelette, became increasingly popular but Lloyd also plagiarised works which had been successful with middle class audiences. Dickens suffered as a consequence of this practice. *Oliver Twiss* and *Nickelas Nicklebery* were thinly disguised versions of Dickens's novels adapted for a working class readership. The highly successful *Pickwick Papers* reappeared in Lloyd's edition as the *Posthumous Notes of the Pickwick Club*. In this version the major differences were that the level of comedy was altered and Sam Weller became the true hero.[39].

The number of magazines and periodicals produced increased rapidly in the second half of the century, as did the circulation figures. The *Weekly Budget*, which had commenced publication in 1860, had by 1885 a circulation of 350,000 and in that same year the *Penny Illustrated Paper* sold 200,000 copies per week.

The spread of literacy played a vital part in facilitating the dissemination of news and information throughout the country, but also did much to break down beliefs in witchcraft and the super-natural and in the old oral traditions. Britain in 1800 was a country where superstitions abounded. The countryside was, as John Clare wrote, an area where one could not walk for more than half a mile without coming across a place where an apparition had been seen by 'old women or someone else in their younger days'.[40] Of course, in many rural areas all manner of superstitions continued throughout our period but in the new urban areas, despite the popularity of almanacks and books dealing with predictions and the supernatural, there was a marked difference. Joseph Lawson, writing in the 1880s but looking back at his own home town of Pudsey much earlier in the century, commented: 'If we consider the dense and widespread ignorance of the people in past times, together with the dark lampless streets and lanes, the very little light even in the houses, we may easily see what a flourishing time boggards would have.'[41] The spread of literacy and education, the development of towns and gas lighting in streets and houses, and the improvement in communications brought about by developments in printing and the railway system, all played their part in bringing about these changes. But as with all changes, not everybody regarded them as necessarily beneficial. James Burn writing in 1855 argued that modern popular pastimes were much less attractive or worthy: 'When ghosts, fairies, and witches cease to live in the belief of a people, the character of such a people will lose much of its poetry.' All that had occurred, he argued, was that 'the superstitions of the last century, with their train of supernatural agencies, had been substituted by the vilest trash imaginable'.[42]

In the eyes of Burn, and many other self-improving workmen, this 'trash' included the numerous and popular penny novels and romances which were bought on street-corners, from newsagents and from railway book stalls. An observer at the end of the century commented:

> The clerks and artisans, shopgirls, dressmakers and milliners, who pour into London every morning by the early trains, have, each and everyone, a choice specimen of penny fiction to beguile the short journey, and perhaps the few spare minutes of a busy day. The working man who slouches up and down the platform waiting for the moment of departure, is absorbed in some crumpled bit of pink-covered romance. . . . [43]

Railways, as well as giving an enormous boost to the publishing trade, played an important part in the development of other popular pastimes. They enabled brass bands and choirs to perform much further afield and to enter the mushrooming number of music competitions organised around the country. The first brass band festival was held in 1845 near Hull; by the 1890s there were 222 band festivals[44] throughout the country. Some sports, legal and illegal, received a similar fillip from the railways. Attendances at many sporting events, especially race-meetings, increased and it became possible to organise inter-club tournaments and leagues in a variety of sports as the railway network spread.

It would be wrong, however, to ascribe these developments entirely to the railways: beliefs in 'muscular Christianity' and a growing conviction among the middle classes in the 1860s that organised sports were ideal instruments for developing self-discipline and team-spirit; and, more importantly, the increased amount of leisure time which was becoming available to the working classes from the 1850s on, were factors which must also be taken into account when discussing the development of organised sports. Where railways can claim the credit is in providing extensive opportunities for cheap mass travel. Although very few working class families could afford holidays in the middle years of the nineteenth century, an increasing number could take advantage of the cheap railway day excursions which were offered by most companies. Although Londoners had had the opportunity of taking steam boat trips down the Thames to Gravesend for just 6d from early on in the century, and similar trips were available to Glaswegians along the Firth of Clyde, the railways made day excursions possible for the working people living in most of the provincial towns and cities.

Trips to the seaside or countryside at Whitsun or at the weekends was for many people, in Disraeli's words, 'a great revolution'. The *Banbury Guardian* in 1857 commented on a Mechanics' Institute railway outing to Warwick Castle and contrasted this occasion with earlier in the century when 'boys and girls were shut up in the little towns and villages they were born in till close upon twenty years of age'.[45] All sorts of excursions were arranged both by local clubs and by professional agents like Thomas Cook and Stanley and Marcus. By the 1850s, at least in industrial Lancashire and the West Riding of Yorkshire, many excursions were not confined to day trips but were arranged so that trippers left on the Saturday and returned on the Monday or Tuesday. The numbers involved in excursions were often staggering. During Whit week in 1850 it was estimated that 200,000 trippers left Manchester by train. Blackpool in the 1850s would regularly receive up to 12,000 excursionists at week-ends in the summer, and on August Monday in 1854 had 5,000 visitors.[46]

The effects of such numbers descending on a seaside resort did not go unnoticed by newspapers and magazines. Invariably working class trippers were portrayed in cartoons as loutish figures out for drunken and boisterous fun, accompanied by sluttish wives and children who were likely to break windows or trample on flower beds. James Ewing Ritchie wrote after spending four weeks at a resort on the east coast, 'I begin to tremble at the very sight of an excursionist'.[47] There were complaints both from respectable middle class families, who bemoaned the declining standards and falling social tone of certain seaside resorts, and from the inhabitants who feared that trippers would disrupt their tranquil lives. The latter soon realised, in any case, that there was not much money to be made from people who had spent nearly all they had on the excursion fare and who tended to bring their own food and drink with them. Even some railway companies were dubious about carrying large numbers of working class trippers. For example, when a direct line to Brighton was opened in 1841, the railway company concerned, although in considerable financial difficulties, opposed cheap excursions on the grounds that they would lose their 'superior traffic' as a result. Partly for these sorts of reasons, some other railway companies were prepared to meet the demands of the Anti-Sunday Travelling Union and stopped running cheap Sunday excursions; by the mid-1860s parts of 40 railway lines were closed to Sunday traffic.[48] By this time, however, the novelty of excursion trains had waned somewhat and they were, rather than being exceptional events, just one further leisure outlet for working people.

Despite the alarm expressed at the behaviour of working class excursionists, many improving organisations saw merits in the development of such activities. The *Manchester Guardian* in 1845 numbered among the advantages, that

> they are greatly conducive to health, by combining pure air with the active exercise of field sports; that they are not less productive of cheerful, sober, and insouciant enjoyment, and that they are eminently social and domestic in their character – and in all these respects are infinitely preferable to the tumultuous, disorderly and intemperate scenes of the racecourse – scenes in which wives and children cannot and ought not to participate.[49]

Unfortunately many people wanted to use excursions for that very purpose of going to the racecourse, or to what the *Manchester Guardian* would have regarded as equally questionable activities. On occasions in 1859 and 1860 the South East Railway Company, the secretary of which was the great apostle of self-help, Samuel Smiles, ran trips to prize fights; Smiles gave as the company's excuse the simple truth that the demand was irresistible.[50]

Nevertheless, the respectable Victorians who had been suspicious and indeed frightened of the working class excursionists in the 1840s were by the late 1850s less inclined to complain about their behaviour. One reason was that very often there was little of which to complain. Also, the image of working men and women had greatly improved as a result of their behaviour during the Great Exhibition in 1851. When the Exhibition was first mooted, and again when it was clear that organizations like Thomas Cook would be bringing operatives and workmen from Leeds to London by train for just 5 shillings return, a whole range of fears was expressed about the effects of so many of the lower orders descending on London. Madame de Lieven predicted violent political disorders, if not revolution, and

Colonel Sibthorp M P foresaw that 'All the bad characters at present scattered over the country will be attracted to Hyde Park. This being the case I would advise persons residing near the Park to keep a sharp look out for their silver forks and spoons and servant maids'.[51] The organisers themselves were concerned and made sure that neither tobacco or alcohol was sold on the Exhibition site. As it happened, despite the fact that 4½ millions (165,000 of whom came on rail trips organised by Thomas Cook) attended the Exhibition on days when the entrance fee was only one shilling, during the whole period of the Exhibition the number of offences committed inside the building for which persons were prosecuted amounted to only 25.

Respectable Londoners were surprised at the good behaviour of the working people who visited the Exhibition, especially those who came from the still mysterious industrial north. The experience of the Great Exhibition contributed to the growth in a feeling of optimism that at least some elements within the working classes were becoming civilised. This view was most clearly expressed by Gladstone in a speech to Parliament in 1866 in which he argued that skilled workers should be enfranchised. He stated that large sections of the working community were taking advantage of 'the civilizing and training powers of education'. He also pointed out that many working men no longer spent their wages wantonly but invested in Post Office savings banks. They also took an interest in public affairs by reading the daily press and, not without considerable sacrifices, studied to improve themselves:

> Take, for instance, the Working Men's Free Libraries and Institutes throughout the country; take, as an example of the class, Liverpool; who are the frequenters of that institution? I believe that the majority of the careful, honest, painstaking students who crowd that library are men belonging to the working classes. . . . [52]

In the parliamentary debates for electoral reform it was the 'self-improving men' who were singled out as being worthy for enfranchisement and, as was so often the case in the nineteenth century, the role played by women in the home and at work was entirely ignored.

Partly for this reason working class women have proved something of a problem for historians of the nineteenth century working classes. Their lives and recreations were more private and domestic than those of their menfolk and they rarely, unlike their upper and middle class counterparts, left written records. Their lives overlapped with those of men but were separate for much of the time; in particular they did not participate to the same degree in the collective leisure activities which took place outside the home and, of course, their work experience was different. One effect of industrialisation and urbanisation was, at least initially, to deepen the division between male and female life experiences. Women had always been excluded from much of the recreational culture of the labouring classes; the inn was largely a male preserve while many of the physical recreations of pre-industrial England were for young men only. Nevertheless, women would have attended most festivals even if only as spectators. The urban popular culture of the nineteenth century saw an increased sexual demarcation as the leisure industry sought to cater for primarily male 'taste publics'. At the same time there was a smaller percentage of women in paid employment during the nineteenth century than had been the case in the eighteenth, while those who were in paid work tended to work for shorter periods of their lives. The type of employment they found was in general very different to that of men. Only a small minority of women have ever worked in factories and a disproportionate amount of attention has been directed towards them by historians. Throughout the Victorian period the vast majority of working class women were domestic servants, while the next largest category of employment was dress-making, done largely at home until the last decades of the century. The production of textiles was the only factory industry in which female workers were ever employed in large numbers.

Whereas for men work values permeated private and leisure life, for women domestic and personal values appear to have determined their working experience. Women rarely set out to work for their whole adult lives; they intended to work until marriage and for the most part they did cease employment after marriage. Patricia Branca has claimed that 'a desire for a warm human relationship at work'[53] characterised female choice of employment. Women were also drawn to work where marriage opportunities were high, and to jobs with higher status even if the wages were low. Lacquering and metal burnishing had high social standing, with wages which reflected the skill of the work, but work in warehouses, while socially prestigious, paid depressed wages. Shop assistants, especially those who worked in department stores or dress shops, were considered a cut above most working women and by 1914 there were to be half a million of them in Britain; but again the hours were long and the wages low.

One obvious characteristic of female employment was that many working class women were in intimate contact with the middle and upper class worlds. It has become a commonplace of nineteenth century history that there was an increased separation between the classes; towns were divided into class specific suburbs and their inhabitants rarely ventured into the territory of other classes. Working-class women were a significant exception to this during their pre-marital years. They worked in large numbers in upper class and middle class homes and served in shops and department stores, hotels, restaurants and tea-rooms. By contrast working class men, or the majority of them, had private and working lives which rarely took them into middle class territory. One result of this was the acculturation of many working-class women by the values of their workplace; another was that women were by and large more sophisticated in their understanding of the wider world than were their menfolk.

Flora Thompson in *Lark Rise* describes the attempts of village girls who had been in service to improve the furnishings and domestic standards of their cottages, in emulation of the houses in which they had worked:

> When the bride bought the furniture, she would try to obtain things as nearly as possible like those in the houses in which she had been employed. Instead of the hard windsor chairs of her childhood's home, she would have small parlour chairs with round backs and seats covered with horsehair or American cloth. The deal centre table would be covered with a brightly coloured woollen cloth between meals and cookery operations. On the chest of drawers which served as a sideboard, her wedding presents from her employers and fellow servants would be displayed – a best tea service, a shaded lamp, a case of silver teaspoons with the lid propped open, or a pair of owl pepper-boxes with green glass eyes and holes at the top of the head for the pepper to come through. Somewhere in the room would be seen a few books and a vase or two of flowers. The two wicker arm-chairs by the hearth would have cushions and anti-macassars of the bride's own working.[54]

Such attempts to create a more genteel atmosphere were often short-lived, especially when the home relied on a farm labourer's wages, but the direction of modest increases in spending power into interior decoration, the acquisition of mass-produced furniture and the hanging of prints and photographs may well have had much to do with the knowledge of middle class standards gained through women's working experiences.

The matriarchal nature of the working class home has been long accepted but the reasons for this have been too little remarked upon. It may seem obvious enough that women did the cooking and the housework and brought up the children but it is less obvious why they should have been the financial managers. The cultural explanation is to be found in the fact that, quite simply, they understood money – how to handle limited budgets, how to barter and how to deal with tradesmen – while men had been denied this knowledge by the narrowness of their life experience. A good proportion of such knowledge would be handed on from mother to daughter but it could be extended by experience in domestic service or as a shop assistant. The gradual decline of domestic manufacturing put pressure on many married women to find some work at or close to home and a wide range of 'penny capitalist' activities were undertaken; these would range from taking in work or putting up lodgers, to opening small shops, but all involved financial calculation. The great expansion in the credit facilities available to working people in the late nineteenth century provided both pitfalls and opportunities for the housewife. A great deal of attention has recently been paid to pawnbroking as a central element in working class budgeting – and it was of course women who looked after the pledging and redeeming of possessions – but the pawnbroker is only one aspect of the credit system. There were the various clubs, such as coal clubs, christmas clubs and boot clubs, the scotch drapers, furniture salesmen, tallymen or 'Johnny Fortnightlies', and the ticket system operated by many shops; all were essentially forms of hire purchase.[55] They could lead to disaster but, used with caution, made possible a more comfortable home and better clad children. One historian has seen the credit system as constituting a subtle pressure towards respectability (because only the respectable could expect credit) and as widening the differences between men and women of the unskilled working class, since the wife had a need '–as purchaser – to maintain a respectable "labour aristocratic" image with the shopkeeper'.[56]

Both the working experience of women and their involvement with domesticity may have made them more susceptible to the preachings of rational recreationalists, and especially to demands for temperance and respectability. As they spent so much time at home they were also likely to greet favourably the concept of home-based recreation. Such tendencies may have further exacerbated the war between the sexes which, half-jocular, half-serious, is a recurring theme in working class life and art. Benjamin Brierley in one of his working-class tales from the 1850s points to the threat that a St Monday holiday could pose to domestic tranquillity:

> I never knew an industrious, striving woman, who liked holidays. She looks upon them as so many opportunities held out to weak-minded men for getting out of the steady path of business; as encouragements to loose principles and spend-thrift habits; as gaps opened by mischievous people to let in a flood of evils which ought never to be known to the domestic hearth. . . . [57]

As in this instance there seemed to be little question of asking the wife to participate in the holiday excursion, her lack of enthusiasm for holidays is perhaps understandable.

Women played a fundamental role in determining whether a family was regarded as respectable or non-respectable. Nevertheless, when in the franchise debates of 1866 Gladstone praised the 'self-improving' working men so lavishly, he well knew that there were still large sections of the working population whom he would be forced to classify as non-respectable. In addition, there were many working class families who, although they would have been called respectable by Gladstone and the middle classes, had not adopted middle class values of respectability.[58] The leisure pursuits of the majority of working men were by no means what Gladstone would have hoped for. In 1856, only ten years before Gladstone's speech on parliamentary reform in which he praised the working men of Liverpool so highly, the town was being described as a place where, apart from the Saturday evening concerts, there were no improving entertainments. At the Royal Casino there was 'an undisguised display of vice in its grossest features' and outside the theatre 'gaudily attired girls use their best endeavours to entrap the unwary and make assignations with the fully initiated'. Milling-cribs, betting-houses and Sunday morning dog-fights were the main entertainments in the town.[59] In addition, despite the efforts of reformers and the authorities, prize-fighting continued. Just one of many instances was the prosecution in Shropshire of two men who pleaded guilty to participating in a prize-fight. They were given seven days' imprisonment, fined £5 each and bound over to keep the peace for twelve months.[60] Many different sorts of illegal bloodsports were also perpetuated. In 1850 there were seven prosecutions in South Northumberland for cockfighting and the sport continued in that area until the 1870s at least.[61]

Despite these instances, changes were taking place. Cruel blood sports were now the exception rather than the rule. Leisure patterns were altering as railways were extended, public building programmes undertaken and new technologies harnessed by an emerging leisure industry. Understandably, therefore, the social history of the common people is often seen as the adaptation of the working classes to the new urban environment. Adaptation there certainly was but we should not ignore the degree to which the working classes, not least in their leisure life, helped create their own environment.

SIX

Popular culture and the Victorian middle classes

> Rest is not idleness; in a very true sense it is a part, an integral part of work. . . . If we really work when we work, we need not be ashamed of periods of sheer inaction. . . . For nature is not idle with us at such times; she coils the uncoiled springs of action, screws up the wires which have been out of tune, tightens the rigging of our ship, sets the grass growing over the worn and bare places in the pastures of our minds, overhauls the lumberroom of our memory, and puts the sap of life through a moral change. . . .
>
> *The Leisure Hour*, 6 July 1872

Although the term 'middle class' encompasses a heterogeneous assortment of people, from professional men and manufacturers to clerks and shopkeepers, this grouping was growing more rapidly than the rest of the population. In addition many of them in the middle years of the century were, as incomes rose, finding more time and money for leisure activities. Perhaps not surprisingly, considering their concerns about how the lower orders should spend their spare time, they viewed these increased opportunities not so much with enthusiasm and delight as with concern and anxiety. For in leisure time man could succumb to a whole range of temptations. As Peter Bailey has written, for much of the Victorian middle class 'Leisure was less the bountiful land in which to site Utopia, than some dangerous frontier zone which outran the writ of established law and order.'[1] Certainly leisure was a subject which was continually being discussed in the press and the ever growing number of weekly and monthly magazines. Also, much time was devoted by parsons and preachers in their sermons to what they regarded as the 'problem' of leisure. Invariably the response of the various churches was that leisure time could be of value only if it was used either as a complement to work or devoted to activities of an improving nature. Largely for this reason, Victorians were much happier talking of recreation than leisure. For recreation could be viewed more easily as a virtue; it could be a time in which one 're-created' one's strength for the more important aspects of life, such as work. Even a magazine with the title *The Leisure Hour* regarded itself as 'A family journal of instruction and recreation' and at the front of every issue quoted Cowper's lines,

> Behold in these what leisure hours demand,
> Amusement and true knowledge hand in hand.

The Leisure Hour not only associated recreation with instruction but emphasised that these activities should take place within the ambit of the family. This was a commonly held belief. The emphasis on the importance of home and family was present throughout the century. It was no accident that 'Home! Sweet Home!' was the most popular of all Victorian songs and sold over 100,000 copies in 1823, the first year of its publication. Even towards the end of the century that propagandist for self-improvement, Samuel Smiles, was writing that 'Home is the first and most important school of character. It is there that every human being receives his best moral training, or his worst. . . . Law itself is but the reflex of homes'.[2] This emphasis on the value of the home as a moral force coincided with a rise in the standard of living for many of the middle classes. Their improved financial resources enabled them to make material improvements within the home and a substantial proportion of their spending went into buying the ever-widening range of domestic furnishings which were appearing on the market.

Home-buying and moving to properties which were on the fringe of the urban areas and further away from the work environment was also something which became more frequent, at least among the more prosperous of the middle classes. The move into the suburbs developed with the century and as improvements in transport occurred. All the major cities had their fashionable suburbs; Clifton for Bristol, Alderley Edge and Wilmslow for Manchester, and Edgbaston for Birmingham. By the 1840s Edgbaston was being rapidly but carefully developed and the preservation of the high 'tone' of the area was ensured by attaching restricted leases to the properties which prevented the building of workshops in gardens or the opening of shops on the premises.

One of the most important features of these new suburban properties was the private gardens which were attached to them. Gardening had always been a favoured leisure occupation for those who could afford it but in the nineteenth century it was becoming, as the first edition of the *Gardener's Chronicle* in 1841 claimed, 'an indispensable part of the domestic establishment of every person who can afford the expense.' It was an activity which, as we saw in chapter 4, the Victorians regarded as an acceptable and rational recreation. As well as being health-giving it involved both physical and mental labour and was therefore a worthy pastime. Many middle class families spent much of their time not just sitting but working in their gardens and although in some of the larger gardens full, part-time or casual gardeners were employed, very often the husband and wife did the bulk of the work. Their interest was stimulated and developed by a whole host of gardening books and magazines which appeared in growing numbers from the 1820s on. *The Gardener's Magazine* (1826), *The Magazine of Natural History* (1828), *A Manual of Cottage Husbandry, Gardening and Architecture* (1830), *An Encyclopaedia of Gardening* (1835), *The Suburban Gardener and Villa Companion* (1838) and *The Suburban Horticulturalist* (1842) were all the work of John Claudius Loudon. Loudon was the most prolific of gardening writers but there were many others, including Joseph Paxton who, at the time that he started the periodical *The Horticultural Register* in 1831, was gardener to the Duke of Devonshire at Chatsworth. The appeal to the middle classes of copying some of the methods used in one of the great gardens of England was clear. Just as so many aristocratic fashions were followed, albeit modified, by their social inferiors, so some of the wide range of flowers, herbs and bushes grown in Chatsworth and other imposing gardens were now planted in the gardens of suburban villas. But although, just as with the aristocracy, a large garden was a symbol of wealth and status, to the middle classes it was also a place of seclusion and privacy. In that sense, as Stephen Constantine has pointed out, 'The garden was regarded as an extension of the private house, requiring the same preservation from public gaze. It was in effect a private retreat, garden and house together forming a home environment as distinct as possible from the head of the household's place of work. Within this shelter the Victorian middle class would practise and preserve the domestic values they held dear.'[3]

A significant consequence of this concentration on the house and garden was that much of the leisure time of the middle classes was increasingly spent within the family unit. This was a development viewed with alarm by some reformers, who argued that unless leisure time in some degree was shared by all classes, then the activities of the lower orders, without the beneficial influence of their social superiors, would deteriorate. The trend in drinking habits was held out as an example of this. Whereas in the late eighteenth century it was not uncommon for all classes, both men and women, to drink in public houses, in the nineteenth century the middle classes frequented these places less and less. One result of this was that the tone declined and by the 1850s no respectable townsman, let alone townswoman, would enter a public house. It was not that the middle classes no longer drank, but that drinking was now very often done in the privacy of the home. Wines and spirits were often bought from local off-licences and grocers well-positioned in the middle class suburbs. It was a profitable business, as Messrs. Gilbey soon proved after starting up in the trade in 1857.

Many other middle class leisure activities were not vastly different from those of the lower classes, but they tended to be pursued in a quite different environment. Singing, reading aloud and partaking in games were common to all but in the case of the middle classes these pastimes took place in the drawing room. There was one other important difference. In the middle class home, especially in the first half of the century, there was often much heart-searching about what songs should be sung, what books should be read and what games should be played. Games invariably had to be improving as well as amusing and in many cases there was frequently no choice. Not until well into the second half of the century were jigsaw puzzles made purely for pleasure, 'untainted with didacticism'.[4] Also, just as there was deep concern about the reading habits of the lower classes, so there was a continual debate about what should be read in the middle class home. Some Victorians refused to read anything but religious books on the grounds that 'trashy' books were not only a waste of time but were morally harmful; in the first half of the century, the number of religious publications greatly outnumbered those in other subject areas. In the years between 1816 and 1851 somewhere around 45,000 books were published in England and Wales, of which 10,000 were religious works and only some 3,500 were works of fiction.[5] Nevertheless, as the century progressed, and despite all the breast-beating, the growing number of circulating libraries throughout the country found that by far the most popular reading matter was novels. In fact, some of the smaller circulating libraries concentrated only on providing novels. Even Edward Mudie, who set up in 1842 what was to become the most famous of circulating libraries, stocking a vast range of book titles, recognised that fiction would become the main source of his income. Of the 391,000 volumes which Mudie added to his shops between the start of 1858 and the end of 1859, 42% were works of fiction, 22% histories and biographies, and 13% travel and real adventure stories.[6]

The cost of first editions of novels, largely because the circulating libraries had a stranglehold on the market for most of the century, was high. So those people who wished to read new novels usually did so either by reading them in serial form in a weekly or monthly magazine or – and this would appear before the serial was actually completed – in a three-decker library edition. Only after this library edition had been in circulation for about a year would the novel be reprinted at a cost which varied but was often around the sum of six shillings. At the height of its success Mudie's, with a minimum subscription charge of one guinea per annum, had around 50,000 subscribers. But there were many other similar, if less famous, circulating libraries including of course W.H. Smith. Smith had been a newsagent for many years before he saw the advantage that the rapid building of the railway would bring. In 1848 he started his railway bookstall business and modelled his libraries along the same lines as those of Mudie. By 1862 he possessed some 185 bookstalls in prime sites on railway stations around the country.[7]

Of course it is impossible to measure the extent of reading that occurred in the nineteenth century, but it was a common practice, and not just among the middle classes, for novels and magazines as well as the Bible to be read aloud in the family circle. It was partly for this reason (but only partly, as Humphry House has shown) that such popular writers as Dickens employed a constant self-censorship and why it could be said of him that despite the subject nature of many of his novels, 'you will not find a page which a mother need withold from her grown daughter'.[8] But this could not be said of all novels or novelists popular with sections of the middle classes. In the third quarter of the century especially there appeared a large number of novels, often with very similar plots and story lines, which were aimed specifically at middle class women. The reasons for the massive popularity of writers like Mary E. Braddon, Rhoda Broughton and Mrs Henry Wood have recently been re-examined.[9] Many of these novels deal with unhappy marriages and often, as in Wilkie Collins's, *The Woman in White*, the major female character is anything but the sickly, weak, helpless person so often put forward as the stereotype of the Victorian woman. Again, Sally Mitchell has pointed out that in the novels of the 1860s pain, suffering and alienation are the emotions that are most easily identified. There are numerous 'fallen women' stories along the lines of *East Lynne* and it is these characters with whom the readers identify. In addition, many of the men characters, and often the heroes, were in some way or other physically disabled. As one contemporary male novelist lamented in 1866, heroes were limited to 'the consumptive, the insane, the inane, the hunchbacked, the lame and the blind'.[10]

Why these novels took the form they did is open to differing interpretations. But they were undeniably successful in catering for an expanding market of women readers. As suburbs were extended and travelling to work from a distance became easier, many middle-class Victorian housewives spent less time with their husbands. They not only had more leisure time but also more money at their disposal, so that novel reading became an increasingly popular pastime. The conclusion reached by Sally Mitchell – that many of the novels written particularly for women in the 1850s and 60s reveal a deep female discontent with the institutions of family life, especially the dullness and monotony of the day-to-day routine – is a persuasive one; but it is important to remember too that although women's fantasies may have been reflected in these novels, the growing number of magazines devoted to capturing the middle class women's market concentrated on the much more practical and home-based subjects of child-rearing, the control of servants and the problems of managing the home.

Many of these magazines had a large readership. *The English-woman's Domestic Magazine*, for example, which was first produced in 1852, had by 1861 a circulation of 61,000. But while nearly all of the magazines aimed at the middle class housewife laid a great stress on economy in household accounting, they also included many articles on high fashion. Cookery books followed a similar format. Included alongside plain, economical recipes were those which required all manner of expensive ingredients and which were only within the price range of a few. In a young, competitive, industrial, capitalist society it is understandable that hints on household economies should appear alongside articles on how to follow the ways and customs of the gentry. This was an age where there were increasing inducements to spend surplus wealth on conspicuous consumption, whether on a carriage or merely on bric-á-brac for the mantelpiece. Many families could now afford an increasing number of luxuries. The stereotypical image is of the middle class housewife leaving more and more of the domestic chores to the servants and spending most of her time having babies and cultivating the accomplishments of piano-playing, needlework and drawing. This was the 'perfect lady', the Victorian ideal of the 'completely leisured, completely ornamental, completely helpless and dependent middle-class wife or daughter, with no function beside inspiring admiration and bearing children'.[11] Whether this is not a caricature of even the more prosperous middle class wife is questionable: as Patricia Branca has made clear[12] there were many middle class families living on about £100-£300 per annum. Although the standard of living was rising they would not have had much money to spare for amusements or luxuries. These families would, at the most, employ one servant as a maid of all work, and their concern would be to acquire goods which, as the century progressed, were regarded more as essentials than luxuries. Piped water in the house, a fixed bathtub, a coal-burning cast iron range, a washing machine and, towards the end of the century, a sewing machine, were the immediate objects of desire rather than pianos, carriages and sumptuous dresses.

What does become evident from an examination of women's magazines and journals is that by the second half of the century the extent and influence of religious publications had declined. Whereas in the early part of the century most publications aimed at women had a mainly religious content, by the 1850s this was not the case. Indeed *The Englishwoman's Domestic Magazine* specifically stated that it was their policy to exclude all religious articles, and they even refused to print religious poems. Even *The Leisure Hour*, which was published by the Religious Tract Society, made few overt references to religion.

Nevertheless, although many magazines may have been more secular in tone in the second half of the century, it is equally true that as each year went by they and the newspapers devoted an ever increasing amount of space to that supposedly religious festival, Christmas. Articles giving advice on cooking the Christmas dinner and on decorating the house and the tree, and suggestions for numerous family amusements for that special day, abounded. Readers were left in no doubt that Christmas was a time both for family gatherings and for showing goodwill and benevolence to all men. Home, family and charity were all held in deep regard by the Victorian middle classes and it was no accident that they were highlighted. Much in the celebration of this festival stemmed from a romanticised version of Christmas amongst the aristocracy and gentry, recreated and renovated in a middle class setting.[13]

Of course Christmas celebrations date back many centuries, and from the time of the Norman Conquest right up to the seventeenth century the 'twelve days' of the Christmas festival (between the Nativity and

Epiphany) became established as the major annual holiday of the year. But during the dominance of Puritanism in the sixteenth century there was a strong reaction against the festival, which on the one hand was considered to have too many close connections with the Roman Catholic church and, on the other, contained too many secular activities such as drinking, dancing and gambling. For a time it was not permitted to keep Christmas day either as a religious or a secular holiday. With the Restoration the laws against Christmas were relaxed but although it was observed by many people as a holiday, it was not held in any special esteem. Many Dissenters still refused to acknowledge Christmas. In an age when the Bank of England was closed for 47 days of the year Christmas was, whilst still kept as a holiday in many parts of the country, much less observed than for example, the New Year. *The Times* newspaper in the eighteenth and early part of the nineteenth century rarely referred to Christmas and when it did the items were invariably extremely brief. It was not just the press which ignored Christmas in these years. Charles Knight writing about his childhood in the 1800s mentions the excitement of St Valentine's Day but fails to comment on Christmas at all and, again, in 1820 Leigh Hunt remarked that Christmas was 'scarcely worth mention'.[14] But some sections of society, such as the aristocracy and gentry, did observe Christmas, at least to the extent that they went to church, partook of a Christmas dinner and very often held house-parties over the Christmas period. Also, many of them continued the age-old custom of giving presents of clothing, blankets and coals to their tenants and the poor of the district. But there is no evidence to suggest that Christmas in the early nineteenth century was celebrated to anything like the extent or with the same keen interest that pervades the pages of the middle class magazines of the second half of the century.

This transition occurred largely because Christmas as a festival was taken up with enthusiasm by the middle classes. Some reasons for this are fairly obvious. After all, this was a section of the community which was growing not only in numbers but in prosperity, thus having money to spend on goods and celebrations. In this sense they were in a favourable position to treat Christmas as a special occasion, particularly as the number of official holidays were rapidly reduced in the early part of the century, so that by 1834 Christmas Day was one of only four days regarded as a holiday. Also, it is not particularly surprising that in deciding how Christmas should be celebrated they looked to, and aspired to copy, some of the customs and manners of their social superiors. What is important is that they not only copied but added extensively to the festival and reinterpreted it in the light of their own preoccupations. So during the nineteenth century Christmas once again became a festival of great importance, consisting of a mixture of old and new traditions.

The Christmas dinner had always been a traditional part of the festival and this remained central to the celebration.[15] In addition, many new traditions were introduced, often from other countries. Christmas crackers, for example, the use of which grew in popularity from the 1840s onwards, were a modification of a French custom of giving sweets as presents wrapped up in a cracker. The Christmas tree also came from Europe, being introduced by German cotton and woollen merchants who settled in the new industrial towns of Manchester and Bradford. The idea spread rapidly and was given widespread publicity when Prince Albert insisted on a tree at Windsor for the Christmas of 1841. Other innovations such as Christmas cards were British. Although first manufactured soon after the introduction of the penny post in 1840 these cards did not catch on at first; only when cheaper methods of colour lithography were introduced in the 1860s did the Christmas card begin to challenge the New Year and Valentine's card in popularity. By 1880, however, when Messrs de la Rue were publishing Christmas cards at twopence each, something in the region of five million letters and cards were being posted over the Christmas period.

Carol singing was revived and became increasingly popular as the century progressed, but the most popular development was in the exchanging of presents on Christmas Day itself. Early in the century the giving of presents among friends and family had usually taken place on New Year's Day, and only the giving of 'boxes' or gifts to the poor had occurred on Christmas or Boxing Day. But from the 1860s there was a gradual switch of present giving from New Year to Christmas Day and this was connected to some extent with the idea imported from the United States of Santa Claus being a bearer of surprise gifts. Of course, Father Christmas was by no means a new creation. He had appeared in 'mumming' plays and masques long before the Puritan revolution, but he was not at that time associated particularly with present giving. Indeed, there was not even one set image of Father Christmas. His physical features and costume varied widely from illustration to illustration and it was not until the 1860s, when he was introduced into this country from the States as Santa Claus, that he became something more than merely a vague seasonal character. Within a very short time from this date Father Christmas became a standardised and enormously popular figure.

Of course, the growth of the habit of present giving at Christmas time had important economic consequences. The Christmas market for most of the century had been one consisting mainly of food and drink, but this widened to include all sorts of goods. The period of preparation before Christmas gradually lengthened. Whereas in 1856 Nathaniel Hawthorne noted on 20 December that the London shops were beginning to show 'some tokens of approaching Christmas', in 1867 *The Times* of 11 December was devoting columns to advertising and reviewing books for children; by the end of the century *The Times* was advertising Christmas presents at the end of November. Also in the last decade of the century, Father Christmas was appearing in many of the recently built large department stores in towns throughout Britain, in the weeks preceding Christmas.

Although there was an enormous increase in spending during the Christmas period and a large proportion of the money spent came from middle class pockets, it would be wrong to describe the middle classes' contribution to the festival as a purely material one. Indeed, they attached many other values to the celebration of Christmas and these elements appear time and time again especially in the writings of Charles Dickens, a man whom George Orwell described as 'a fine specimen' of the 'small urban bourgeoisie'.[16] His very first novel, *Pickwick Papers*, published in 1836, described a 'good humoured Christmas' and, of course, *A Christmas Carol* had an immense impact on its readers and was an instant success. The book sold 15,000 copies in 1834, its first year of publication, and in the following year nine London theatres staged dramatised versions of the story. The reasons for the book's success are not hard to find. For one thing the story emphasised the importance of those factors so close to the hearts of middle class Victorians, namely home and family. As Dickens wrote in *Sketches by Boz*:

> Who can be insensible to the outpourings of good feeling, and the honest interchange of affectionate attachment, which abound at this season of the year? A Christmas family-party! We know nothing in nature more delightful! There seems a magic in the very name of Christmas. Petty jealousies and discords are forgotten; social feelings are awakened, in bosoms to which they have long been strangers; father and son, or brother and sister, who have met and passed with

averted gaze, or a look of cold recognition, for months before, proffer and return the cordial embrace, and bury their past animosities in their present happiness.

Of course the Christmas house-parties of the gentry included the family but now the role of the family, and particularly the children of the family, was made much more central. In one sense this was yet another example of the tendency of the urban middle classes to lead a more private social life and have their celebrations within the home.

The Christmas ethos was more complex than this however, because, once again, the great unease about the use of leisure time was present, was mingled with other feelings of guilt, fear and genuine philanthropy about the plight of the less well-off. It was for this reason that Scrooge was such a hated figure when he treated the Cratchits so badly and why it was important for the readers that Marley should teach him the important lesson about the spirit of benevolence and goodwill. Again, the first Christmas edition of *Punch* in 1840 contained Thomas Hood's 'Song of a Shirt', a fierce attack on and denunciation of the sweated industries. The deserving poor had to be remembered and the middle classes, like their predecessors, contributed to and established all manner of Christmas charities. The problem of reconciling the traditional virtues of benevolence, charity and good neighbourliness with the poverty and inequalities which were apparent in Victorian society was partly resolved by the middle classes adopting a vision of Christmas which looked back to bygone days. In fact they invented an idealised Christmas – a typical picture was painted by the anonymous writer of *Christmas in Olden Times*, published in 1859:

> . . . the frost was on the pane, and snow lay thick upon the ground, when all the chimneys smoked and all the ovens were full; . . . when all were full of gladness and both serf and squire, baron and retainer did their best to keep their companions happy. All classes gave themselves up to frolic and revelry, with a thoroughness of spirit.[17]

This was only one of a whole host of books and articles which appeared from the 1840s onwards telling the stories and legends of pre-Puritan Christmases. G.K. Chesterton later on in the century described the Victorian Christmas as a determined search for the old 'feudal Christmas' and Dickens too played his part in this. He urged in his *Sketches by Boz* that the reader should adhere to these old values and should not heed those people

. . . who will tell you that Christmas is not to them what it used to be; that each succeeding Christmas had found some cherished hope, or happy prospect, of the year before, dimmed or passed away; that the present only serves to remind them of reduced circumstances or straitened incomes – of the feasts they once bestowed on hollow friends, and of the cold looks that meet them now, in adversity and misfortune.

Of course the imagery of Christmas created by Victorian writers, painters, producers of Christmas cards and so on is not a real depiction or re-creation of a medieval or feudal festival. It is much more an idealised picture of Merrie England or Olde England; an eighteenth century England with an idealised medieval ethic. It is a world of benevolent squires, stagecoaches, inns and ruddy-faced, hospitable landlords. This looking back to the past, and invariably an idealised past, was not merely confined to Christmas. Asa Briggs in his study of Victorian cities remarks on how many Victorian writers were much more interested in the distant history of Victorian cities than in their 'contemporary significance', and this tendency was not confined to the older, more well-established towns. 'Some of the new cities, indeed, made more of their remote medieval origins than they did of the "facts" of their economic progress.'[18] The popularity of works of antiquarianism and history in the nineteenth century was widespread among the middle classes, together with a tendency towards the idealisation of the countryside. It is difficult not to conclude, as many writers have done, that these were specific responses proceeding from the concerns and unease of the middle classes about the effects of urbanisation and technological progress.[19]

By the end of the century, in most but by no means all parts of England, Christmas had largely superseded the New Year as the major annual celebration, and had spread to most sections of society. Standish Meacham writing of the Edwardian years states that 'Christmas was, even for the poorest families, the most important celebration of the year for children – even more important than birthdays'.[20] But how one celebrated Christmas naturally depended on the financial means of individual families. Most accounts give the impression that families soon developed their own traditional ways of spending Christmas Day. The young Robert Roberts for example received no presents, but his mother did cook a turkey dinner for eight on Christmas Day.[21] In an account of the festivities in a middle class home in London in the 1870s, however, a picture is drawn of a much more regular routine. Indeed the writer even mentions the word 'ritual':

> Christmas Day itself followed a regular ritual. Service at St. Paul's was exactly the same as it is now . . . The post was the next excitement, and we displayed our cards on the mantel-piece. The traditional dinner of turkey and plum pudding and dessert was followed by a comatose afternoon.[22]

Church going was important for some, but cards, presents, dinner, home and family were the essential ingredients for most. Christmas had by the end of the century become such an established institution that some Victorians such as the Grossmiths were able to poke fun at these middle class 'traditions'. *The Diary of a Nobody* for 19 December:

> The annual invitation came to spend Christmas with Carrie's mother – the usual family festive gathering to which we always look forward. Lupin declined to go. I was astounded, and expressed my surprise and disgust. Lupin then obliged us with the following Radical speech: 'I hate a family gathering at Christmas. What does it mean? Why, someone says: "Ah! we miss poor Uncle James, who was here last year", and we all begin to snivel. Someone else says: "It's two years since poor Aunt Liz used to sit in that corner." Then we all begin to snivel again. Then another gloomy relation says: "Ah! I wonder whose turn it will be next?" Then we all snivel again, and proceed to eat and drink too much; and they don't discover until *I* get up that we have been seated thirteen at dinner.'[23]

Another target for the Grossmiths' humour was the Pooters' annual summer holiday at Broadstairs. For by 1900 not only were Christmas, Easter, Whitsun and August Bank Holiday times for relaxation but the yearly seaside holiday had also become something of an institution. By the middle of the nineteenth century most of the salaried middle classes received at least a fortnight's paid holiday and by 'the 1860s even ordinary bank clerks could expect at least a week's holiday after only a year's service'[24]

At first glance it may seem that here was an activity which would work against the tendency for the middle classes to make their leisure activities more private, and would ensure that, instead of spending their time solely in a family unit and within the home, they would inevitably mix freely with all classes on the beaches and promenades of the seaside resorts of Britain. To an extent this was the case but it would be wrong to exaggerate the point. In many ways the hotel or boarding house simply became a second home 'and people merely transferred to the resorts . . . the style of life they led at home'.[25] So Pooter on holiday felt quite justified in reproving his son Lupin for going out 'to a common sort of entertainment' rather than spending the evening with the family in the boarding house reading.[26] Indeed this desire for privacy and distaste for mingling with the lower classes has led one social historian to suggest that, if anything, the seaside holiday accentuated the considerable class differences which already existed:

> The class-consciousness of the Victorians, which showed itself in the segregation by class and sub-class in the social zoning of towns and suburbs, in the refined grading of schools, clubs and societies, and in the different pew-rents within the churches and chapels, was nowhere more evident than in their pleasure resorts. People of different status might be forced to meet and mingle in factories and markets, city streets and even political meetings; some might still wish to in the surviving deferential society of rural village and country town. But most of the English in that age took their pleasures separately, in the company of their social equals, and each resort had its own 'social tone', finely adjusted to the exact status of its clientele.[27]

Social zoning within seaside resorts developed rapidly in the last quarter of the nineteenth century as the rise in real wages and the increase in leisure time enabled, for the first time, large numbers of the working classes to visit the seaside – not only as day trippers but also, particularly in the north west of England, as holiday makers. However, social zoning had been present throughout the century in some form or other. Even in the late eighteenth century Brighton, which boasted of its royal visitors, was regarded as a most fashionable resort whilst Margate, which was comparatively accessible to London by cheap boat transport, was seen as less respectable. Again, in 1788 Catherine Hutton wrote of Blackpool that in addition to the Lancashire gentry and respectable professional men visiting the resort there was 'a species called Boltoners, that is, rich, rough, honest manufacturers of the town of Bolton, whose coarseness of manners is proverbial even among their countrymen'.[28] This sort of unpleasant experience meant that it was necessary for the better classes even then to search for more exclusive and less accessible resorts.

In 1780, the high cost of travel, let alone the accommodation charges, tended to exclude the 'plain unrefined' tradesmen[29] so that seaside holiday makers were confined primarily to the aristocracy and gentry, together with the more affluent of the professional classes and merchants and manufacturers. In any case spas were still far more popular among the better classes than seaside resorts, although there was an ever increasing interest in sea-bathing. This had first started around the middle of the eighteenth century, largely as a result of a number of medical writers advancing their opinions that sea-water had certain recuperative and regenerative powers, and that both the drinking of sea-water and sea-bathing were potential cures for a variety of ailments. These views were made even more acceptable to those wishing to follow fashion when George III and his court were converted to the pleasures of sea-bathing. His visits to Weymouth, together with the Prince of Wales's predilection for Brighton, did much to ensure that these towns became major and fashionable resorts.

Most early seaside resorts depended on the custom of the 'leisured classes' and of Londoners, so not surprisingly the resorts along the Kent and Sussex coast, especially Brighton, Margate and Ramsgate, were the most popular. The development of resorts which occurred in the early part of the century was again largely in the south of England along the coastline from Southend to Weymouth. In fact, apart from Scarborough, which was also a spa town and which had attracted the Yorkshire gentry since the mid-seventeenth century, all the major seaside resorts in the first quarter of the nineteenth century were along the south coast. But as the number of people such as manufacturers, tradesmen and clerical workers who could afford, and wanted, to take holidays increased, so resorts grew in numbers and size. Provincial resorts such as Great Yarmouth, Cleethorpes and Southport were developed, helped by the great railway boom of the 1840s which not only made travel faster and cheaper but provided opportunities to visit places which had hitherto been virtually inaccessible.

By the 1860s white collar workers and small tradesmen were taking their families on holiday; the same decade saw the establishment of the Victorian middle class family holiday. This tremendous boom in holidays meant that seaside resorts were playing an increasingly important role in the social life of the country and were also important as economic growth areas. The construction of hotels gave a great boost to the building industry and there was also a very large investment in pleasure piers. Blackpool's North Pier, costing around £13,000, was opened in 1863, and the West Pier in Brighton was completed three years later at a cost of £30,000. By the end of the decade at least 21 piers had been completed – 'piers had fully established themselves as independent attractions of the seaside resorts and no resort worthy of the name could be without one'.[30] Manufacturers and retailers also took advantage of the growing seaside market, producing articles of seaside wear for adults and catering for upper and middle class children by manufacturing buckets, spades and shrimping nets.

As more and more of the lower middle class adopted the holiday habit, so the 'better classes' sought to avoid the company of their social inferiors by exploring either the more remote parts of the British coastline or by going abroad. The Riviera was a particular attraction, as was Switzerland, especially for those who liked walking or winter sports or who sought a cure for tuberculosis. But overseas travel was confined to a very small proportion of the population and the 'better classes' were still attracted to some of the larger British resorts like Bournemouth, Folkestone and Eastbourne. Indeed, some resorts catered for specific clienteles. So while 'Fashionable Folke-stone' 'was one of the most aristocratic watering-places on the English coast' and competed with Eastbourne in this league, a resort such as Broadstairs was regarded as 'a middle class haunt' which attracted in particular 'the quite, respectable, and not too highly cultured middle class taste'; while Herne Bay by the end of the century had gained the reputation of catering in particular for the young middle class Victorian family and was known as 'Baby Bay'.[31] Elsewhere most resorts reached a series of compromises and a social zoning took place within the resort itself, as in Blackpool, where the working classes crowded on to the central pier, while the more respectable sought out the select north shore area.

Out of season holidays also were becoming fashionable and resorts were looked upon more and more as attractive and healthy places to which the wealthy could retire. A change in medical opinion was partly responsible for these developments. In the eighteenth century doctors had started to favour seaside resorts because of the supposed health-giving properties of the sea, but by the mid-nineteenth century the fortunes of resorts were enhanced still further as theories about the beneficial qualities of invigorating sea breezes were propounded. The medical view that fresh air not only aided health generally but would help fight TB, the greatest of all Victorian killer diseases, became prevalent and was, quite understandably, underlined and advertised by those with commercial interests in seaside resorts. The *Blackpool Visitor's Guide* for 1897 confidently asked the question 'Who has not heard of the fame of Blackpool's Breezes and their miraculous recuperative qualities?' and went on to assert that 'Muscular, nervous and pulmonary diseases are cured as if by magic'.[32]

Partly because of medical opinion, seaside resorts grew and overtook in popularity the old spa resorts. But there were other reasons for the decline of the spa towns. By and large seaside holidays, which did not involve the highly organised social activities associated with stays at spas, were cheaper. But, even more important for the Victorian middle classes, who above all regarded seaside holidays as family holidays, the beach was a much more exciting place for children than the pump room. Indeed, the seaside resort was able to cater more easily than the spa town for most ages and tastes. In addition, for the Victorian the sea held its own magic. Its grandeur and its potential wildness were major attractions. Walking along a pier over a rough sea at high tide was a thrilling experience and it was no accident that one of the very first photographs in the 1897 Blackpool guide was that of the lifeboat going out in rough seas to the wreck of the 'Bessie Jones'. Once again, the *Guide* proudly asked, 'Who has not heard of Blackpool and its Dashing Sea – which swells majestically to our feet?'[33]

Certainly, seaside resorts were regarded as places where for one or two weeks the urban middle class family could get away from the smoky, dirty town air and restore their health in the invigorating atmosphere of the seaside. But it would be wrong to overemphasise this particular aspect. John Walton, in his excellent examination of English seaside resorts in the nineteenth century, concluded that the major motivations for the Victorian middle classes in going on holiday were 'the pursuit of status and enjoyment as well as, or instead of, health'.[34] Undoubtedly 'keeping up with the Joneses' was important to middle class Victorians, and so increasingly was the idea of enjoyment, but this latter factor was only developed after a great deal of uncertainty and uneasiness. As late as 1872 a writer in *The Leisure Hour* was 'loth to commend a visit to the seaside as it is generally paid', on the grounds that these resorts are 'monotonously oppressive. There is often a toyshop look about them, and a donkey-driving, band-listening, telescopic weariness of pertinacity which is soon tiresome'. Instead the writer recommended a more improving and invigorating holiday: 'If you want to combine sea air and exercise in a short holiday, take a walking tour by the seaside, and use the frequented watering-places only as stations in which to rest for a night or for a meal.'[35]

Once again the mid-Victorians found the answer to the dangers inherent in leisure by recommending a whole host of improving activities while at the seaside. Most seaside guides provided lists of local churches, museums and libraries as well as pointing out places of historical interest. They also stressed the geological and botanical interests of their coastline and during these years, aided by the writings of Philip Henry Gosse and others, the search for flora and fauna and collection of shells and fossils from the seaside became very fashionable as well as popular hobbies. Charles Kingsley, that great advocate of rational recreations, enthusiastically extolled the delights of these pastimes and urged them upon the 'army of idlers who saunter about the cliffs and sands and quays'.[36] This idea of improvement and the suspicion of artificial entertainments was partly present in the minds of some of the investors in piers. The North Pier at Blackpool was not built, it was proclaimed, to provide base amusements but rather to give access for the landing and boarding of boats as well as providing an 'extensive and agreeable promenade' at high tide.[37] Again, in the 1870s, a number of aquaria were built at resorts where not only were all sorts of fish displayed but informative talks and musical accompaniments were provided. But their success was limited for, despite the concerns of Kingsley and others, there was a growing determination on the part of the middle classes to enjoy themselves. Punch and Judy shows, donkey-rides and bands on the piers were becoming increasingly acceptable, available and preferred to more improving activities. Nevertheless there were sections of the population, and not just extreme dissenting groups, who were still unsure of how leisure time should be spent. *The Saturday Review* in 1870 upbraided its readers, 'We really do not know how to amuse ourselves'. Seven years later the same journal again noted judiciously that 'Many people are manifestly incapable of enjoying repose and light diversion except on the understanding that they have a right to do so'.[38] In a society where bodies of men could meet and agree that, while English country dancing which did not involve pushing, squeezing or kissing, and Scotch reels which gave 'the maximum of disciplined exercise with the minimum of familiarity'[39], were acceptable pastimes, but that in general dancing should be super-vised, obviously the spending of leisure was still a serious business.

As the century progressed, however, attitudes towards leisure did change and it became much more easily accepted as part of life's normal pattern. By the third quarter of the century there was a middle class generation which was quite different from its fathers and grandfathers. Mark Girouard has noted that 'Fathers who had spent their lives reading the Bible and making money with equally dedicated intensity very probably had agnostic children who were suspicious of the effects of money, and of the commercial society which produced it'.[40] So also, these children were probably much more desirous of spending their money on luxuries and entertainment than their predecessors.

The new public schools which catered primarily for upper-middle class boys also played an important part in altering some of these attitudes. First, the 'gentrification' of these schoolboys led to a much wider acceptance of the life style of the gentry. *Tom Brown's School-Days*, published in 1857 and selling over 11,000 copies in its first year, typified the process, extolling the virtues of Christian and manly behaviour. Second, although this was by no means entirely due to the public schools, organised games and exercises enjoyed a growing popularity. These games contained ingredients which developed the virtues praised by Hughes and others. The Church Congress of 1869, for example, asserted that 'the salt of good manners, good morals, and every manly virtue is to be found in the cricket field, and gives a tone to every good cricketer.'[41] Sports clubs of all descriptions became the rage in the 1860s. Peter Bailey's researches in Bolton have shown a succession of associations being formed from the mid 1860s on: 'A rowing club was in existence in 1865, the year of the foundation of Bolton's cricket club (whose membership grew from 30 to 220 in six years); an amateur athletic club formed in 1870, followed by an amateur swimming club in 1871. . . . Bolton FC was born in the following year. Subscriptions were beyond the range of any but a middle-class pocket.'[42] The participants were not just ex-public schoolboys but were, as the *Bolton Chronicle* pointed out, from 'the recent wave of professional and commercial men now assuming middle-class status.'

The growth in the popularity of a large number of sports in the second half of the nineteenth century was phenomenal. Active participation in and viewing of these sports was not confined solely to the middle classes. Indeed, the rational recreationalists saw the playing of sports by the lower classes as having all sorts of beneficial consequences for them, making them stronger and healthier but also developing in them sound attitudes towards discipline and team spirit. In addition the playing of the same sports by all classes revived old hopes that the privatisation and class specificity of leisure activities would be broken down and that class harmony would be established. These hopes were far from being fully realised. In sport, just as with holidays, a considerable degree of social zoning took place. Despite this, or perhaps because of it, by the end of the century there was much more tolerance shown in sport and at the holiday resorts towards the working classes. One reason was that both classes had much more in common than they had earlier in the century. They now played together or against each other in football and in other matches and went to see the same football games, albeit very often in different parts of the ground; and although they stayed in different hotels at the seaside, the resorts which they went to provided many new commercial entertainments which were proving attractive to middle as well as working class audiences. By the end of the century, popular culture was once again becoming popular across a wide spectrum of society.

SEVEN

Popular culture in a mature class society

It would be impossible to form a better idea of the advance made by Englishmen of all classes, whether in town or country, in the art of 'popular amusement' than from a comparison of the advertisements relating to sports, pastimes, and recreations in a newspaper of today with those which made their appearance less than half a century ago. One would look in vain now for the announcements of pugilistic encounters between bruisers of established and growing reputation, cock-fights, dog-fights, and performances of terrier dogs, backed for large sums to kill several scores of rats within a limited space of time. One would have looked in vain then for the accounts of cricket-matches, and the scores made by their players, in different parts of England, which now occupy entire pages of the sporting journals; for the notices to excursionists that are a regular feature in every newspaper during the summer season; for the miscellaneous programmes of picture exhibitions, lectures, theatres, music-halls, entertainments of all kinds, places of amusement of every variety, which have become an essential part of the machinery of our social life.

T.H.S. Escott, *England: Its People, Polity and Pursuits,* 1885

In 1883 Blackburn Olympic, a soccer team consisting of 3 weavers, a loomer, a gilder, 2 iron foundry workers, a clerk, a master plumber, a licensed victualler and a dentist, defeated the Old Etonians in the English FA Cup Final. They were the first team from a northern industrial town to win the Cup since it was inaugurated in 1872. The significance of the result was not merely that a team composed very largely of working men had defeated the amateur gentlemen of England but that a considerable amount of thought, training and money (most of which had come from a local iron foundry owner),[1] had gone into the preparation of the Blackburn team for the final. The week before the match the team had stayed in Blackpool and had undergone special training as well as embarking on a carefully chosen special diet composed of:

6 a.m.	Glass of port wine and two raw eggs followed by a walk along the sands
Breakfast	Porridge and haddock
Dinner	Two legs of mutton (one for each end of the table)
Tea	More porridge and a pint of milk each
Supper	Half a dozen oysters each[2]

By the time of the 1883 Cup Final, football was beginning to be not only a national spectacle but an important business. Money was needed to finance the 1000 clubs which by 1888 were affiliated to the Football Association. Wages had to be paid to the growing number of men who after 1885 openly were making their living, or at least supplementing their wages, by playing the game. But more importantly, money had to be found to finance the special grounds and stands which were needed to accommodate the growing number of football spectators. Although exceptional, in 1901 the Cup Final played at Crystal Palace attracted a gate of over 100,000. For those who did not play or watch the game, the opportunities to read about the teams and matches grew as the number of sporting journals proliferated and as an increasing amount of space in the national and local presses was devoted to sport in general.

C.E.B. Russell observed that for most boys in Manchester 'outdoor games have only one meaning, and that is football, as played under the Association Code'.[3] Certainly football was the most popular of all sports but it was by no means the only one for which there was a growing tide of enthusiasm. A bewildered foreign visitor to this country in 1899 concluded that 'All is sport in England. It is sucked in with the mother's milk'.[4] By 1890, 15 sports had a following such that they could be organised on a national scale. Fifty years earlier only horse-racing, golf and cricket had any form of national organisation.

There was an enormous explosion in the popularity of sports in the last quarter of the century. But it would be wrong to overemphasise this and neglect the fact that sports of one sort or another, especially horse racing, pedestrianism and cricket, had throughout the century a popular following and played an important part in the leisure activities of many men. Cricket, in particular, very early on in the century exhibited some of the features which were characteristic of the sports developed later. In 1835 for example, a crowd of 20,000 attended the Notts v Sussex cricket match; in the 1840s William Clark's All-England XI toured the country, and he and other professional cricketers attracted a large following. Pedestrianism too was a popular sport in certain parts of the country. In Northumberland there were so many races that the authorities in 1844 felt that they were proving a hazard to the public, and the local magistrates imposed 40 shilling fines on people taking part in races on the roads to Morpeth.[5] Even in the case of football, it is hard to believe that the legislation in the early part of the century, designed to put an end to the more unruly and violent games played in villages, eliminated the game entirely. The kicking around of a ball or tin on rough areas of ground by youths and men was a pastime which never disappeared. So the enormous interest generated in sports from the 1860s on was based on long-established and solid foundations. What was new was that for the first time many of these sports were codified and organised on a national scale.

The reasons for the vastly increased interest in sport are many. As we have seen, rational recreationalists believed that participating in organised sport developed the acceptable social and moral qualities of self-discipline, courage, loyalty and teamwork whilst at the same time diverting minds from drink, gambling and other wasteful activities; from the 1850s on they worked strenuously in advocating sport for all classes in the country. The headmasters of both old and new public schools also promoted this idea and the rules of football and many other games were drawn up and codified in these institutions. It was amongst the ranks of ex-public schoolboys and university men that the chairmen and members of national sporting organisations, and the legislators of Victorian sports, were to be found.

Although sport was seen as fundamental in developing moral qualities it was also increasingly envisaged as an appropriate means of reaching the non-believing working classes. Charles Kingsley and other advocates of 'Muscular Christianity' argued that a healthy mind was dependent upon a fit body, and later on in the century a healthy and fit population was to be seen as an essential national asset; an asset which could be nurtured and refined by the playing but not the mere watching of sport.

'Muscular Christians' advocated taking sport to the masses with an enthusiasm equalled only by their missionary zeal overseas. Church and chapelmen promoted all manner of games and played an important role, especially in the early stages, in the organisation of a number of sports. Many football clubs, including Aston Villa, had close ties with churches and chapels. One estimate concluded that church and chapel teams and Sunday School football clubs made up a quarter of all organised football clubs in the 1860s.[6] Similar figures are given for cricket teams. In Bolton one third of the cricket clubs in the towns in 1867 had connections with religious bodies.[7] At times the enthusiasm of churchmen reached the point of absurdity. The Reverend J.F. Jones, for example, went on record as believing that 'St Paul was such an admirer of physical games that, were he alive now, he would exercise his diligence to complete his week's work by midday on Saturday in order to witness a football match'.[8]

Despite the lead given by the public schools and the enthusiastic promotion of sports by many of the clergy, it would be misleading to conclude that they were entirely successful in promoting *their* ideas of the virtues of sports. As Hugh Cunningham has aptly concluded, in reality they proved to be 'sponsors more than missionaries' and although, because of the 'lack of alternatives', the working class 'was prepared to accept for as long as necessary, the fact of middle class sponsorship' they were not prepared to accept its ideology.[9] This became disturbingly clear to the moral reformers by the end of the century. By then professionalism had become firmly established in the game of football and football supporters appeared not so much interested in fair play as in seeing their own side win. Even worse, as C.E.B. Russell pointed out,

> Where leagues are formed for youths of a particular age it is a common practice for those of a higher age to lie and cheat in order to join, and so endeavour to make certain of winning whatever trophies may be offered. The play is frequently unfair, and too often foul and violent tactics take the place of strenuous play.[10]

Sport did in general play an important part in developing a sense of community and loyalty but it was not the same loyalty as that conceived of in the public schools. It was a loyalty which led football crowds often to be abusive to opponents and on occasions violent. In one sense it involved a much deeper commitment than public school men had ever expected or desired. For whereas to them sport was just one factor, albeit an important one, in building character, to many working men it was a central element in their lives.

POPULAR CULTURE IN A MATURE CLASS SOCIETY

Alan Metcalfe in his study of the Northumberland mining community has asserted that 'For the submerged majority of miners, sport provided the meaning of life; it was more important by far, after survival needs had been met, than any other aspect of life'. It is hard to disagree with this when faced with the evidence. In 1870, for example, on the death of Harry Clasper (a miner who had become a popular professional oarsman), a crowd of between 100,000 and 130,000 turned out to line the streets of Newcastle for his funeral, which was held on a Sunday 'to meet the convenience of numerous bodies of working men'. These crowds were gigantic compared with the 12,000 who went to the Sunderland v Blackburn football match in 1890, but this crowd in its turn was much larger than the 2,000 who greeted the Prince and Princess of Wales when they visited Sunderland on the same afternoon.[12]

Even the extent to which the public schools sponsored the sport of football needs to be questioned. Although the Football Association was dominated by the southern clubs, most of which were run by and contained a large proportion of amateur gentlemen players, very many clubs, especially in the midlands and north of England, were promoted by publicans and local factory owners and by religious organisations. These teams were composed largely of skilled workingmen and the initiative for the formation of the teams on occasion even came from these groups. The origin of Tottenham Hotspur is a case in point. The team was sponsored by the YMCA but only after a number of players had asked the local branch for assistance, which then took an active role.[13] In fact, rather than an institution being essential to the development of a sport, an interest in sport was at times crucial to the survival of an institution. For example, the Bristol branch of the YMCA, founded in 1853, had after an initial success fallen into decline; only in the late 1870s, when it turned to providing sporting facilities and opening local branches which ran their own sports teams, did its fortunes revive and membership figures rose.[14]

Many football clubs had their headquarters in that long-established working man's social and recreational centre – the pub. In 1865 in Sheffield 11 out of the 13 clubs listed in a local directory had public house addresses.[15] Pubs possessed the great advantage of being able to provide changing facilities – and in some instances publicans also provided grounds on which to play – as well as being ideal for entertaining after the match.

A small proportion of clubs was started at the workplace. Woolwich Arsenal and West Ham are perhaps two of the most famous examples. But whereas in the former the workmen received no assistance from the management, West Ham owed much to A.F. Hills, a shipyard owner, who as well as being interested in football, believed that promoting a works team would go a long way towards achieving peaceful industrial relations.[16]

Very often there was a variety of interests within a single club. Although at one time Aston Villa had connections with a Wesleyan chapel, the football field was provided by a local butcher and the dressing rooms by a local publican.[17] Perhaps not unexpectedly the larger, more ambitious clubs which after 1885 were permitted to employ professional players and which attempted to attract large crowds, became increasingly the preserve of those businessmen and industrialists who were willing to put considerable sums of money into them. Some elite clubs like Sheffield United, whose ordinary shares in 1899 were worth £20 each, had no working class share-holders, but the majority of clubs listed shares at £1 and some were even as low as 5 shillings. In a survey of the directors of 46 professional clubs in the period 1885-1915, Tony Mason concluded that small employers, wholesalers and retailers, publicans and hoteliers pre-dominated. However, 5.7% of the directors were skilled manual workers and 1.9% engineers. Directors who were unskilled manual workers amounted to only 0.5%.[18]

Nevertheless, football was a game which particularly attracted working men and boys. For it was cheap to play: apart from a ball very little equipment was needed. It was an advantage to have football boots, but they were not essential and in any case were comparatively cheap compared with equipment for cricket, tennis and other sports. Football spectators often watched local matches free and charges even at the highest level were only 3d or 6d.

Football, unlike many other sports, was within the financial scope of a considerable section of the working population. It was played everywhere and working people had more time for it as half-day Saturday working gradually became established. Textile workers were given a statutory Saturday half-holiday in 1850, and three years later in Birmingham 30 of the largest firms in the town, partly in the hope that the tradition of St Monday would be broken, introduced half-day Saturday working. But, in some areas of the country and particularly for certain groups such as clerks, shopworkers and shipworkers, the Saturday half-day was a long time coming, and whereas the Northumberland miners attained a 5 day week in 1872 Liverpool dockworkers were not awarded a 5½ day week until 1890. The importance of this half-day in enabling working men to participate in or watch a variety of sports was enormous. For example, Mason has pointed out that from October 1879 to March 1880 in Birmingham, where the Saturday half-day was widely observed, 811 football matches were listed in the local papers, whereas in Liverpool, where the half-day was not established, only two matches were listed during the same period.[19]

The shortening of the working week, together with the Bank Holiday Acts of 1871 and 1875, were major factors in contributing to the growth of sport. Railways too played their part in enabling both teams and spectators to travel further afield, thus facilitating the playing of matches between distant teams on a regular basis. Football specials were being organised from the 1880s onwards, but maybe more important than the train for many football spectators was the growth of urban tram and bus transport.

Central to all these developments however was an ability to pay for either taking part in or travelling to and watching particular games. From the early 1860s to 1875 average real wages in the country rose by some 40%[20] and they increased still further in the period of falling prices between 1880 and 1895. With enhanced spending power not only were many working people able to purchase goods and services which previously had been out of their price range but, also, there was a wider range of goods coming on to the market aimed specifically at this new and potentially fruitful range of consumers.

To cater for the phenomenal growth in all kinds of sports in this period, sporting goods firms made increasing demands on the leather, rubber and timber industries. In addition, newspaper owners, both national and local, gave greater coverage in their papers to sports. The few sporting papers which had existed earlier in the century faced competition from a growing number of provincial and national papers which either gave wide sports coverage or specialised in particular sports.

By the 1880s Saturday evening sports papers concentrating on the afternoon's football results were common to many towns. This new, comparatively cheap press, by giving more space to sport, was at the same time responding to public demand and helping to stimulate that demand, by popularising sports and sporting personalities and advertising sporting events.

Most popular of all among the sporting newspaper columnists were the horse-racing and, in the 1890s, the football tipsters. For gambling was, and always had been, intimately connected with most sports. Alan Metcalfe has pointed out that Northumberland miners 'rarely competed just for the fun of competition. They competed for a prize, usually side stakes that were placed by the two protagonists and their supporters. Gambling by the spectators accompanied most competitions'.[21] It was a pastime indulged in by all sections of the population and, if we are to believe many of the witnesses who gave evidence before the Select Committee on Gaming in 1844, had been on the increase for most of the century. Vincent Dowling, editor of *Bell's Life in London*, pointed out to the Committee that not only were large sums spent in betting on horses but that betting on boat races on the Thames went on to 'a very great extent'. Whilst he admitted that the Oxford versus Cambridge boat race was rowed 'more frequently for the Honour than for Money' most other races were not entered into unless there was some prize at stake.[22] The same can be said for the rowing competitions on the Tyne, where large amounts of money changed hands, races varying from individual challenge matches with stakes ranging from £5 to £100, to rowing championships where professional oarsmen, watched on occasions by crowds numbering 100,000, competed for prizes from £200 to £1,000.[23]

In every town in the country gambling on a wide range of sports took place. In 1885 T.H.S. Escott commented on the popularity of pedestrianism in Sheffield and then described how 'All the approaches to the ground which is the scene of the contest – many of them miserably squalid and dirty – are densely crowded. Hundreds of men throw up work for the day in order that they may get a glimpse of the sport, and make their books, or have an opportunity of backing their fancy'.[25]

Escott went on to voice the concern of many respectable Victorians about the gambling habits of working men. They seemed to have no conception of thrift and their wages were 'recklessly squandered in betting.' With the intention of making off-course betting illegal and thus to a great extent preventing working men from gambling, legislation was passed in 1853. It was not very successful. The street bookmaker, despite being harassed by local Watch Committees, flourished. The advent of the electric telegraph and the consequent rapid publication in the newspapers of racing results and starting odds prices, gave a tremendous stimulus to off-course betting. So too did the increase in real wages that occurred in the last quarter of the century. By the 1890s gambling seemed endemic. A London club steward told L.H. Curzon that 'everyone bets . . . everyone from the City to the West End; the cabman who brought you from the railway station, the porter who took your hat, the man who sold you that copy of the Special *Standard*, all bet'. Similar evidence came from Manchester. A newsagent living on the outskirts of the city told an enquirer that among the poor people, gambling is 'all they live for.'[25]

The government, alarmed at the evidence presented before the House of Lords Select Committee on Gambling in 1902, attempted four years later to plug the loopholes in off-course betting by passing the Street Betting Act. But competitions of all sorts, not just betting, caught the public imagination in the last decades of the century. Both *Tit Bits* and *Pearson's Weekly* were magazines which reached enormous circulation figures largely because of the various competitions which they promoted. A Salford newsagent in 1906 remarked that although people bought papers, 'Reading don't matter that much. What does count is the chance of getting something for nothing, £10 notes from tram tickets, gold watches for naming football winners'.[26]

Betting and competitions were indulged in by both men and women. In a society where hire-purchase and obtaining goods on credit were becoming more common and more socially acceptable, there was an obvious attraction in having a flutter on the horses or entering a treasure trail competition in the hope that a small windfall would solve a financial problem. Even if a successful gamble did not produce enough to pay off debts, 'A lucky win', as Standish Meacham comments, 'might enable the workman to indulge with his wife in an evening at the local music hall. "A night out for a shilling" meant two seats at the hall, 6d; a pint of beer, 3d; 4 ounces of sweets, 1d; and either two tram fares or a packet of cigarettes, 2d. Performances, twice a night, lasted two hours or so, and depending on the talent, were wretched or sublime or something in between.'[27]

Although some women did attend football matches, race meetings and other sporting events, sport was primarily male dominated. The vast majority of spectators and players were men. This was not true to the same extent in the music halls where, especially towards the end of the century, the numbers of women in the audience increased as did the proportion of female performers to men. By that time music halls were the most well attended of popular amusements. The London halls alone sold around 25 million tickets annually. It was an industry capable of making huge profits. As much as £5 million was invested in the music halls in London in 1900, and in the provinces new halls were being built and some of the larger ones were being syndicated into large entertainment empires such as the one run by Edward Moss.

The music halls of the late nineteenth century drew upon the traditions of the old travelling theatre companies, the fashionable London song-and-supper clubs and, above all, the free-and-easies. However, the financial structure of the halls, their physical appearance and the activities which went on inside were markedly different from the establishment described by Disraeli in *Sybil* in 1845. The publican had been replaced by shareholders and a theatre manager, and instead of a simple stage or platform there was now a well-lit curtained stage. Whereas in the 1840s the emphasis had been on drinking, with the entertainment a secondary consideration, by the end of the century the roles had been reversed. Ill-organised evenings of entertainment supplied very often by voluntary performers had been superseded by tightly scheduled, twice nightly, performances from professional artists, many of whom had a countrywide reputation. Finally, instead of gaining entry by purchasing set price tickets and then sitting informally at tables, later nineteenth century music hall audiences sat in fixed seating facing the stage and were segregated by varying admission prices.

The transition from free-and-easies to music halls gathered pace in the 1850s and 60s. In these decades the number of music halls increased at a much faster rate than the traditional theatres. Charles Morton's purpose-built music hall in the West End of London, the Oxford, was opened in 1861. It was followed quickly by many others, as the Limited Liability Act passed in the following year encouraged investors to back this expanding area of entertainment. By 1866 there were 33 large halls in London with an average seating capacity of 1,500. In the provinces the number of halls doubled in the 1860s[28] and many of the larger ones were modelled on the Oxford with its fully equipped stage and fixed seating.

The mid-1880s witnessed a further acceleration of investment in music halls; during this decade the percentage of their income derived from the sale of liquor declined sharply. One obvious reason for this was that a fixed seating system meant it was more difficult for members of the audience to buy drinks. But in any case, many proprietors, especially those owning the larger halls, were very keen to improve the image of the halls and one way of accomplishing this was by reducing the emphasis on drink. Throughout the period music halls came under attack from religious and temperance organisations. In the minds of many respectable Victorians the halls were associated with noisy, unruly audiences, gambling, prostitution and, of course, drink. Peter Bailey has emphasised the pressure under which music halls were placed: 'Next to the pub the music halls became the most embattled institution in working-class life, as reform groups strove variously to close them, censor them or reproduce their essential appeal in facsimile counter-productions purged of vulgarity.'[29]

In their attempts to counter these attacks music hall proprietors used a number of devices which, whilst going some way towards pacifying their critics, did not significantly harm their takings. Charles Morton, being an astute businessman as well as a life-long gambler, went to great pains to present a public image of respectability and he, like a number of other music hall proprietors, joined the socially acceptable Volunteers.[30] He advertised his halls as family entertainment; other managers, also keen to appear acceptable, attempted to censor both audiences and performers by prohibiting any sort of vulgar jokes, songs or exchanges between audience and artistes. Some managers went so far as to ask performers to sign contracts stating that they would not indulge in badinage with the audience, and, in an attempt to prevent audiences becoming unruly, paid for members of the police force to be present at performances. Later, uniformed commissionaires were introduced. Finally, an increasing number of halls, including the two 3,000 seater ones built in Bristol in the 1890s[31], did not sell alcohol.

These actions certainly had some effect. As early as 1866 a number of witnesses giving evidence to the Select Committee on Theatrical Licences and Regulations said that they approved of music halls. The Chief Commissioner of the Metropolitan Police, Sir Richard Mayne, giving evidence on the music halls in London, stated:

> There are a great number in some parts of the town, especially in the eastern parts, where the audiences are a very low class of people, and many of them are very young, but they are well-behaved. There are police, I believe, employed in every house; the usual course is for the manager to apply for the police to attend to prevent any disorder or indecorum, and I think the system works satisfactorily so far.

The author Frederick Guest Tomlins also spoke in favour of the halls to the Committee. He approved of them largely because they were places where men could take their wives without the women being demeaned:

> I think that the model music hall . . . is the Canterbury Hall,
> where you see artisans and small shopkeepers, with their
> wives and families, and it is a piece of actual humanity to the
> wife to take her there; it is quite a godsend to the wife and
> family to get out of their dull homes, and to go occasionally to
> these places, and it would be most cruel to interfere with
> them.[32]

Unfortunately, a majority of the writings on music halls have concentrated on what F. Anstey called 'the aristocratic variety theatre of the West End'.[33] It can be misleading to draw evidence solely from these London halls because they, together with some of the larger provincial halls in the 1890s, had a different clientele from most halls in the country. On the other hand, although the audiences may have been varied, much of the entertainment would have been similar. Artistes worked more than one hall in an evening and consequently their work schedules were both complicated and exhausting. The itinerary of the 'Great' MacDermott for an evening in 1878 was as follows: '8.15 Royal Aquarium, 9.10 Metropolitan, 10.00 London Pavilion, 10.50 Collins'.[34] Many musical hall artistes became household names and, as they began to tour the halls, not only in London but around the provinces, some received nationwide adulation. Provincial artistes, like the Tynesider Ned Corvan, often complained that they had been pushed from star billing by London-based singers and comedians.[35]

Music halls attracted men and women primarily from the working and lower middle classes. They attended halls ranging from vast 3,000 seaters to small establishments holding around 200. It was estimated that some 200 to 300 small halls, some of which exacted entrance by the old refreshment check, existed in London in the mid-1850s; although some of these later disappeared, partly as a result of stricter licensing regulations, there was a total of 328 places 'licensed for music' in 1900.[36]

Ewing Ritchie, visiting the music hall at Hungerford Market in the late 1850s, gives a vivid description of one of the smaller, more disreputable halls.

> On the night of my visiting the place there might have been
> above a hundred and fifty persons there; the hall seemed
> about half full. On each side of the room were highly-

coloured paintings, representing Alma, Sebastopol, Inker-
mann and Balaklava, and before me was the stage. The
audience consisted chiefly of young persons of both sexes,
and while the males had each their yard of clay, the ladies
indulged in bottled stout. One or two awful young swells
with excruciating all-rounders were present, but they,
though they were evidently got up on economical principles,
notwithstanding the general splendour of their appearance,
were not in keeping with the character of the place, which a
candid regard to truth compels me to denominate as seedy,
to say nothing of the damp, tunnel-like atmosphere which
not even the fumes of tobacco and grog and gas could
overpower.[37]

In every town in the country small halls existed alongside
their larger brethren, although many were eventually squeezed out of
existence[38] by those rich enough to attract the bigger stars. It was at
these places that the audience consisted of 'labourers, artisans,
porters, navvies, street-sellers of all kinds' and 'their wives, their
sisters and their sweethearts.'[39] Nevertheless, as at the larger halls,
very strong lines of social demarcation were drawn up within these
audiences, encouraged by varying entrance charges. Robert
Roberts's father refused to attend the Mayor's Charity Show at the
local Prince of Wales theatre because prices had been raised
especially for the occasion and he would not be seen sitting in the
cheaper seats. He considered 'the cost of his usual seat in the pit . . .
far too high and the company on the "top shelf" much too low'.[40]

Despite the attempts to make music hall respectable both audiences and performers at times overstepped the line which many
managers would have thought acceptable. There is also evidence that
within some audiences there were organised groups of 'chirrupers'
who threatened that unless they received payment from the artistes
they would disrupt their acts, and also 'gallery boys' and 'slogging
gangs' who harassed audiences and demanded money from them.[41]

Although many of the audiences remained aggressive and gave
nervous and weak performers a hard time, the songs and material
served up to them, it has been argued, were nowhere near as class-
specific or socially conscious as the old broadside ballads. The
commercialisation of the music halls and the wider social mix of the
audience inevitably meant that as the century progressed the artistes'
material became homogenised. To see such developments, as one

writer has done, as 'pernicious instruments of propaganda'[42] is to judge the late nineteenth-century working class by the criterion of 1970s radical romanticism. While accepting that the history of the music halls and their development from the old free-and-easies can be seen in terms of the growth of market forces, it is hard not to observe a cultural continuum between the two. Music halls did not provide a class-based entertainment in the way that broadsides did, but then in the years between the height of the popularity of broadsides and the growth of a mature music hall, Britain had developed into a highly industrialised, urban nation and inevitably there was bound to be some shift from a class-based to a mass-based entertainment. One fact remains clear – music halls were immensely popular. They attracted the working and the lower middle classes in large numbers and, towards the end of the century, an even wider section of the population.

For the development of larger and more luxurious music halls large scale capital investment was needed and was invariably obtained. The surplus spending power of the labouring population was clearly apparent by the 1880s and hence it was now worthwhile to invest in ventures which thirty years earlier would not have paid dividends. This is true not only of the music halls but in other areas of entertainment. More elaborate and expensive equipment and re-sources were put into the old traditional circuses and fairs; in seaside resorts much more consideration was given to the entertainment needs of working class day-trippers and, at least in the case of Blackpool, to holiday makers from the textile towns. Whereas in Blackpool in the 1860s it had been comparatively difficult to raise capital for leisure ventures, and what companies were formed were composed mostly of local businessmen, by the 1890s the numerous projects – including those for a Tower, a giant Ferris Wheel and the Alhambra – attracted money not just from the locality but also from Manchester and London.[43] Not all these schemes were financial successes, but money was available for investment in the entertain-ment industries to an extent unknown earlier, and new technologies were applied to them in the knowledge that there was an ever-widening audience which had both leisure time and money to spend.

Although sport, the music halls and other entertainments are an important element in the popular culture of the last quarter of the nineteenth century, they should not be dwelt on to the exclusion of other activities, especially those home-based ones which took up the greater part of people's lives. The 10 hour day and the 5½ day week meant that more time was spent in the home, which probably for many working men was becoming the centre of their leisure activities. Spare time was occupied now by making improvements to the home and pursuing hobbies, many of them home-based. In some instances men chose to take up hobbies which were closely associated with their full-time work but what is noticeable is that so many hobbies contained a serious competitive element. Pigeon and whippet racing and the showing of birds and dogs were among the many pastimes in which men gambled but also competed for prizes and cups. In most urban and rural areas there were flower and vegetable shows but these varied considerably in content from region to region, depending on the local enthusiasms for particular strains of flowers and vegetables. For although there were serious limitations on space, the interest of working men in gardening was still strong. It was hoped that Colling's Small Holdings Bill, passed in 1892, which gave local authorities powers to allocate land for allotments, would go some way towards meeting the obvious need of land for cultivation. Unfortunately, few authorities evinced much interest in the legislation and by 1910 only some 31,000 acres had been added to the 445,000 acres of allotments already in existence in England and Wales[45] at the time when the bill was passed.

Music remained throughout the century a central form of entertainment, although for many working families it was confined either to listening to street performers, visiting the music hall or having a sing-song in the local pub. The extension of credit facilities meant that in some cases it was possible to purchase a secondhand piano or some other instrument, and the possession of musical instruments, or indeed any articles of household furniture, did much to give the home a certain status and an aura of respectability. To maintain this respectability, however, much depended on the attitude and hard work of the women in the household. Their abilities as good housekeepers played a vital part in determining the position of the family in communities which in most cases were extremely complex and hierarchical structures.

The major way in which respectability was achieved was by demonstrating that the family possessed financial security. Hence the importance of the well-furnished Sunday parlour and the 'Sunday best' clothes.[45] But there was a myriad of other seemingly trivial factors which came into play. Robert Roberts described the disgrace felt by mothers on receiving from the school the 'green card' which indicated that their children were verminous, and he stresses how above all else, 'nonconformity in sex could do more than anything else to damage one's prestige'. Most matters concerning the upkeep of the home, including when one did one's washing, were coded and commented upon. Roberts recalled the old rhyme,

Them as wash on Monday have all the week to dry,
Them as wash on Tuesday do little that's awry,
Them as wash on Wednesday are not so much to blame,
Them as wash on Thursday are folk that wash for shame,
Them as wash on Friday most likely wash in need,
But them as wash on Saturday – they are sluts indeed.[46]

By the end of the century it would be common to find some form of newspaper or magazine being read in a working class home. The reading habit may have been further encouraged but was by no means formed by the implementation of the 1870 Education Act; even by mid-century the majority of working people were literate. In addition to the enormously successful *Tit Bits* (1881), *Answers* (1888) and *Pearson's Weekly* (1890), sporting papers and 1d women's magazines like *Forget-Me-Not* were now rivalling the old penny novelettes in popularity. Comics too, although by no means new, attained large readership figures. *Ally Sloper's Half-Holiday*, first published in 1884, was not only a great success but began the development of the front page cartoon character, Ally Sloper, into a household name. He became as well-known as any leading music hall star, inspiring the production of a whole host of Ally Sloper publications, while other branches of commerce took advantage of his popularity by manufacturing a range of Ally Sloper products – umbrellas, plates, mugs and so on.[47] Later comics owed much to *Ally Sloper's Half-Holiday* but *Chips* and *Comic Cuts*, produced by the Harmsworth press had the advantage of costing only ½d.

By 1900 the ½d comic and the ½d newspaper were attracting a substantial working and lower middle class readership. Harmsworth's *Daily Mail*, started in 1896, had by 1900 circulation figures of well over 500,000. The paper contained a section for women readers and its layout was markedly different from that of the more traditional papers. Produced by new rotary presses and Linotype type-setters this 'revolution' of Harmsworth's was 'less an innovation in actual journalism than a radical change in the economic basis of newspapers tied to the new kind of advertising'.[48] Harmsworth, realising the growing importance of advertising as a major source of newspaper income, sold entire pages of the *Daily Mail* to advertising agencies.

Display advertising became more and more prominent in the press with firms like Bovril taking up a whole page spread in the *Daily Mail* in 1900 to explain 'Bovril's Part in the South African War'.[49] As well as manufacturers, the new large department stores and chain stores, which were being built in most towns, used display advertising on a large scale in both the national and local press. Newspapers, however, were only one medium used by an advertising industry which by the 1880s had become big business.

Despite the popularity of the *Daily Mail* and Pearson's *Daily Express*, which was started in 1900, it is necessary to put their readership figures into some sort of perspective. The reading of national dailies remained far from being a majority habit. Sunday newspapers, which throughout the century had been far more popular, had much larger circulations. There was, however, a considerable expansion of the number of regional newspapers in the period and these papers competed with the older established press of the *Daily Telegraph* and the *Daily News* for an essentially middle class readership.

Although many leisure interests were shared by members of the working and lower middle classes,[50] the middle classes, if they did participate in similar activities, did so at some distance. Just as there were 'better' residential areas within most seaside resorts, so there were more expensive seats for sporting and other events which ensured that the space between the middle and the lower classes was maintained. In some instances, however, there were tendencies towards excluding the lower classes altogether from certain leisure activities. The theatre is perhaps the best example, for in the last years of the century an increasing amount of time was devoted to plays which can justly be termed products of a 'high' culture. Of course, this move can be overstressed and the theatre's links with the music halls and the working classes were to some extent maintained throughout the century. For example, music hall stars often went into theatre pantomime at Christmas and the less successful artistes, in efforts to earn a reasonable living, obtained work both on the halls and in the legitimate theatre. Nevertheless, the number of theatre productions of tragedies and melodramas, especially popular among the poorer classes who stood or sat in the theatre 'gods', declined as interest in the problem plays of Wilde, Shaw and Pinero developed.

In the late 1860s Thomas Wright described the spectators who sat in the galleries of theatres as 'passionately fond of the drama' and as entering into the spirit of the occasion with enthusiasm. 'The roughs' sitting in the 'gods' are

> . . . those who come to the theatre with unwashed faces and in ragged and dirty attire, who bring bottles of drink with them, who *will* smoke despite of the notice that 'smoking is strictly prohibited', and that 'officers will be in attendance'; who favour the bad with a stamping accompaniment, and take the most noisy part in applauding or giving 'the call' to the performers. The females of this class are generally accompanied by infants, who are sure to cry and make a disturbance at some interesting part of the performance.[51]

By the 1880s, however, many theatres had become much more respectable establishments. Theatre prices had been raised, the theatres themselves had been restructured and the content of many of the plays presented was markedly different from that of the old farces and melodramas.

Hugh Cunningham has observed that this attempted 'middle class appropriation of leisure' occurred not just in the theatre but in sports like rowing and athletics which once were the domain of working men. In 1866 middle class legislators within the associations for these sports obtained agreement that not only should no professionals be permitted to take part in events organised by the associations but also that anyone who 'is a mechanic, artisan or labourer' should be excluded.[52]

Although the attempt to exclude working men did not last long, it does reveal that for some at least the idea of the amateur gentleman meant much more than merely not being paid for playing sport. Rather, as was argued in the *Sporting Gazette* in 1872,

> Sports nominally open to gentlemen amateurs must be confined to those who have a real right to that title, and men of a class considerably lower must be given to understand that the facts of their being well conducted and civil and never having run for money are NOT sufficient to make a man a gentleman as well as an amateur.[53]

The socially important idea of the amateur sportsman was retained in most sports and, of course, introduced into the new sports which were invented around this time. Tennis, hockey and badminton were new middle class games and they remained the preserve of the middle classes until well into the twentieth century. It has been pointed out that, ironically – at a time when 'muscular Christians' were extolling team games because they promoted the virtues of trust, companionship and interdependence – many of the new games, together with golf which was taken up by the middle classes in England about this time, were for individuals rather than teams.[54]

It is noticeable that within a short space of time all these games were taken up by women. This is true also of cycling, which was made much more comfortable and attractive by the introduction of the 'safety' bicycle in the 1880s and the patenting of Dunlop's pneumatic tyre at the end of the decade. The cost of the machines, however, limited cycling to the middle classes for the remainder of the century. H.G. Wells's Mr Polly and his friends could not afford bikes and 'found boots the greatest item of their skimpy expenditure'[55] but a growing second-hand bicycle trade in the early years of the new century began to enable him and other lower middle and working class men and women to participate.

For the late Victorian middle classes leisure continued to remain something of a dilemma. To those people who wished to distance themselves from the lower orders it was becoming perfectly clear that they would need higher walls and hedges to preserve the privacy of their homes from the eyes of working class day trippers or cyclists; they needed to discover coves and fishing villages further and further afield in order to avoid the ever-increasing number of working class holiday makers; and playing in exclusive clubs was the only way of ensuring that they did not have to compete against rough and ungentlemanly players. The situation was just as unsatisfying, however, for those Victorians who had striven hard to effect class conciliation, for the lower orders did not seem to want to play the game according to middle class rules. To them, winning, and an uncritical support of the home side, were more important than 'playing the game'; dancing on the pier was more enjoyable than bracing sea walks; and drinking and gambling were still more popular than rational recreations.

EIGHT

The civilisation of the crowd

You may see it in the Saturday football crowds in all the manufacturing cities: see it in concentrated form when a selection of all the Saturday football crowds has poured into London for the 'final contest' for the 'cup', which is the goal of all earthly ambition. All the long night overcrowded trains have been hurrying southward along the great trunk lines, and discharging unlimited cargoes of Lancashire and Yorkshire artisans in the grey hours of early morning. They sweep through the streets of the metropolis boisterous, triumphant. They blink round historic monuments. They all wear grey cloth caps; they are all small men with good natured undistinguished faces. To an oriental visitor they would probably all appear exactly alike, an endless reproduction of the same essential type.

C.F.G. Masterman, *The Condition of England*, 1909

Those who wished to change and elevate the life-styles and leisure habits of the populace in the mid-nineteenth century, were, for the most part, sturdy optimists. Faced with the gin-palace, the rat-pit and St Monday, they both envisioned and willed the tea-room, the debating society and the diligent and moral employee. History was, they considered, on their side and their moral and religious ideals would meet with wider acceptance; respectability, self-improvement and rational recreation were, indeed, the natural accompaniment to steam power and economic progress. It was true that to such reformers the bulk of the working classes appeared unregenerate, with gross and brutish appetites, but this was largely a hangover from an earlier age, exacerbated by lack of proper supervision and moral care in urban environments, but susceptible to reform. Middle class reformers such as John Bright placed their faith in the respectable and self-improving section of the working classes which seemed to many in the 1860s to be the vanguard of the future. To Matthew Arnold that part of the working classes looked forward

> . . . to the happy day when it will sit on thrones . . . to survey, as Mr Bright beautifully says 'the cities it has built, the railroads it has made, the manufactures it has produced, the cargoes which freight the ships of the greatest mercantile navy the world has ever seen', – it is obvious, I say, that this part of the working class is, or is in a fair way to be, one in spirit with the industrial middle class. It is obvious that our middle class liberals have long looked forward to this consummation, when the working class shall join forces with them, aid them heartily to carry forward their great works, go in a body to their tea meetings, and, in short enable them to bring about their millenium.[1]

Many of the leaders of that minority of the working classes designated by historians of the left as 'the working-class movement', would probably have quarrelled with the likes of Bright as to who should take the chair at the tea-meeting of the millenium and some would have questioned whether employers should be invited to the party at all; however, all would have agreed that it should be a sober and respectable affair. As we have seen, working class radicalism and proto-socialism shared with middle class radicalism and liberalism a belief in the individual's capacity for self-improvement, provided he was set the right example, given proper opportunities for education and imbued with the correct doctrines. Those who argued the case for the extension of the franchise in the 1860s pointed to the increasing numbers of respectable artisans: men with decent Sunday suits and watch-chains who took heed of the morrow and attempted to make it secure with their savings, their friendly societies, trade unions and burial clubs. Such paragons seemed to be epitomised in the persons of radicals and trade union leaders like George Howell, Henry Broadhurst and Thomas Burt. These men would surely become more typical as working-class prosperity increased and as Mechanics' Institutes and Working Men's Clubs combined with chapel as the focus for their education and recreation. Even the small minority of extreme radicals and socialists, whether middle or working class, who looked back on Chartism and forward to a class-conscious workforce, envisaged a working class culture that was essentially rational and sober.

The concept of respectability is an important one and many historians have seen the distinction between those who were and those who were not respectable as the most significant one in Victorian society. Ideals of respectability changed, however, as one moved up or down the social ladder, and one should not take the ideas of one section of the middle classes as necessarily representative of those in other social strata. A working class concept of respectability emerged which, although it paralleled middle class notions, was yet distinctive in its own right. Far from being a weak-kneed obeisance to middle class values, it was very often an assertion of personal dignity in the face of adverse circumstances. That respectability should have been seen to become more widespread among the working classes when it had already become well established among the middle classes is not surprising. Only after 1850, when rising living standards began to percolate down to sections of the working classes, did middle class observers become aware of the respectable working man. However, the working class desire for respectability sprang from the same root as it did in the middle classes, namely a realisation of the sheer brutality of much of contemporary life and, even more so, of life in the recent past, and a corresponding desire to assert one's distance from it. We may distinguish three kinds of working class respectability: that which corresponded closely to what was expected from working men by the middle classes and was often, as Peter Bailey has pointed out, a charade, 'a kind of exploitation in reverse for its actors, who assumed respectability to meet the role demands of their class superiors';[2] that found particularly among nonconformists which was very similar to its middle class equivalent but was not deferential and often buttressed independent political attitudes; and, by far the most widespread, an innately working class respectability, misunderstood by middle class employers and reformers, which often went hand in hand with attendance at the pub, the music hall or even the race track.

Thus, overt and often clumsy attempts to reform and improve working-class attitudes and behaviour, such as Mechanics' Institutes, the early Working Men's Clubs and the encouragement of rational sports were rejected or transformed by perfectly respectable working men. The victory for those who wished beer and gambling to be permitted in the Working Men's Clubs, although reluctantly supported by the Reverend Henry Solly, represented a defeat for a certain ideal of working-class behaviour but did not mean that the clubs ceased to be respectable. The Sunday School as an institution became central to the lives of working class churchgoers. Many football clubs quickly severed their early assocation with church or chapel.

Working-class respectability was by no means standardised nationally; it was, for instance, quite acceptable for a wife to go out to work in parts of Lancashire whereas in a Durham mining village it would have been an occasion for shame. In the urban villages, demarcated from each other by railway line or main road, which made up the working class sectors of late nineteenth century towns and cities, there were infinite gradations of status, and local mores could differ considerably, but common criteria for respectability do seem to have included decent clothing, a clean and burnished doorstep and the avoidance of frequent or ostentatious drunkenness or of public family brawling.

In 1881 A.J. Mundella, addressing a breakfast meeting of the British and Foreign School Teachers Society, commented on an article in *The Times* of 25 December 1880 which had asserted that there was no substantial difference between the working man of 1880 and his predecessor of 1830:

> [He] cited the late Mr Charles Knight's picture of London on the Christmas Day of 1824, with its 'rampant, insolent, outrageous drunkenness', drunkenness such that 'no decent woman could, even in broad daylight, at the holiday season, dare to walk along in the Strand or Pall Mall, much less in the regions into which flowed all the filth of the Seven Dials'; and contrasted that picture with what he had himself observed on the Boxing Day of the present year, when he had carefully watched the crowds of respectable working men and their families, visiting the National Gallery, the South Kensington Museum and the Tower; and he declared that there was real and substantial progress, in both the mental and moral scale.[3]

Mundella was of course selective in his sampling. Had he gone to a pub and not to the National Gallery, he might have reached different conclusions. But it is undeniable that a profound change in cultural mores and a blurring at the edges between the worlds of the middle and of the working classes had taken place.

Only a very small section of the working classes spent their leisure time in the improving way described by Mundella, but the general behaviour of working men and their families in the public space they

shared with other sections of society no longer aroused the appre-
hension of former years. Matthew Arnold's concern about the
unredeemed and unorganised populace which

> ... raw and half-developed, has long lain half-hidden
> amidst its poverty and squalor, and is now issuing from its
> hiding place to assert an Englishman's heaven born privilege
> of doing as he likes, and is beginning to perplex us by
> marching where it likes, meeting where it likes, bawling what
> it likes, breaking what it likes ... [4]

was as a political fear already something of an anachronism
in the circumstances of the sixties. It is, perhaps, something of a
tribute to the essential stability of England in that decade that
Arnold's 'moral panic' should have been excited only by the unusual
disturbances attendant on the debate over parliamentary reform and
their coincidence with Fenian outrages and religious riots. Such
incidents occurred in a society which was getting used to what was, by
any historical comparison, a high degree of public order and social
and political stability. Fear of the working classes was, indeed, not a
common upper class reaction. Masterman, early in the twentieth
century, considered that 'The Rich despise the Working People; the
Middle Classes fear them'[5], but it would have been more accurate to
conclude that the rich condescended to them and the lower middle
classes feared they were not distant enough from them.

The world of leisure was one in which the classes, often obeying
very similar instincts and pursuing similar pleasures, yet kept their
distance from each other and followed different codes of conduct; they
occasionally observed each other and sometimes mingled warily. In a
sense they were on the same train but travelling in different
compartments, each reserved for their own kind, just as the seats and
boxes at music halls or circus were graduated by price and therefore,
to some degree, class. As we have seen, many holiday resorts came to
cater for working class and middle class visitors alike. Although it is
easy to point to the extremes of the social spectrum in such a setting as
the sea-side resort (those who stayed at the most opulent hotels and
those who slept several to a room at the cheapest boarding houses),
the fuzziness of the dividing lines and the inadequacy of blunt class
terminology must always be borne in mind. That fear of the unknown
but probably violent and seditious working class that had characterised upper class thought in the forties had largely disappeared by the
eighties; observation of the lower orders at play had much to do with

this change of attitude. The *Spectator*'s comments on holiday-makers on the Isle of Man illustrate both the urbanity with which an upper-class journal regarded them and the degree to which distinctions of great importance to those directly involved could appear of little consequence to those more removed:

> Those who flock thither are almost all persons of the lower middle-class, and operatives from the thickly populated towns of Lancashire and Yorkshire. They make but a short day, they ramble over the island, and their loud, provincial tones are heard in boisterous merriment. In themselves these people are a study. You see the best of the working-class of the North away from their factories and workshops, and though your taste may be sometimes offended at rude jokes, and noisy merriment, yet they are essentially an independent and hardworking class even in their amusements.[6]

In one very important respect, and one reflected in the way in which people spent their leisure time, working class life had become closer to that of the middle classes. It has become conventional for historians to contrast the private and domestic lives of the Victorian middle classes with the public and communal lives of their working class counterparts; the public house was, we are told, the working man's front parlour, and the social stage for women was the street and corner shop. Such a distinction is broadly true but it became less pronounced towards the end of the nineteenth century, with the development of a greater emphasis upon the family and upon private leisure pursuits among the working classes. This development, encouraged by some improvement in housing, was reflected in the increased expenditure upon household furniture, in the importance attached by respectable families to the footwear and clothing of wife and children as well as of the husband, in the centrality of the institution of the Sunday dinner in the working class weekend and in family outings and holidays. Greater domesticity and more affectionate attitudes towards children were made possible by greater security and important, though patchy, increases in real income and leisure. They may well have also been facilitated by state and, later, compulsory education which had the ancillary effect of prolonging childhood and economic dependence upon parents and thus strengthening the influence of mother and household. Fondness for home and family should not be appropriated to any particular class or century but clearly a modicum of security and prosperity provide a fertile context for such affection, and different sections of society have at different stages of modern history achieved such a context. Acculturation to the values of superior social groups may have played a part in changing the cultural patterns of working class life and in making domesticity more central to it; the greater resources available were probably more decisive. The desire for domestic comfort and harmonious family life was no new phenomenon among working people, as witnessed by the traditional samplers and ornaments bearing such phrases as 'East, West, Home is best' or 'Bless this house' which graced even the meanest homes.

What made such developments possible was a general rise in real wages paralleled by a fall in basic living costs. The improvements in transport technology that made possible the import of cheaper grain and frozen meat from other continents, together with the activities of such retail revolutionaries as Thomas Lipton and Jesse Boot, did more for the standard of living of the British working classes than the combined efforts of the 'working-class movement'. Although a considerable section of the population still lived in poverty at some stage in their lives, mere sufficiency was no longer the order of the day for the majority and greater choice and variety led to rising expectations. It is true that, even for the skilled worker, a degree of insecurity remained which the network of trade unions and friendly societies could not quite overcome, for ill health and old age still brought attendant poverty. Nevertheless, for most working men and their families, for most of their lives, there was increasingly some excess spending power after basic needs had been met. If much of this spending power went into the purchase of more and better food, decent clothing that enabled the family to withstand with confidence the gaze of the world, and the furnishings practical and symbolic that graced front parlours, a considerable proportion also was spent on pleasure, on 'having a good time' and on entertainment, sport and holidays.

The demands of the more exacting middle class reformers were not fulfilled and those who were foremost in attempting to direct or cajole working people towards improved lifestyles themselves represented a rarefied and self-conscious version of an ethos which was only whole-heartedly subscribed to by a minority of their own stratum; missionaries and reformers are, after all, rarely typical of their own milieu. Slum clearance and philanthropic housing schemes, the work of the Charity Organisation Society and the efforts of armies of missionaries and temperance advocates, failed to bring about a sober and

Christian working class society in which leisure time was spent in a relentless search for self-improvement. Indeed, in the eyes of many clergymen and philanthropists, the manifest signs of working-class respectability and domesticity could appear as wasteful expenditure, heedless extravagance and rash improvidence. That a working-class family could enjoy a sumptuous Sunday dinner and then pawn its best clothes on a Sunday morning, that ornate furniture could be acquired for a parlour that was hardly ever used, and that a family could return penniless from an annual holiday, were not only incomprehensible but reprehensible actions in the eyes of the reformers. Despite great regional variations the majority of working people proved recalcitrant in the face of successive efforts made from within and without their ranks to make church or chapel central to their lives, and crusades for temperance were no more successful. Public parks, municipal art galleries and museums and, later, subsidised libraries did not fulfil the hopes of reformers that they would transform working-class life. Indeed, the very concept of 'working-class life' was inherently a view from without and it is doubtful whether many skilled workers saw themselves in the same class as the poor or considered that in their leisure and recreation they had much in common with them. Although parks were made use of by a wider social spectrum, it was only a minority of working people who frequented, even occasionally, art galleries, museums and libraries; amongst that minority the unskilled worker and his family were unusual and the poor rare. It was, overwhelmingly, to the highly market-conscious commercial leisure industry that the more affluent working class of the late nineteenth century looked for diversion and self-fulfilment in their leisure time.

The notion of a sharp break between a world of pre-commercial leisure and a more exploitative commercial one is, as we have seen, mistaken. For centuries the provision of popular amusements had been a commercial activity, and in the nineteenth century the multiple effect of small individual increases in spending power, the sheer expansion of the population and the significant increase, on Bank Holidays and free Saturday afternoons, of time reserved for leisure resulted in a colossal expansion of the industry, making it a major national economic force. Perhaps because the spokesmen for the entrepreneurial ethic and the proponents of free trade had so often been of a puritan persuasion in their private lives, it had taken a long time for Adam Smith's dictum that the high price of labour was the very basis of public opulence to be accepted. In the latter decades of the nineteenth century its truth was revealed as the satisfaction of mass consumer demand became a major engine of the economy. While Thomas Lipton and the Maypole Dairy Company were providing for the nation's dietary needs, Hepworths and Freeman Hardy and Willis for its need to be clothed and shod, entrepreneurs of leisure and entertainment were active on a vastly increased scale in satisfying its need to be amused. As James Walvin has written:

> At times it must have seemed that any capital investment in leisure facilities could reap a rich return, as financiers and entrepreneurs, often local men but also drawn from metropolitan circles of finance, stumbled over each other to give the public what they wanted.[7]

Such expectations were often confounded and many late nineteenth-century entrepreneurs of leisure went bankrupt, after starting up in the wrong place or with the wrong product or because they were under-capitalised, as had many hopeful cotton manufacturers in the late eighteenth century. Many a Plaza or Wintergarden dominating a bleak sea-shore has in a hundred years of existence never made a decent profit for its innumerable succession of proprietors, attempting over the decades to attract a fickle public with the fancies of the day; while entire towns testify to their unsuccessful attempt to become holiday resorts, their promenades, parks and piers laid out, like the air-strips of a cargo cult, for a public which never came. But the public and its money were there in plenty for those who could attract them. At its fringes the world of commercial leisure was still somewhat raffish, since the fairground, the sporting publican and the street-entertainer were still important; while any sea-side resort, slow in the imposition of its bye-laws, could find its streets, links and even the beach itself overrun by winkle-stalls, musicians, Punch and Judy shows and the cavalry of competing donkey-owners. The small business-man or business-woman continued to thrive, and indeed the number of petty entrepreneurs expanded, but popular reading habits and enthusiasms for dancing and for the stage could now potentially make substantial profits for large and well-organised businesses.

If the hopes of those who had worked for the emergence of a sober, Christian, self-improving but deferential culture of the people were disappointed, so were those of individuals who had wished to see the secular radical sub-culture, that had characterised a small section of the working classes in the early nineteenth century, become a general culture. In many respects the socialist critique of popular culture echoed that of the rational recreationalists. Whereas the latter wished the people to become Christian, domestic and rational in their recreations, the former hoped they would become socialist, communal and rational, but both berated popular culture for its hedonism and cynicism. The rush to the sea-side, the giddy throng on Bank Holidays and the cultural parameters of the music-hall could not be the foundations of a new Jerusalem. Unable to believe that popular recreations and entertainments reflected genuine tastes and free choices, they found the source of contamination in the commercialisation of leisure which had, they considered, an innate tendency to appeal to and sometimes even to shape the lowest appetites. Imprisoned within the attender at the music-hall, the spectator at the football match and the reader of *Tit Bits* was, they believed, a worthy socialist trying to get out. William Morris, John Burns and Tom Mann all bewailed the new opium of the people. As Chris Waters has argued with a wealth of quotation from such socialist journals as *Justice*, *The Clarion* and *The Labour Leader*,

> Socialists argued that while the excitement and frivolity offered in music halls, at football matches, and on Bank Holidays wasn't really leisure at all, the proprietors of these amusements tried to claim that it was ... [it is difficult to see] that socialists actually developed a new critique of the commercial leisure industry that transcended the moral homilies of rational recreation.[8]

Belfort Bax thought that:

> A well-conducted English workman, 'thrifty and industrious' is no doubt kept in a state of dogged contentment by never knowing what leisure intelligently occupied means, by his tastes being carefully kept under and by his weekly holiday being 'empty, swept and garnished' of all relaxation.[9]

The popularity of spectator sports and in particular the craze for watching football matches was a particular worry. Some complained of the fact that enthusiasm for a local team distracted workers from what should have been their proper preoccupations: politics and agitation. Norman McCord in his study of North-East England cites the following report of a speaker's words at a Northumberland Miners' Picnic early in the twentieth century:

> ... he remembered seeing a great crowd in Newcastle. The

Lord Mayor was out, and the bands were playing amid general excitement. He was told that Newcastle United has beaten Barnsley, and had won the English Cup! Thousands of people were there talking about the football match, yet that very day a father of three children had gone out on to the moor and cut his throat because he had been out of work for eighteen months and could not obtain bread for his family ... yet the thousands were more interested in the football match than they were in one human soul who wanted their help and aid so much. In conclusion, he would urge them to keep their heads right, and remember that a crust of bread to a starving being was of more value than all the Cups and the Leagues in the country.[10]

John Burns almost pre-empted Oswald Spengler in his fear that the poor, 'over-specialised in their work, over-athleticised in their play' were becoming mere spectators of sport, like 'the Greeks and Romans in the days of their degradation'.[11]

Thomas Cooper, the old Chartist, had earlier detected a decline from an earlier radical culture:

In our old Chartist time, it is true; Lancashire working men were in rags by thousands; and many of them lacked food. But their intelligence was demonstrated wherever you went. You would see them in groups discussing the great doctrine of political justice ... or they were in earnest dispute respecting the teachings of socialism. *Now* you will see no such groups in Lancashire. But you will hear well-dressed working men talking of co-operative stores, and their shares in them, or in building societies. And you will see others, like idiots, leading small greyhound dogs, covered with cloth, in a string! They are about to race, and they are betting money as they go![12]

The historian Gareth Stedman Jones has argued that in London a radical secular culture flourished among artisans for the first three-quarters of the nineteenth century but had all but died out by 1900:

For the most prominent developments in working class life in late Victorian and Edwardian London were the decay of artisan radicalism, the marginal impact of socialism, the largely passive acceptance of imperialism and the throne, and the growing usurpation of political and educational interests by a way of life centred round the pub, the race course and the music hall.[13]

Stedman Jones's artisanate was, of course, a sector in decline, and his skilled workers in traditional London trades such as silk weaving, watch making and clothing, footwear and furniture making, who largely worked in small workshops, were atypical of the group usually known as artisans in the late nineteenth century. They were certainly very different from such artisan élites in engineering and shipbuilding as those described by Geoffrey Crossick in his study of Kentish Town[14] and it is dubious whether, however influential they may have been, their numbers even at mid-century were sufficient for their decline to be central to the 'remaking of the English working class'. There is, as we have seen in Chapter 2, evidence that the old popular radicalism made a special appeal to artisans whose skills and traditions were threatened, and the tendency of many older skills and patterns of employment to survive in the special circumstances of London, with its large market for luxury goods, may have ensured the greater longevity of that radicalism there. One may question, on the other hand, how persuasive the popular radicalism nostalgically remembered by Cooper and rediscovered by Jones ever was, and how central it was in the lives of all but a handful of devotees; whether, in short, there ever was a golden age of radical secular culture. There is little evidence that explicit atheism or republicanism were ever professed by more than a handful of working men, while popular culture has usually been not only conservative and monarchist in its sympathies but also deeply cynical about the claims of political and social visionaries.

Historians and sociologists influenced by the Italian Marxist Antonio Gramsci have viewed the major developments in popular culture during the late nineteenth century as part of the consolidation of a bourgeois hegemony. Such a view sees 'popular culture as an *area of exchange* between the culture and ideology of the dominant classes in society and the cultures and ideology of subordinate classes'.[15] In this exchange the commercialisation of popular culture is seen as of decisive significance, and Cunningham has written:

The strength of popular demand was such that many direct efforts to control leisure failed, yet that demand was contained within a world of commercialised leisure which provided its own controls. From the point of view of authority this commercialised leisure was increasingly acceptable, for if what was offered within it was hardly uplifting, at least it posed no threat. On the contrary, leisure was shorn of many of its political and social associations, and while the way it was spent might be individually damaging, it was no longer politically or socially dangerous.[16]

It is certainly true that the recreations of the lower orders had been viewed by many in the eighteenth and early nineteenth centuries as a threat to public order and social stability and that by the late nineteenth century they were no longer perceived in this way; but the commercial exploitation of leisure was no new phenomenon, as Cunningham's work itself suggests, and its expansion into a mass industry was as natural a response to increased spending power as Thomas Lipton's shops. Like Lipton, leisure entrepreneurs such as Edward Moss studied their market as Barnum and Bailey, Philip Astley and many an obscure publican had done before them. What made leisure less threatening to authority and respectable society was not that it was more commercial but the changed circumstances and mores of its crowds of consumers. Working people were more prosperous, they were better dressed, their homes were more comfortable and they had a little more control over their own lives and immediate futures; they no longer needed to snatch at their pleasures or to gulp them down quite so swiftly.

Class was certainly an important social factor but the characteristics of the culture and ideology of late nineteenth century society were not the prerogative of any one class nor dictated by the interests of any class. Exchange there was in plenty between different interest groups and the proponents of different values, but not between classes, for there was no homogeneity or conformity of interests or values within classes. Values which transcended class were interpreted differently by various sections of society, and this interpretation was influenced by tradition and circumstances, but they were common values nevertheless. The movement towards privacy, domesticity and respectability did not result from middle class influences or 'bourgeois values'; rather, in a general historic process, the middle classes were the predecessors. Bound up with the process was the rise in living standards and life expectancy, and the shift through which work became more public and family and leisure life more private and individualistic; women were able to focus more exclusively on the home and ties of affection between couples and their children to flourish more freely. Inevitably this process had an impact on the character of more public and gregarious leisure activities.

Popular leisure pursuits became less violent and riotous. Cock-fighting, dog-fighting and even ratting were no longer general pursuits though they continued, as they do today, to be followed by an underground of aficionados. Boxing, wrestling, football and cricket had all undergone a considerable transformation and were now characterised by the rule book and the association, the league or board of control. The standards of the workplace continued to permeate many leisure pastimes, especially in small towns and villages, and much recreation was still community-based, but individual predilection became even more important. Drinking was still central to the leisure of many and was the natural accompaniment to other enjoyments for most people, while gambling surmounted the legal restrictions placed in its way; but 'boisterous' and 'giddy' were the kind of adjectives used to describe holiday throngs where once they would have been called 'drunken' and 'brutalised'; the appearance of a train load of day trippers was now more likely to make shop keepers rub their hands than put up their shutters.

As we saw in Chapter 4 the cultural barriers which had seemed to divide the middle and working classes at mid-century were beginning to come down. The height of such barriers can be explained by three factors: the different time scales by which the majority of the different strata achieved the economic basis for more private, domestic and respectable cultural mores; the impact of the religious revival which began in the late eighteenth century; and the pressures for ostentatious respectability and the exaggeration of social differences upon an expanding middle class in which so many were socially and economically insecure.

The late eighteenth century had witnessed a steady expansion of the middle orders of society and an increase in their relative prosperity. It was perhaps to be expected that they should seek recognition of their new status both by emulating aspects of the life styles of those above them and by accentuating the gulf between themselves and those below them. The latter preoccupation was given more urgency by the turbulent and often brutal nature of much of common life and popular culture. Of course many working people already aspired to respectable status and made valiant and heroic efforts to achieve it, but their numbers were inevitably limited by economic constraints. The further and more rapid expansion of the middle classes in the early nineteenth century and the new awareness of the importance of this section of society coincided with a great religious revival. This revival, especially in its Evangelical and Methodist forms, moulded the outlook not only of merchants and manufacturers but large numbers of the landed élite, the lower middle class and sections of the working classes. A respectable station in life and a demeanour of piety, sobriety, chastity, thrift and industry became for many indissolubly linked. The importance which Evangelicalism attached to the family, its emphasis on the paternal role, its demand for discipline and its suspicion of the world and its pleasures influenced the attitude to leisure and recreation of great swathes of Victorian society, and above all of the middle classes.

The degree to which such an outlook ever dominated Victorian society can, of course, be exaggerated. It was, for instance, far from universally accepted by those who possessed the greatest wealth, sat in the Palace of Westminster and provided the dignitaries and office holders of the departments of state and the major national institutions. Even among the business and professional communities many did not subscribe to its values; there were plenty of hard-drinking solicitors, adulterous factory owners and horse-racing merchants, just as there were whole communities of temperate and God-fearing miners.[17] Nevertheless the tone of high seriousness and moral earnestness which so many have seen as dominant did have a basis in fact and was most widespread among spokesmen in the middle classes, amongst whom psychological and social pressures to conform were strong. In the mid-Victorian decades, in seemingly natural alliance with economic individualism, and incarnate in provincial liberalism, such attitudes were at their most influential. In the late 1860s Matthew Arnold, drawing heavily upon the work of the Manchester School and on the views of leading nonconformists, inveighed in *Culture and Anarchy* against the 'Philistines' with their narrow and arid social vision, their concern with a plain but intense religiosity and their equally plain and mechanical view of social progress; but even then, such men were becoming less typical of the middle classes. The traditions of high seriousness, earnestness and a desire for self-improvement continued to colour middle-class Victorian attitudes to leisure, but by the eighties they were a colouring rather than an essence. Those who, like A.J. Mundella, continued to preach the mid-century ideals in their pristine purity were an important section of opinion, the nonconformist backbone of Gladstonian Liberalism; they were but one section nonetheless.

Middle class concern for the improvement of the working classes occurred, paradoxically, precisely when greater psychological security threatened, from within the middle classes themselves, the very values they sought to inculcate in the lower orders. Just as middle class missionaries sought, through Sunday Schools, Mechanics' Institutes and Working Men's Clubs, to convince working men of the virtues of toil, self-help, industry and sobriety, so the siren voices of enjoyment, entertainment and sport were beguiling the increasingly receptive middle classes. The railways and Thomas Cook suggested holidays; and sport, instead of being time misspent, began to accord with muscular Christianity; while music, dancing and even the theatre became less suspect. There was no sudden change, for pleasure could be taken seriously, holidays made educational and sport hard work, but the dam had been breached.

This was followed by a more relaxed attitude towards leisure and recreation among most of the middle classes, perhaps reflecting the more relaxed atmosphere in their homes, as the discipline and formality of mid-century gave way to more permissive attitudes, a more overt display of affection and a greater interest in children. The search for a wider world of pleasure gathered pace.

The pattern of leisure activities and the timetable of the recreational calendar for the great majority of the population increasingly converged during the last decades of the nineteenth century as working and middle class entertainments came to overlap. Recreations, sports and institutions showed an ability to move up and down the social scale. The family Christmas, as we have seen, spread from the middle to the working classes and holidays at the seaside followed a similar path. Football, having risen from being the turbulent and disorganised pastime of the people to a respectable public school game, returned reorganised to the common man. Pedestrianism and rowing, low pastimes of the people in the early and mid-nineteenth century, were, as athletics and sculling, acceptable to the Oxford man at its end. If the music hall continued to attract its main audience from the working classes, it also catered for clerks and, in the west end of London, at the Empire, Trocadero and the Tivoli, for young aristocrats as well; while pantomime became part of the Christmas routine for families from all classes.

As befitted a society with many jealously guarded social divisions, different sectors of society took their pleasures as separately as possible, even when the pleasures were identical. The superior, select bar at the local in a working class neighbourhood could be reserved by custom for the labour aristocrat while the sea-side resorts which catered for a wider range of clientele were divided into class-specific areas. A whole town could support its local football club but the working men watched from the stand and the middle-class directors from their boxes. The acme of class consciousness was reached on the county cricket field where amateurs and professionals emerged from their different dressing rooms and passed through separate doors on to the field in order to play for the same team.

Harold Perkin has observed that the mature class society is one in which the relations between the classes are those of 'a familiar kind of marriage in which the partners cannot live together without bickering but are perfectly aware that apart they cannot live at all'.[18] Bickering is an apposite word for the class tensions that periodically interrupted the development of mass sport in the late nineteenth century, and accompanied the wary intermingling of the classes at the seaside, a bickering made querulous by the very real problem of asserting status in a society where prosperity was more widely diffused and social gradation becoming ever more complex. At the same time as working people had more leisure, and a considerable proportion of them the means to dress well, take holidays and participate in national sports, the numbers of those claiming middle class status were expanding. The desire to assert caste exclusivity and to buttress it against those immediately below by emphasising the importance of style and codes of behaviour was no new phenomenon but, the greater the material equality of a society and the higher the degree of social mobility, the more self-conscious and inventive such an assertion becomes. The British social system achieved a Byzantine complexity in the late nineteenth century and, if education and residential neighbourhood were essential criteria for its infinite gradations, so leisure activities and sport in particular were an arena for its public display.

Some developing sports like golf and lawn tennis were specific to the upper and middle classes and were retained within clubs whose membership was carefully confined to peer groups. Within those sports which were accessible to all classes, internal divisions would be maintained by the organisation of, for example, Old Boys' clubs which retained the social groupings of school days and played only against socially acceptable opponents. But such exclusivity could be maintained only up to a point, for as sports became national and leagues and cups proliferated, the desire to win and the need to attract ability and skill could militate against social divisions.

The sports field showed status consciousness at its most acute, rarefied and hypocritical level. Although the opposition to professionalism was in part based on genuine fears that enthusiasm for the game for its own sake, genuine regional connections and the link between the 'rabbit' and the expert would be lost, it was also based on a determined exclusivity and the association of amateurism with higher social status. From the division of rugby into league and union in the nineties, to the abolition of the gentleman and player distinction in cricket in the 1960s and the continued wrangling in athletics, the battle was to be a long one. It is worth noting that the prince of amateurs, W.G. Grace, made more money out of his distinguished career than any professional of his day.

Such arguments should not disguise from us that national sports had developed in which all classes were involved. Local and county club teams were supported by a wide cross-section of society, match results published in most newspapers, and the sporting heroes of the day idolised because of their ability in a common sport rather than because of their social background. There were still discernible differences between the classes at play: by and large the middle classes remained more private and domestic in their leisure life and more decorous in their behaviour, while the working classes were typically more public, gregarious and rowdy. Such differences had, however, been eroded considerably and this facilitated the emergence of a more national leisure culture in which mass spectator sports and the entertainments industry had the effect of homogenising many regional and social distinctions.

For some the emerging mass culture of leisure was a primary focus for their lives, while for others it took second place after work and domestic and private interests. For a minority of intellectuals it was a threat and a cause for cultural despair. Both conservative and socialist critics saw standardised, commercial entertainment as undermining, with its cheap emotional appeal, high culture, and as smothering genuine cultural experience. The Edwardian observer Charles Masterman asked:

Are the main lines set as at present, and later developments confined to variations in length and direction along these lines? In such a case progress will mean a further repetition of the type; two cotton factories where there is now one; five thousand grey-capped men where there are now three; perhaps in some remote millenium, fourteen days of boisterous delight at Blackpool where there are now only seven.[19]

His pessimism has been echoed by literary critics and mass society theorists ever since.

A more optimistic view of the emergence of a mass culture is that of J.H. Plumb who considers that, 'from the late seventeenth century a mass culture, belonging essentially to the middle classes, developed, which if it did not quite obliterate the other two [the aristocratic and the bucolic], drove them into smaller and smaller social enclosures'.[20] We would suggest, however, that two cultures – a common culture, and a high culture which is the articulate expression of it – existed at both the beginning and end of our period. This is not to underestimate the role of the middle orders of society nor of the commercial exploitation of leisure. High culture was no longer an aristocratic preserve by 1900: it had acquired the ethos of moral earnestness which suggested that a taste for the arts led to improvement and refinement; it had indeed come to embrace most intellectual and artistic pursuits. As Roger Scruton has reminded us:

> . . . high culture includes not only the aristocratic art of Racine and Molière, but also the bourgeois art of Dickens and Mann, the popular moralism of Bunyan and the folk poetry of the Aegean.[22]

Nor must we lose sight of the continuity of popular culture. If the nineteenth century witnessed a taming of its cruder and more violent manifestations, as working class people followed the middle classes in the direction of domesticity, privacy and respectability, many leisure pursuits remained in essence the same and were simply modified to suit a society which had become more prosperous, more humanitarian and less disorderly. People have always liked to sing, to get drunk in company, to enjoy competitive and violent games, to be entertained by story tellers or dramatists, to goggle at the unusual and to gamble. In the nineteenth century they found different and, on the whole, more amusing ways of doing this than in the past and a commercial leisure industry was anxious to assist.

The anarchic figure of Punch still personified much of popular culture, mocking dignity and authority and applauding those who by their wit cheat both the rent collector and the hangman. A late nineteenth century incarnation of Punch was Ally Sloper. This shabby scarecrow of a swell, his phallic umbrella recalling the slapstick humour of the Harlequinade, celebrated the undeserving common man, his sexual fantasies and his desire for life to be a perpetual half-holiday. He was no threat to society but neither was he a suitable subject for reform.

Bibliographical note

During the course of this book the authors have referred to a wide range of secondary sources. Authors, titles and publication dates of these works are included in the following 'Notes and references' section. Many of the books and articles cited deal with specific aspects of popular culture, but there are a small number of key books which deal generally with the questions of popular culture and leisure and which are valuable especially to those readers who are new to this branch of social history.

Two general social history books which contain interesting chapters on popular culture are R. Porter, *English Society in the Eighteenth Century* (1982), especially Chapters, 4, 6 and 7, and G. Best, *Mid-Victorian Britain, 1851–75* (1971). Chapter 3 deals with Education, Religion and the Uses of 'Leisure' although it is only leisure in the towns which is discussed. Two books which are important for the early part of the period are P. Burke, *Popular Culture in Early Modern Europe* (1978) and R.W. Malcolmson, *Popular Recreation in English Society 1700-1850* (1973). Malcolmson's thesis, that the attack on popular recreations in the late eighteenth and early nineteenth centuries resulted in the disappearance of many traditional practices and pastimes, has recently been questioned by H. Cunningham, *Leisure in the Industrial Revolution* (1980), which covers the period roughly 1780 to 1880, J. Walvin, *Leisure and Society* (1978), and P. Bailey, *Leisure and Class in Victorian England* (1978). Bailey examines the transformation of popular leisure in the period 1830 to 1885, especially in relation to the textile town of Bolton. Another town which is well documented with regard to the changes in the leisure activities of its inhabitants is Bristol, in H. Meller, *Leisure and the Changing City, 1870-1914* (1976). M. Vicinus, *The Industrial Muse* (1974) is well worth a mention and although it concentrates primarily on working class literature in the nineteenth century, there is a good final chapter on the development of the music hall. Finally, R. D.

Storch (ed.), *Popular Culture and Custom in Nineteenth Century England* (1982) contains a number of good articles on particular aspects of popular activities, as does J.K. Walton and J. Walvin (eds.), *Leisure, in Britain 1780-1939* (1983) which became available just as this manuscript was being handed over to the publishers.

Notes and references

Introduction (pages 9–15)

1 'Ways of seeing: Control and Leisure versus Class and Struggle' by Eileen and Stephen Yeo in *Popular Culture and Class Conflict 1590–1914*, 1981, edited by Eileen and Stephen Yeo, p. 137.
2 Tony Bennett, 'Popular Culture: themes and issues (2)', in the Open University *Popular Culture* Course, Block 1, Unit 3, 1981, p. 10.
3 *The Birth of a Consumer Society: the Commercialization of Eighteenth Century England* by Neil McKendrick, John Brewer and J.H. Plumb, 1982.
4 Bennett, op. cit., p. 32.

Chapter 1 (pages 17–40)

1 R. Williams, *The Long Revolution*, 1961, p. 63.
2 Ferdinand Tönnies, *Community and Society. Gemeinschaft and Gesellschaft*, translated and edited by Charles P. Loomis, 1957.
3 Robert Redfield, 'The Folk Society' *American Journal of Sociology*, 52, January 1947.
4 Peter Burke, *Popular Culture in Early Modern Europe*, 1978.
5 Ibid., p. 28.
6 Ibid., p. 16.
7 See Alan Macfarlane, *The Origins of English Individualism*, 1978, and *The Justice and the Mare's Ale*, 1981.
Harold Perkin, *The Origins of Modern English Society 1780–1880*, 1969.
For a debate between Marxists on this subject see Perry Anderson 'Origins of the Present Crisis', *New Left Review*, 1964, and E.P. Thompson, 'The Peculiarities of the English', *The*

Socialist Register, 1965.

8 Macfarlane, *The Origins of English Individualism*, 1978.

9 Perkin, op. cit., p. 104.

10 For detailed descriptions of holidays, fairs and popular recreations in eighteenth century England see Robert W. Malcolmson, *Popular Recreations in English Society 1700–1850*, 1973. Similar ground but with a greater emphasis on custom and ritual is covered by Bob Bushaway, *By Rite: Custom, Ceremony and Community in England 1700–1880*, 1982.

11 Keith Thomas, 'Work and Leisure in Pre-Industrial Society', *Past and Present*, No. 29, 1964.

12 Peter Laslett, *The World We have Lost*, 2nd. edn., 1971, and *Family life and illicit love in earlier generations*, 1977.

13 Lawrence Stone, *The Family, Sex and Marriage in England 1800–1900*, 1977, p. 146.

14 See for instance: Edward Shorter, *The Making of the Modern Family*, 1976, and Lloyd de Mause (ed.), *The History of Childhood*, 1974.

15 Ferdinand Mount, *The Subversive Family*, 1982, p. 57.

16 Malcolmson op. cit., p. 170.

17 E. Kerridge, *The Agricultural Revolution*, 1967.

18 Christopher Hill, 'A Changing Economy' in Block 1 of *Seventeenth Century England: A Changing Culture*, Open University Course A203, 1980, p. 24.

19 Keith Wrightson, 'Alehouses, Order and Reformation in Rural England 1590–1660' in *Popular Culture and Class Conflict*, Eileen and Stephen Yeo (ed.) 1981, pp. 15–20.

20 From, *A Brief Defence of the several Declarations of King James the First and King Charles the First, Concerning Lawful Recreations on Sundays*, 1708, quoted by Malcolmson, op. cit., p. 158.

21 Henry Bourne, whose *Antiquitates Vulgares*, 1725, is an important source for such information, combined the zeal of a reformer with a relentless antiquarianism which made him write down a wealth of detail on activities, most of which he disapproved of.

22 Perkin, op. cit. p. 20. Perkin uses Gregory King's estimates. See W.A. Speck, *Stability and Strife in England 1714–1760*, 1977, on the usefulness and the shortcomings of King.

23 J.H. Plumb, *The Commercialisation of Leisure in Eighteenth Century England*, 1973, pp. 2–3.

24 Ian Watt, *The Rise of the Novel*, 1957, p. 53.

25 Speck, op. cit., p. 54.

26 Watt, op. cit., p. 56.

27 Plumb, op. cit., pp. 17–18.

28 Alan Everitt, 'Social Mobility in Early Modern England', *Past and Present*, No. 33.

29 E.M. Butler (ed.), *A Regency Visitor. The English Tour of Prince Pückler-Mushau described in his letters 1826–1828*. From the original translation by Sarah Austin, 1957, p. 114.

30 *Public Advertiser*, 5 September 1785. Quoted by Thomas Frost, *The Old Showman*, 1881.

31 Bushaway, op. cit., p. 176.

32 Frost, op. cit., pp. 151–152.

33 'Two cultures? Uses and abuses of the two-tier model'. Paper read to the Annual Conference of the Social History Society, 1981.

Chapter 2 (pages 41–62)

1 Peter Burke, *Popular Culture in Early Modern Europe*, 1978, p. 218.

2 For a summary of the views of a number of anthropologists on the lack of differentiation between work and leisure in primitive societies see Keith Thomas, 'Work and Leisure in Pre-Industrial Society', op. cit., pp. 51–2.

3 Christopher Hill, *Society and Puritanism*, 1964, p. 506.

4 Lawrence Stone, *The Family, Sex and Marriage in England 1500–1800*, 1977, p. 678.

5 Ibid., p. 27.

6 Edward Shorter, *The Making of the Modern Family*, 1975.

7 E.A. Wrigley and R.S. Schofield, *The Population History of England 1541–1871. A Reconstruction*, 1981.

8 J.M. Winter, 'The Demography of Dorian Gray' (Review of Wrigley and Schofield above), *Historical Journal*, 26 January 1983, p. 217.

9 Peter Laslett, *The World We Have Lost*, 2nd edn., 1971, p. 152.

10 *Jackson's Oxford Journal*, 22 July, 1979. We are grateful to Bridget Hill for this reference. Her book, *Eighteenth Century Women. An Anthology* is to be published in 1984. The fullest treatment of the subject of wife-selling is Samuel Pycatt Menefee's *Wives For Sale*, 1981.

11 John Brand, *Observations on Popular Antiquities including the whole of Mr. Bourne's Antiquitates Vulgares*, 1777, p. 21.

12   Ibid., p. 27.

13   Quoted by Stone, op. cit., p. 658.

14   Brand, op. cit., p. 193.

15   Ibid., pp. V, VI.

16   G.M. Young, *Portrait of an Age*, O.U.P. (paperback edn.), 1973, p. 2.

17   Quoted by Stone, op. cit., p. 667.

18   Quoted by Malcolmson, op. cit., p. 98.

19   Ibid., p. 97.

20   Bernard Mandeville, *The Fable of the Bees*, Penguin 1970.

21   Brand, op. cit., p. 234.

22   Malcolmson, op. cit., Chapter 7, pp. 127–35.

23   *Thomas Babington Macaulay*, Everyman's Library Edition, 1910, p. 248.

24   Quoted in Malcolmson, op. cit., p. 107.

25   William Cobbett, *Rural Rides*, Penguin, 1967, pp. 188–9.

26   Craig Calhoun, *The Question of Class Struggle. Social Foundations of Popular Radicalism during the Industrial Revolution*, 1982, p. 43.

Chapter 3 (pages 63–87)

1   Norman Gash, *Aristocracy and People. Britain 1815–1865*, 1979, p. 36.

2   There seems little reason to believe that large scale manufacturing and the division of labour militated against such permeation, as Patrick Joyce has demonstrated in his study of later nineteenth century textile towns, *Work, Society and Politics*, 1980.

3   Malcolmson, op. cit. and Michael R. Marrus, *The Rise of Leisure in Industrial Society*, 1974.

4   Michael R. Marrus (ed.), *The Emergence of Leisure*, 1974, pp. 4–5.

5   E.M. Butler (ed.), *A Regency Visitor. The English Tour of Prince Pückler-Mushau described in his letters 1826–1828*. From the original translation by Sarah Austin, 1957, p. 238.

6   Ibid., p. 89.

7   Ibid., p. 91.

8   Ibid., p. 143.

9   Thomas Frost, *The Old Showman and the Old London Fairs*, 1881, p. 258.

10   *A Regency Visitor*, op. cit., p. 83.

11 Frost, op. cit., pp. 239–240.
12 Arnold Rattenburg, 'Methodism and the Tatterdemalions' in *Popular Culture and Class Conflict 1590–1914*, Eileen and Stephen Yeo, ed., pp. 51–2.
13 Frost, op. cit., pp. 239–40.
14 See D. Harker, 'The Making of the Tyneside Concert Hall' in *Popular Music. A Year Book*, 1982. We are indebted for information on Purvis to Mr. Vincent Arthey's unpublished paper 'Billy Purvis and Ned Corvan'.
15 F.M.L. Thompson, *English Landed Society in the Nineteenth Century*, 1963, p. 144.
16 E.W. Bovill, *The England of Nimrod and Surtees 1815–1854*, 1959, p. 11.
17 Gash, op. cit., p. 38.
18 Bovill, op. cit., p. 9.
19 Hugh Cunningham, *Leisure in the Industrial Revolution*, 1980, p. 27.
20 Bovill, op. cit., p. 9.
21 Newcastle MSS, Diaries, 17 November 1829.
22 Hugh Cunningham, *Leisure in the Industrial Revolution*, 1980, p. 27.
23 J. Rule, 'Methodism, Popular Belief and Village Culture in Cornwall', in R.D. Storch, *Popular Culture and Custom in Nineteenth Century England*, 1982, p. 55.
24 Hugh Cunningham, *Leisure in the Industrial Revolution*, 1980, p. 23.
25 P. Joyce, *Work, Society and Politics*, 1980, p. 286.
26 G.M. Trevelyan, *English Social History*, Pelican, 1976, p. 423.
27 R.D. Storch, 'Persistence and Change in Nineteenth Century Popular Culture', in R.D. Storch (ed.), op. cit., pp. 2 and 9.
28 R.D. Storch, ' "Please to Remember the Fifth of November": Conflict, Solidarity and Public Order in Southern England, 1815–1900', in R.D. Storch (ed.), op. cit., pp. 89 and 98.
29 P. Bailey, *Leisure and Class in Victorian England*, 1978, p. 12.
30 J. Walton and R. Poole, *The Lancashire Wakes in the Nineteenth Century*, in R.D. Storch (ed.), op. cit., p. 103.
31 J. Walton, 'The Demand for Working-Class Seaside Holidays in Victorian England', *Economic History Review*, 1981, p. 254.
32 Walton and Poole, in R.D. Storch (ed.), pp. 115–16.
33 F.M.L. Thompson, 'Social Control in Victorian Britain', *Economic History Review*, 1981, p. 198.
34 Walton and Poole, in R.D. Storch (ed.), p. 118.
35 J. Ewing Ritchie, *The Night Side of London*, 1857, p. 33.
36 D.M. Downes, B.P. Davies, M.E. David and P. Stone, *Gambling, Work and Leisure*, 1976, p. 30.

37 Brian Harrison, 'Religion and Recreation in Nineteenth-Century England', *Past and Present* No. 38, Dec. 1967, p. 121.

38 Norman McCord, *North East England, The Region's Development 1760–1960*, 1979, p. 72.

Chapter 4 (pages 88–110)

1 S. De Grazia, *Of Time, Work and Leisure*, 1962, p. 6.

2 R.W. Malcolmson, *Popular Recreations in English Society 1700–1850*, 1973, pp. 170–1.

3 J. Walvin, *Leisure and Society 1830–1950*, 1978, pp. 9–10.

4 J. Walton and R. Poole 'The Lancashire Wakes in the Nineteenth Century', in *Popular Culture and Custom in Nineteenth Century England*, ed. R.D. Storch, 1982, p. 130.

5 De Tocqueville, *Journeys to England and Ireland*, ed. J.R. Meyer, 1958, p. 108.

6 Cited in J. Walvin, *Leisure and Society 1830–1950*, 1978, p.6.

7 P. Bailey, *Leisure and Class in Victorian England*, 1978, p. 36 but see the whole of Chapter 2 for an excellent survey of the reasons for rational recreations. He assesses the various attempts which were made to reform working men's leisure habits and examines the reasons why these attempts were often successfully resisted. Another first rate book dealing with this problem is H. Cunningham, *Leisure in the Industrial Revolution*, 1980. For a more formal account of the adult education movement in this period see J.F.C. Harrison, *Learning and Living 1790–1860*, 1961.

8 Report from the Select Committee of Enquiry into Drunkenness with Minutes of Evidence 1834, *British Parliamentary Papers*, 1968, (4), xii.

9 Cited in W.L. Burn, *The Age of Equipoise*, 1964, p. 106.

10 T. Bennett, 'Popular Culture: Themes and Issues', in Open University *Popular Culture* course Unit 3, p. 13.

11 B. Harrison, 'Teetotal Chartism', in *History*, vol. 58, 1973, p. 197.

12 J. Lawson, *Progress in Pudsey During the Last Sixty Years*, 1887, p. 42.

13 D. Vincent (ed.), *Testaments of Radicalism*, 1977, p. 129. This book includes the memoirs of five working men – Thomas Hardy, James Watson, Thomas Dunning, John James Bezer and

Benjamin Wilson. There was a surprisingly large number of working men's autobiographies published in this period and in *Bread, Knowledge and Freedom*, 1981, David Vincent lists 142 such publications which cover all or some part of the period 1790–1850.

14 D. Vincent, *Bread, Knowledge and Freedom*, 1981, p. 138.

15 *The Baptist Children's Magazine*, October 1831, p. 317.

16 D. Vincent, *Bread, Knowledge and Freedom*, 1981, p. 138.

17 J.F.C. Harrison, *Learning and Living 1790–1960*, 1961, p. 29.

18 *Report from the Select Committee on Public Libraries, 1849. Session I*, 1976–8, 2000–2012.

19 H. Cunningham, *Leisure in the Industrial Revolution*, 1980, p. 97.

20 J.F.C. Harrison, *Learning and Living 1790–1860*, 1961, pp. 75–6.

21 B. Harrison and B. Trinder, 'Drink and Sobriety in an Early Victorian Town: Banbury 1830–60', *English Historical Review* Supplement 4, 1969, p. 51. Although it concentrates on the drink question, this impressive extended article provides a first-rate account of the leisure activities available to the people of Banbury during the period 1830–60.

22 P. Bailey, *Leisure and Class in Victorian England*, 1978, p. 46.

23 S. Alexander, *St. Giles' Fair 1830–1914*, 1970, p. 38.

24 G. Hawkins, 'The Taming of Whitsun', in E. and S. Yeo, (eds.), *Popular Culture and Class Conflict*, 1981, pp. 195 and 197.

25 See Eric Hobsbawm, 'Introduction: Inventing Traditions' in Hobsbawm E. and Ranger T. (eds.), *The Invention of Tradition*, 1983, for a discussion of the distinction between invented tradition and custom.

26 Bob Bushaway, *By Rite. Custom, Ceremony and Community in England 1700–1880*, 1982, p. 274.

27 Cited in H. Cunningham, *Leisure in the Industrial Revolution*, 1980, p. 92.

28 S. Martin Gaskell, 'Gardens for the Working Class', *Victorian Studies*, Summer 1980, p. 490.

29 D.A. Reid, 'The Decline of St. Monday', *Past and Present*, No. 71, 1976, pp. 83 and 99.

30 F. von Raumer, *England in 1835*, 1836, 3 vols., ii, 263.

31 H. Cunningham, *Leisure in the Industrial Revolution*, 1980, p. 96.

32 S. Martin Gaskell, 'Gardens for the Working Class', *Victorian Studies*, Summer 1980, pp. 481–2.

33 S. Constantine, 'Amateur Gardening and Popular Recreation in the 19th and 20th Centuries', *Journal of Social History*, Spring 1981, pp. 394 and 398.

34 J. Walvin, *Leisure and Society 1830–1950*, 1978, pp. 100–1.

35 Cited by V. Gammon, 'Babylonian Performances: The Rise and Suppression of Popular Church Music 1660–1870', in *Popular Culture and Class Conflict*, E. and S. Yeo (eds.), 1981, pp. 75 and 78.

36 J. Walvin, *Leisure and Society 1830–1950*, 1978, p. 102.

37 J. Lawson, *Progress in Pudsey During the Last Sixty Years*, 1887, pp. 103 and 106.

38 *Report from the Select Committee on Public Libraries 1849. Session I*, 1262–65 and 2782–85.

39 B. Trinder, *A Victorian MP and his Constituents*, Banbury 1969, p. 116.

40 P. Bailey, *Leisure and Class in Victorian England*, 1978, p. 50.

41 B. Harrison and B. Trinder, 'Drink and Sobriety in an Early Victorian Town: Banbury 1830–60', *English Historical Review*, supplement 4, 1969, pp. 57–8.

42 R. Currie, *Methodism Divided*, 1968, p. 138.

43 D.A. Reid, 'The Decline of St. Monday', *Past and Present* No. 71, 1976, p. 99.

44 P. Bailey, *Leisure and Class in Victorian England*, 1978, p. 51.

45 J. Walvin, *Leisure and Society 1830–1950*, 1978, p. 102.

Chapter 5 (pages 115–43)

1 A.E. Dingle, 'Drink and Working Class Living Standards in Britain 1870–1914', *Economic History Review*, 2nd series, v. 25, 1972, p. 612.

2 J. Burnett, *Plenty and Want*, 1966, p. 199.

3 J. Rule, 'Methodism, Popular Beliefs and Village Culture in Cornwall 1800–50', in *Popular Culture and Custom in Nineteenth Century England*, ed. R.D. Storch, 1982, p. 55.

4 B. Harrison and B. Trinder, 'Drink and Sobriety in an Early Victorian Town: Banbury 1830–60', *English Historical Review*, supplement 4, 1969, p. 2.

5 N. McCord, *North East England*, 1979, p. 185; *Leisure Hour*, 1872, p. 170.

6 G. Best, *Mid-Victorian Britain 1851–75*, 1979, p. 243.

7   B. Harrison, *Drink and the Victorians*, 1971, p. 298. This study is by far the best and most thorough account of drink and the temperance movements in the nineteenth century.

8   B. Harrison, 'The Drunken Committee of 1834', *Historical Journal*, 1968, p. 283.

9   F. von Raumer, *England in 1835*, 1836, 3 vols., v. 2, p. 122.

10 B. Harrison, *Drink and the Victorians*, 1971, p. 32.

11 Thomas Wright, *Some Habits and Customs of the Working Classes by a Journeyman Engineer*, 1867, pp. 68 and 73.

12 C. Behagg, 'Secrecy, Ritual and Folk Violence' in *Popular Culture and Custom in Nineteenth Century England*, ed. R.D. Storch, 1982, p. 166.

13 B. Harrison and B. Trinder, 'Drink and Sobriety in an Early Victorian Town: Banbury 1830–60', *English Historical Review*, supplement 4, 1969, p. 14.

14 L.L. Shiman, 'The Band of Hope Movement: Respectable Recreation for Working Class Children', *Victorian Studies*, v. 18, 1973, p. 51.

15 B. Harrison and B. Trinder, 'Drink and Sobriety in an Early Victorian Town: Banbury 1830–60', *English Historical Review*, supplement 4, 1969, p. 3.

16 A.E. Dingle, 'Drink and Working Class Living Standards in Britain 1870–1914', *Economic History Review*, 2nd series, v. 25, 1972, pp. 618 and 620.

17 B. Harrison, *Drink and the Victorians*, 1971, p. 340.

18 *The Nineteenth Century*, Jan-June 1893, pp. 690–701 and 1046–1061.

19 D. Vincent, *Bread, Knowledge and Freedom*, 1981, p. 141.

20 L. James, *Print and the People, 1819–51*, 1976, p. 38.

21 M. Vicinus, *The Industrial Muse*, 1974, p. 96.

22 D. Vincent, *Bread, Knowledge and Freedom*, 1981, p. 113.

23 M. Vicinus, *The Industrial Muse*, 1974, p. 43 and pp. 289–90.

24 L. James, *Fiction for the Working Man: 1830–50*, 1974, pp. 14–15. This book is central to a study of popular fiction in the first half of the nineteenth century. A more general introduction to the subject of popular literature is provided by the same author in *Print and the People 1819–51*, 1976. Another good readable survey is V. Neuberg's *Popular Literature*, 1977.

25 R.K. Webb, *The British Working Class Reader*, 1955, p. 22.

26 R. Williams, *The Long Revolution*, 1965, p. 187.

27 D. Vincent, *Bread, Knowledge and Freedom*, 1981, pp. 110–11.

28 L. James, *Fiction for the Working Man: 1830–50*, 1974, p. 9 and D. Vincent, *Bread, Knowledge and Freedom*, 1981, p. 119.

29 R.D. Altick, *The English Common Reader*, 1957, p. 246.

30 G. Best, *Mid-Victorian Britain 1851–75*, 1979, p. 234.

31 L. James, *Print and the People, 1819–51*, 1976, pp. 17 and 23.

32 D. Reed and E. Glasgow, *Fergus O'Connor*, 1955, pp. 59–61.

33 T. Bennett, 'Popular Culture: Themes and Issues' in *Popular Culture*, Open University Course, 1981, Unit 3 p. 17.

34 J. Curran, 'The Press as an agency of social control', in *Newspaper History*, ed. G. Boyce, J. Curran and P. Wingate, 1978, p. 68.

35 L. James, *Fiction for the Working Man: 1830–50*, 1974, pp. 31 and 49.

36 Evidence to *Select Committee on Public Libraries*, Session I, 1849, 2785.

37 R. Williams, 'The Press and Popular Culture', in *Newspaper History*, ed. G. Boyce, J. Curran and P. Wingate, 1978, p. 41.

38 N. McCord, *North East England*, 1979, p. 183.

39 L. James, *Print and the People 1819–51*, 1976, p. 57.

40 D. Vincent, *Bread, Knowledge and Freedom*, 1981, p. 168.

41 J. Lawson, *Progress in Pudsey During the Last Sixty Years*, 1887, p. 52.

42 D. Vincent, *Bread, Knowledge and Freedom*, 1981, p. 189 and L. James, *Print and the People 1819–51*, 1976, p. 21.

43 V. Neuburg, *Popular Literature*, 1977, pp. 189–90.

44 J. Walvin, *Leisure and Society*, 1978, p. 104.

45 B. Harrison and B. Trinder, 'Drink and Sobriety in an Early Victorian Town: Banbury 1830–60', *English Historical Review*, supplement 4, 1969, p. 2.

46 J. Walton, *The English Seaside Resort*, 1983, p. 197. This is the latest and most thorough study of the growth of the seaside holiday industry in the nineteenth century. Two other general books on this topic deserving of mention are J.A.R. Pimlott, *The Englishman's Holiday*, first published in 1947 and reprinted in 1976, and J. Walvin, *Beside the Seaside*, 1978. For an amusing but scholarly study of one particular aspect of the history of the seaside see J. Walton, *The Blackpool Landlady*, 1978.

47 P. Bailey, 'The Victorian Middle Class and the Problem of Leisure', *Victorian Studies*, 1977, v. 21, p. 13.

48 J. Walvin, *Beside the Seaside*, 1978, p. 43.

49 J.A.R. Pimlott, *The Englishman's Holiday*, 1976, p. 95.

50 H. Cunningham, *Leisure in the Industrial Revolution*, 1980, p. 59.

51 *Parl. Deb*, 3, cxii, p. 903.

52 *Parl. Deb.*, 3, clxxxii, pp. 1132–3.

53 Patricia Branca, 'A New Perspective on Women's Work: A Comparative Typology', *Journal of Social History*, v. 9 no. 2, 1975, p. 141.

54 Flora Thompson, *Lark Rise to Candleford*, Penguin edn. 1976, p. 170.

55 W. Hamish Fraser, *The Coming of the Mass Market 1850–1914*, 1981, pp. 85–93.

56 John Forster, *Class Struggle and the Industrial Revolution*, 1974, p. 238.

57 Benjamin Brierley, 'A Day Out in Daisy Nook', *Daisy Nook Sketches*, 1982, p. 3.

58 See P. Bailey's excellent article '"Will the real Bill Banks please stand up?" Towards a role analysis of mid-Victorian working class respectability', *Journal of Social History*, v. 12, 1979.

59 Cited in W.C. Burn, *The Age of Equipoise*, 1964, p. 130.

60 Court of Quarter Sessions for Shropshire, in *Shropshire County Records*, v. IV, 1840–89, p. 174.

61 A. Metcalfe, 'Organized Sport in the Mining Counties of South Northumberland 1800–1889', *Victorian Studies*, Summer 1982, p. 475.

Chapter 6 (pages 144–63)

1 P. Bailey, 'The Victorian Middle Class and the Problem of Leisure', *Victorian Studies*, v. 21, 1977, p. 18.

2 S. Smiles, *Character*, 1882, pp. 31–2.

3 S. Constantine, 'Amateur Gardening and Popular Recreation in the 19th and 20th Centuries', *Journal of Social History*, Spring 1981, pp. 388 and 390. This article is complemented well by S. Martin Gaskell, 'Gardens for the Working Class: Victorian Practical Pleasure', *Victorian Studies*, Spring 1981.

4 L. Hannas, *The Jig Saw Book*, 1981, p. 13.

5 R.K. Webb, 'The Victorian Reading Public' in *The Pelican Guide to English Literature*, ed. B. Ford, 1958, Vol. 6, p. 206.

6 G.L. Griest, *Mudie's Circulating Library*, 1970, p. 38.

7 Ibid., p. 31.

8 Cited in H. House, *The Dickens World*, p. 216.

9 Elaine Showalter, 'Family Secrets and Domestic Subversion: Rebellion in the Novels of the 1860s', in *The Victorian Family*, ed. A.S. Wohl, 1978, pp. 101–116.

10 Cited in S. Mitchell, 'Sentiment and Suffering: Women's Reading in the 1860s', *Victorian Studies*, v. 2, 1977, p. 37.

11 H. Perkin, *The Origins of Modern English Society*, 1972, p. 159.

12 See the first rate article by P. Branca, 'The Modern Homemaker', in P. Branca (ed.), *Silent Sisterhood*, 1975, pp. 38–56.

13 J. Golby and W. Purdue, 'The Making of the Modern Christmas', *New Society* 23/30 Dec. 1982, v. 62, pp. 497–499, and 'A History of Christmas', in Units 1/2 of *Popular Culture*, Open University course, 1981.

14 J.A.R. Pimlott, *The Englishman's Christmas*, 1978, p. 85.

15 Although Pimlott, Ibid., p. 67 points out that it was only in the eighteenth century that Christmas dinner took on the form we know today – i.e. roast beef or poultry plus mince pies and plum pudding.

16 G. Orwell, *Collected Essays*, Vol. 1, 1971, pp. 469–71.

17 *Christmas in the Olden Times*, 1859, p. 1.

18 A. Briggs, *Victorian Cities*, 1968, p. 379.

19 In particular see M. Weiner, *English Culture and the Decline of the Industrial Spirit*, 1981.

20 S. Meacham, *A Life Apart: the English Working Class 1890–1914*, 1977, pp. 151–2.

21 R. Roberts, *A Ragged Schooling*, 1976, p. 26.

22 M. Vivian Hughes, *A London Childhood of the Seventies*, 1934, p. 32.

23 G. and W. Grossmith, *The Diary of a Nobody*, 1979, pp. 128–9.

24 J. Walton, *The English Seaside Resort*, 1983, p. 25.

25 J. Walvin, *Beside the Seaside*, 1978, P. 73.

26 G. and W. Grossmith, *The Diary of a Nobody*, 1979, p. 76.

27 H. Perkin, 'The "Social Tone" of Victorian Seaside Resorts in the North-West', *Northern History*, VII, 1975–6, p. 180.

28 Ibid., p. 183.

29 J. Walton, *The English Seaside Resort*, 1983, p. 13.

30 J. Walvin, *Beside the Seaside*, 1978, p. 50.

31 J.A.R. Pimlott, *The Englishman's Holiday*, 1976, p. 175.

32 *The Blackpool Visitor's Guide*, 1897, pp. 15 and 19.

33 Ibid., p. 15.

34 J. Walton, *The English Seaside Resort*, 1983, p. 20.

35 *The Leisure Hour*, July 6th, 1872.

36 Cited in C.M. Yonge, 'Victorians by the Sea', *History Today*, September 1975, p. 606.

37 J. Walton, *The English Seaside Resort*, 1983, p. 165.

38 P. Bailey, *Leisure and Class in Victorian England*, 1978, pp. 64 and 66.

39 J. Hart, 'Religion and Social Control in the Mid-Nineteenth Century' in *Social Control in Nineteenth Century Britain*, ed. A.P. Donajgrodozki, 1977, p. 129.

40 Cited in M. Weiner, *English Culture and the Decline of the Industrial Spirit 1850–1980*, 1981, p. 30.

41 J. Hart, 'Religion and Social Control in the Mid-Nineteenth Century' in *Social Control in Nineteenth Century Britain*, ed. A.P. Donajgrodozki, 1977, p. 129.

42 P. Bailey, *Leisure and Class in Victorian England*, 1978, p. 78.

Chapter 7 (pages 164–82)

1 T. Mason, *Association Football and English Society 1863–1915*, 1980, pp. 33 and 54. This book is by far the most detailed and scholarly account of the early years of organised association football. For a good general survey see J. Walvin, *The People's Game*, 1975.

2 J. Hutchinson, *The Football Industry*, 1982, p. 39.

3 Standish Meacham, *A Life Apart*, 1977, p. 167.

4 E. Duckershoff, *How the English Workman Lives*, 1899, p. 33, cited in an extremely good article on hobbies by R. McKibbin, 'Work and Hobbies in Britain, 1880–1950' in Winter, J. (ed.), *The Working Class in Modern British History*, 1983, p. 132.

5 A. Metcalfe, 'Organized Sport in the Mining Communities of South Northumberland, 1800–1889', *Victorian Studies*, Summer 1982, p. 477.

6 Mason, op. cit., p. 26.

7 P. Bailey, *Leisure and Class in Victorian England*, 1978, p. 137.

8 Hutchinson, op. cit., p. 12.

9 H. Cunningham, *Leisure in the Industrial Revolution*, 1980, p. 129.

10 Cited in Meacham, op. cit., p. 167.

11 Metcalfe, op., cit., pp. 491–2.

12 Mason, op. cit., p. 257.

13 Bailey, op. cit., p. 139.

14 H.E. Meller, *Leisure and the Changing City 1870–1914*, 1976, p. 146.

15 Mason, op. cit., p. 51.

16 Ibid., p. 29.

17 Cunningham, op. cit., p. 128.

18 Mason, op. cit., pp. 38–9, 42–3.

19 Ibid., p. 8.

20 E.J. Hobsbawm, *Industry and Empire*, 1968, p. 133.

21 Metcalfe, op. cit., p. 474.

22 *British Parliamentary Papers*, 1968, 'Select Committee on Gaming 1844', 218–225.

23 Metcalfe, op. cit., p. 479.

24 T.H.S. Escott, *England: Its People, Polity and Pursuits*, 1885, p. 78.

25 R. McKibbin, 'Working-Class Gambling in Britain, 1880–1939', *Past and Present*, no. 82., pp. 149 and 167.

26 Cited in V. Neuberg, *Popular Literature*, 1977, p. 231.

27 Meacham, op. cit., p. 127.

28 P. Bailey, 'Custom, Capital and Culture in the Victorian Music Hall,' in *Popular Culture and Custom in Nineteenth-Century England*, ed. R.D. Storch, 1982, p. 186. This article by Peter Bailey together with Chapter 7, 'Rational Recreation and the Entertainment Industry: the Case of the Victorian Music Halls' in his *Leisure and Class in Victorian England*, 1978, provide the best accounts of the history of the music hall. Chapter 6, 'The Music Hall: From a Class to a Mass Entertainment' in M. Vicinus, *The Industrial Muse*, 1974 is also very good. For a well-illustrated introduction to the topic see R. Mander and J. Mitchenson, *British Music Hall*, 1965.

29 P. Bailey, *Leisure and Class in Victorian England*, 1978, p. 147.

30 Ed. R.D. Storch, op. cit., p. 187.

31 Meller, op. cit., p. 213.

32 *British Parliamentary Papers* 1968, 'Select Committee on Theatrical Licences, 1866', 969 and 6884.

33 M. Vicinus, *The Industrial Muse*, 1974, p. 249.

34 Cited in B. Waites, 'The Music Hall', Unit 7, *Popular Culture*, Open University course U203, 1981, p. 58.

35 D. Hawker, 'The Making of the Tyneside Music Hall' in *Popular Music I*, eds. Middleton, R. and Horn, D., 1981, p. 54.

36 Cunningham, op, cit., p. 169.

37 J. Ewing Ritchie, *The Night Side of London*, 1857, p. 146.

38 Hawker, op. cit., p. 54.

39 C.E.B. Russell and E.T. Campagnac, 'Poor People's Music Halls in Lancashire', *Economic Review*, x, 1900, pp. 290–1.

40 R. Roberts, *A Ragged Schooling*, 1976, pp. 56–7.

41 Ed. R.D. Storch, op. cit., pp. 193–5.

42 L. Senelick, 'Politics as Entertainment: Victorian Music-Hall Songs', *Victorian Studies*, v. 19, 1975, p. 158.

43 J. Walton, 'Residential Amenity, Respectable Morality and the Rise of the Entertainment Industry: the Case of Blackpool, 1860–1914', *Literature and History*, v. 1., 1975, p. 68.

44 S. Martin Gaskell, 'Gardens for the Working Class: Victorian Practical Pleasure', *Victorian Studies*, Summer 1980, p. 496.

45 P. Johnson, 'Credit and Thrift and the British Working Class, 1870–1939' in Winter, J. (ed.), *The Working Class in Modern British History*, 1983, p. 156.

46 Roberts, op. cit., pp. 86, 89, 91.

47 P. Bailey, 'The Comic Pictorial Press of the 1880s as Mass Culture Prototype', paper delivered to the Social History Society Conference, December 1981.

48 H. Perkin, 'The Origins of the Popular Press', *History Today*, July 1957, reprinted in H. Perkin, *The Structured Crowd*, 1981, p. 56.

49 W. Hamish Fraser, *The Coming of the Mass Market 1850–1914*, 1981, p. 139.

50 For a detailed examination of the lower middle class see *The Lower Middle Class in Britain 1870–1914*, ed. G. Crossick, 1977 and G. Anderson, *Victorian Clerks*, 1976.

51 T. Wright, *Some Habits and Customs of the Working Classes by a Journeyman Engineer*, 1867, pp. 158–9.

52 Cunningham, op. cit., p. 135.

52 E. and S. Yeo, 'Ways of Seeing: Control and Leisure versus Class and Struggle' in E. and S. Yeo, (eds.), *Popular Culture and Class Conflict*, 1981, p. 134.

54 See chapter by E. Hobsbawm, 'Mass-Producing Traditions: Europe, 1870–1914', in Hobsbawm, E. and Ranger, T. (eds). *The Invention of Tradition*, 1983, pp. 263–307.

55 H.G. Wells, *The History of Mr Polly*, 1910, p. 19.

Chapter 8 (pages 183–202)

1 Matthew Arnold, *Culture and Anarchy*, Cambridge University Press edn., 1979, p. 104.

2 Peter Bailey, *Leisure and Class in Victorian England*, p. 178.

3 *Spectator*, 8 January 1881.

4 Arnold, op. cit., p. 105.

5 C.F.G. Masterman, *The Condition of England*, 1960, p. 58.

6 *Spectator*, 1880.

7 J. Walvin, *Leisure and Society*, p. 68.

8 Chris Waters, 'Social Reformers, Socialists and the Opposition to the Commercialisation of Leisure in Late Victorian England', unpublished paper delivered to the Eighth International

Economic History Congress, at Budapest, Hungary, 16 August 1982, pp. 7 and 12.

9 Quoted by Waters in the above, p. 6.

10 N. McCord, *North East England*, pp. 191–2.

11 Waters, op. cit., p. 9.

12 Quoted in M. Beer, *A History of Socialism*, Vol, 1, 1921, pp. 221–2.

13 Gareth Steadman Jones, 'Working Class Culture and Working Class Politics in London, 1870–1900; Notes on the Remaking of a Working Class', *Journal of Social History*, Vol. 7, Summer 1973–74, p. 484.

14 Geoffrey Crossick, *An Artisan elite in Victorian Society. Kentish London 1840–1880*, 1978.

15 Tony Bennett, 'Popular Culture: defining our terms' in *Popular Culture: themes and issues*, Units 1/2 of the Open University course, U203 *Popular Culture*, p. 86.

16 Hugh Cunningham, *Leisure in the Industrial Revolution*, 1980, p. 141.

17 N. McCord, op. cit., p. 185.

18 Harold Perkin, *The Origins of Modern English Society*, 1972, p. 342.

19 Masterman, op. cit., p. 105.

20 J.H. Plumb, 'The Public, Literature and the Arts in the Eighteenth Century', in *The Emergence of Leisure*, Michael Marrus (ed.), 1974, p. 12.

21 Roger Scruton, 'The Politics of Culture' in *The Politics of Culture and other Essays*, 1981, p. 231.

Index